"SO FEW"

THE IMMORTAL RECORD OF THE ROYAL AIR FORCE

OTHER BOOKS BY DAVID MASTERS

WHEN SHIPS GO DOWN
S O S: NEW WONDERS OF THE SEA
ON THE WING
I D: NEW TALES OF THE SUBMARINE WAR
CRIMES OF THE HIGH SEAS
WHAT MEN WILL DO FOR MONEY
DIVERS IN DEEP SEAS
UP PERISCOPE
WITH PENNANTS FLYING
WONDERS OF SALVAGE
Etc., etc.

One of the wonderful Lancaster heavy bombers, designed by Mr. Roy Chadwick, C.B.E., silhouetted against the fires raging in Hamburg during the great raid on January 30, 1943, when it was photographed from another Lancaster flying above it. The weird curves on the left culminating in blobs of light in front and behind the bomber were made by shells bursting very accurately in the path of the Lancaster, but fortunately not at the right height, while the lines and blobs of light above were caused by the terrific barrage put up by the defences.

"SO FEW"
THE IMMORTAL RECORD OF THE ROYAL AIR FORCE

by

DAVID MASTERS
Author of *On the Wing*, etc., etc.

1946

EYRE & SPOTTISWOODE
LONDON

First Impression, September 1941
Second Impression, revised, November 1941
Third Impression, revised, January 1942
Fourth Impression, revised, March 1942
Fifth Impression, June 1942
Sixth Impression, enlarged and revised, July 1943
Seventh Impression, revised, July 1945
Eighth Impression, revised, June, 1946

DEDICATED
TO
COURAGE AND SELF-SACRIFICE

*This book is produced in complete conformity
with the authorised economy standard, and
printed in Great Britain for*
Eyre & Spottiswoode (Publishers) Limited
15 Bedford Street, London, W.C.2

CONTENTS

LIST OF ILLUSTRATIONS

FOREWORD

In the ever-changing kaleidoscope of the war the gallant deeds of the Royal Air Force shone out against the sombre background like beacons which lit up to the world the strength and fortitude and courage of the people of Britain and the British Empire. Fine deeds followed each other in such swift succession that almost before one had been noted there was another to supersede it.

The moving finger of the printing press wrote its glowing tributes in a few words, and having writ, moved on, and what was written one day was forgotten in the new splendour of the deeds of the next. Consequently I strove to place on more permanent record a few of the actions of the R.A.F. which aroused the admiration of all free peoples, and the following pages should reveal something of the spirit animating the airmen who risked their lives against the German air force in order to save our civilization, a civilization which was built up slowly and laboriously over the centuries, to a large extent on British inventions and ideals.

These young men who flew unafraid through darkness and storm, who mounted at dawn through the lowering clouds until they emerged miles above the earth out in the clear sunshine, were modern knights of chivalry, carrying on a greater crusade than mankind had ever known; they sprang from all classes of the population in Britain and the Empire, bus conductors, shop assistants, clerks, aristocrats, insurance agents, farmers, electricians, engineers, men of all creeds, but they were the same breed, running true to type in the face of danger.

Man for man they proved themselves to be better than the Germans. Was this mere chance, depending on better aircraft, and were the better aircraft due to chance, or were there scientific reasons for them? The men of Britain who created the British Empire were the same stock who brought about the industrial and mechanical revolution; they were the inventors of the steam engine, the railway, all the marvellous machines that spun and wove and did a multitude of other things; they were the men who learned to handle engines a generation or two before the rest of the world, whom they taught; and as they had a generation or two start over other peoples, was it surprising if their sons proved a little more adept than the Germans at handling these modern engines of the air? The past accomplishments of the British race may furnish the reply.

And the people of Britain were also a seafaring race; they were used to fighting with the seas for centuries, finding their way in little ships and big all over the globe to far distant points, marking the rocks and shoals on their maps and avoiding them. Thus they not only learned to navigate in the most accurate manner, but they learned to be self-reliant, to act and think quickly in the face of the perils of the sea. These same qualities which enabled the mariners of England to find their way about the oceans were the very qualities which enabled men to become supreme in the air and find their way in the dark to distant places, pin-point a factory on the map and bomb it to destruction. Looked at broadly, there was no great difference between sailing the sea and sailing the skies, and the best seamen should also turn out to be the best airmen.

Nor must I forget that other quality which has so baffled the continental nations and sadly misled them into misunderstanding the British people. I refer to the individualism of the race. The British people are a nation of individuals who prefer to go their own way and do what they like with their own lives. All they ask is to be left alone, and so long as their neighbours do not interfere with them they will not interfere with their neighbours. They air their views in the most outspoken way and will argue and bicker until the foreigner may think the dissension within the nation is so great that the slightest thing will start a civil war. But what the continental peoples unfortunately overlook is the fact that the political freedom so long enjoyed by the British people has bred in them a good-natured tolerance which serves as an effective mask for some of the finer qualities of human nature, a strong courage that may be concealed with a joke, a cold anger against cruelty, and other attributes which become manifest only in times of grave national danger. Tendentious in peace and tenacious in war would be one way of describing the British people, whose anger is so hard to rouse and not so difficult to subdue.

Is it surprising that a nation of individuals who regard the sea as their heritage and who taught the world how to create and use machines should breed a dominant race of airmen? The Royal Air Force in smashing the German air attack on Great Britain in September, 1940, supplied the answer. To me it was obvious that a nation in which individualism had been encouraged for generations should provide a finer air force than the nation in which the initiative of the people had been crushed into following their leader like slaves, learning to do everything at the word of command, relying upon orders and not upon themselves. Nothing can be freer than the aeroplane in the sky. Once the pilot has taken off, he is the captain of his ship and his own soul, and in no other sphere is it possible for individualism and initiative to shine so brilliantly.

As for the better aircraft, the Spitfires and Hurricanes and Defiants and Hampdens and Whitleys and Wellingtons, not to mention those modern miracles, the Stirling, the Halifax, the Lancaster and their secret successors, they offered no surprise to those familiar with the inherent engineering genius of the British race. These aircraft were the direct answer to the question asked by many people in the

days of the Schneider Trophy races—"What is the good of them?"
The intense creative effort which drove Rolls-Royce engineers to
design an aero-engine that was more powerful and lighter in weight
than any the world had ever known and which induced R. J. Mitchell
to create his Supermarine of incredible speed in order to win an
international sporting event furnished invaluable scientific data.
The engineers learned how to use new light alloys such as duralumin
in their engines, the designers learned how to streamline their aircraft in order to increase speed, finding out that a single wire
exposed to the pressure of the air could reduce the speed by several
miles an hour, and the Air Ministry learned how to train men to fly
safely at speeds of 400 miles an hour and more. Who dares to
question the value of the Schneider Trophy races now? The knowledge then gained enabled the aircraft to be designed which prevented
the Germans from destroying London by their fleets of bombers. It
was Mitchell who designed the Spitfire, and future historians may
state with some degree of truth that when Great Britain won the
Schneider Trophy in 1931 she really won the war which saved
Civilization.

Nor should we forget another sporting event, the race to Australia
in 1934, for which de Havillands designed and built the Comet,
with its combination of retractable undercarriage, flaps and con-
trollable-pitch propellers which so largely increased the speed. The
world's fastest long-distance bomber, the wonderful, wooden-
skinned Mosquito, which carried a deadly sting in the way of cannon
and bombs and which outpaced the speediest of German fighters,
was derived and developed directly from the Comet. In a similar
manner Mr. Sydney Camm developed from his earlier masterpiece
the Hurricane—which did so much to help win the Battle of Britain—
his later fighter, the Typhoon, which possessed a far greater speed
and a much heavier armament than the favourite old Hurricane.
The power for this fighter was furnished by the remarkable Sabre
engine of about 2,000 horse-power, designed by Major J. B. Halford,
whose genius produced and packed more power in a smaller engine
than ever before.

We know to-day that the millions spent in building the experimental airships R.100 and R.101 were not entirely wasted, as so
many critics thought when the tragic disaster to R.101 brought the
British Government's airship programme to an end, for, quite apart
from the development of the heavy oil engine, it was while engaged
on the technical work of these airships that Dr. Wallis invented the
geodetic method of construction which was employed in building
many of our heavy bombers. "The strength is phenomenal," said
an expert to me while I examined a Wellington. Designed for the
framework of airships, the geodetic method of construction was
modified to serve equally well for aeroplanes, and thanks to this

invention many a bomber which was so shot about that the experts marvelled at it holding together was able to reach its base and, after repair, carry on the fight against the enemy at a time when bombers were of more importance than armies.

Although I recognized the danger of the German menace, the ultimate triumph of Great Britain and the British Empire was to me never in doubt. I did not know the size of Goering's air force, nor did I underestimate its striking power. But I gained confidence in the fact that it was the first of the modern air forces to be brought into being, and it was therefore the oldest. When Hitler decided to bomb the world into submission or destruction, Goering's air force was four or five years old in design, and it must have been on the way to obsolescence when considered in the light of the technical improvements of those years.

Against this I set the fact that the delay in re-equipping the Royal Air Force made it the most up-to-date air force in the world. Its diminutive size, due to the blindness of politicians and statesmen, was deplorable, but its quality was unsurpassed. It would be ungenerous to the Air Council and to the technical staff of the Air Ministry to underrate the difficult problems they had to solve in the days of peace. They had to select the right moment for putting aircraft into production and the right types to produce. Too early a decision would have provided aircraft which might have been bettered, and by waiting too long they might have had the finest aircraft in the world on the drawing board and none in the air. They did their best in difficult circumstances, and mankind may remember with gratitude that the selected types possessed sufficient superiority to defeat the main German air attacks in 1940.

Future generations will perhaps recognize their debt to Lady Houston for her patriotic gift of £100,000 which made the Schneider Race possible after the Air Ministry had cancelled it for financial reasons; and also to Mr. T. O. M. Sopwith and Sir Frank Spriggs, who, when the Air Ministry were hesitating about placing an order for a few Hawker Hurricanes to equip a squadron or two, had sufficient faith and foresight to order their works to start production of a thousand—which was why the Hurricanes outnumbered the Spitfires by five to one during the Battle of Britain.

The fine quality of British workmanship, derived from the longest engineering experience enjoyed by any nation, played no small part in nullifying the German air attack, for it prevented many aircraft from falling to pieces in the air and their crews from dying. The superior training given to pilots and crews of the Royal Air Force also proved its worth.

The very love of sport, for which the young men of Britain and the Empire were so often taken to task, was another factor making for air supremacy. Rowing and football and cricket have for generations been helping to develop in men of British stock the team spirit which enables them to combine all their talents and energies to achieve victory for their side; they have learned to rely on each other and call out the best in each other during the crisis of a race or game, and this team spirit, bred in the British race by generations of forebears, was seen at its zenith in the squadrons of Spitfires and Hurricanes which defeated the German air force at Dunkirk and Dover and in the Battle of Britain.

The sporting instincts bred in Canadians and Australians and New Zealanders and South Africans were still further quickened by the environment in which they lived. The open spaces gave them a special sense of direction, added a keenness to their vision which enabled them to see and shoot just a fraction of a second quicker than the foe.

Their valour was awe-inspiring, and I count it a privilege to write with first-hand knowledge of these flying crusaders who fought a holy war to preserve Christendom and the lives and liberties of earth-bound mortals. They were the flower of Great Britain and the British Empire, selected in the most scientific manner for the posts of honour which they covered with so much glory. None but the best would do, and those who achieved their desire of becoming pilots and navigators and gunners and wireless operators in the Royal Air Force were in fact the finest specimens of young manhood who walked the earth, young men whose physical fitness, nervous control, mental alertness and swift muscular reactions made them fit to command the giant bombers and handle the darting fighters; they were the knights of the air whose prowess and sacrifice may conjure a new and nobler order out of the ruins created by Hitler and Mussolini.

Behind them, training them, directing their bombing and fighting operations, backing their youthful ardour with mature experience, stood the men of the previous generation, keen-eyed, mentally alert, the flush of health on their cheeks, with hair greying above the ears and thoughtful lines on their lean faces, men who in the last war were emulating the deeds of these younger fighter and bomber pilots in order to bring about the downfall of Germany in 1918. These were the men who first won for Great Britain the supremacy of the air. In the intervening years they used their knowledge and energy in creating an air force to win back freedom for humanity. One day the full story may be told of their heart-breaking task, of the obstacles which they overcame when blind-eyed politicians deliberately sacrificed the dominating air power of Great Britain and all but flung away the British Empire because they were afraid to tell the nation the truth that Germany was re-arming to avenge the defeat of 1918. The Right Hon. Mr. Winston Churchill was one of the foremost to point out the danger and urge the nation to meet it in those days of November, 1936, and earlier, but unfortunately his wise counsel was disregarded.

My own warnings date much farther back. When men and newspapers in Britain were ridiculing the idea of flying, I knew that the Wrights had accomplished the miracle of flight, and a keen study of the rapid developments made me realize that what Wilbur and Orville Wright expected to be one of the biggest blessings ever conferred on mankind might unhappily turn out to be a curse. The manner in which the Germans started to incorporate the aeroplane and airship into their military machine so preoccupied me that in 1912 I wrote about this new air menace and emphasized the danger of London being bombed by the Germans. I went so far as to urge the government of that day to create a strong air force, on the lines of a programme which I formulated, to augment the forty or so experimental aeroplanes and the thirty-eight or forty trained pilots then possessed by the army and navy.

"The sum of £1,000,000 expended as indicated would provide us with the basis of an aerial fleet," I wrote. "At the present time we are helpless. Surely a great country like ours can afford the money. After all, it is a small price to pay for peace. We must remember that the country which rules the air comes within measurable distance of ruling the earth and sea."

The British Governments which came to power after that dire conflict of 1914-1918 chose to ignore this lesson, which was proved up to the hilt.

What Germany failed to do in the last war she plotted to do in this, and the pilots of the Royal Air Force alone saved the British Commonwealth and the world from German domination.

In the messes of Royal Air Force stations all over the British Isles were these modern knights of chivalry whose heroism will ring down the ages and become immortal. They were a modest breed, boyish, clear-eyed, in perfect health mentally and physically, who seldom spoke about the deeds which earned the ribbons on their tunics. They were the generation whose flights and fights and self-sacrifice played so noble a part in frustrating Hitler and Mussolini and in saving for the future the most treasured blessings which have evolved from the past.

Obviously there were many difficulties in obtaining the detailed information in this book, not the least being the extreme reticence of the members of the Royal Air Force concerning their heroic deeds. I am, therefore, particularly grateful to the Air Ministry and to all who assisted me to write these enduring records which are as authentic as any pages of official history.

DAVID MASTERS.

CHAPTER I

THE SCARECROW PATROLS

Now that the enemy has been utterly defeated and the Royal Air Force can fly at will over a ruined and conquered Reich, it is possible to disclose one of the early secrets of the war. That Hitler would rely upon the submarine to strike hard at Great Britain was never in doubt, and the torpedoing without warning of the passenger liner *Athenia* on Sunday, September 3, 1939, a few hours after the late Right Hon. Neville Chamberlain announced over the wireless that German aggression had compelled Great Britain to go to war, indicated that the German submarine campaign would be just as ruthless as before. The first blow struck by Germany was a danger signal to Great Britain.

The ease with which Hitler gained all he demanded at Munich in September, 1938, not only proved conclusively that Great Britain was prepared to go to any lengths to maintain peace, but it indicated to the thoughtful observer that Great Britain was quite unprepared to go to war. With the triumph of Munich and the unopposed occupation of Czecho-Slovakia to convince him that Great Britain was moribund, backed by the misleading advice of Ribbentrop that the English would never fight, Hitler launched his long-planned and treacherous attack on Poland, despite Sir Nevile Henderson's last-minute warning that Great Britain was not bluffing.

However much Hitler was bemused by the opinion that the British Empire was crumbling, he was not so self-hypnotized by wishful thinking as to cease to take precautions in case the imponderable English failed to behave as he hoped. He gave instructions to the German Naval Command that the U-boats were to take up their war stations in the North Sea and the Atlantic where they could hit instantly at British shipping if the British Premier, whom he had deceived and betrayed, had the temerity to accept the German challenge. "It is evil things we shall be fighting against, brute force, bad faith, injustice, oppression, persecution—and against them I am certain that the right will prevail," said Mr. Chamberlain over the wireless on that sunny Sunday morning. The torpedoing of the *Athenia* that night emphasized the truth of his simple words.

Thus in the first hours the submarine menace forced itself upon the attention of the Admiralty and the Air Ministry. In the last war Great Britain was driven to adopt all sorts of measures to defeat the U-boats, some of which, if far from orthodox, were nevertheless effective. One amusing stratagem was to protect Malta by laying a series of mines which, as no mines were available, were simulated by empty barrels, the psychological effect of which kept the U-boats at a respectful distance. On the other hand, the little aluminium-painted airships, popularly known as "blimps," which began their patrols of the British coast in order to discover and stalk and destroy the submarines, played a real part in defending shipping, although the Coastal Command was also wise enough to adopt stratagem to shake the nerves of the U-boat crews.

After the last war, the Admiralty had time to digest some of the lessons of the submarine campaign, with the result that the depth charge, the dread of the U-boat, was developed into a more potent and terrible weapon of destruction; while the hydrophone apparatus, which was invented to detect submarines under water and enable them to be hunted down, was transformed into the secret apparatus known as the Asdic, an instrument sensitive enough to detect at long range the sounds given off by a submerged submarine in order that the submarine hunter could locate the unseen enemy with uncanny accuracy and speed straight to the spot to drop depth charges on the lurking U-boats.

Well-equipped as it was with the scientific means of destroying the U-boats, the Admiralty nevertheless needed as much co-operation from the air as could possibly be obtained. That was the problem of the senior officers of the Coastal Command. If the Coastal Command had been provided with a generous number of squadrons of well-armed, long-range aircraft it would have been a simple matter to send them out on patrol with orders to attack and sink any enemy submarine that was sighted. But the Coastal Command was not so completely equipped. Like the Bomber Command and the Fighter Command of the Royal Air Force, it suffered from the misguided unilateral disarmament policy of the late Mr. Ramsay MacDonald, who hoped by setting other nations a good example to induce them to disarm, instead of which the growing weakness of Great Britain merely encouraged Germany to rearm.

In the circumstances the Commander-in-Chief of the Coastal Command and his senior officers were compelled to do the best they could. They knew that a submarine to be effective had to raise its periscope above water to see its target and judge the speed at which the ship was steaming, before working into position to deliver its torpedo attack. So long as a submarine could be forced under the surface and kept there, it was for the time being rendered practically harmless, and the ships could steam along the surface unmolested.

The problem was how to bring this about. The armed aircraft capable of attacking submarines that were available to the Coastal Command were far too few for the purpose. Yet it was absolutely imperative to organize more intensive patrols for spotting and harrying the U-boats.

As a contribution to the problem, they fell back upon a similar stratagem to that practised in the last war; but whether the idea was directly inspired by the memory of what was done then or whether the idea occurred anew is not known.

"Why not use Tiger Moths?" it was suggested.

Now, the Tiger Moth was purely a training aircraft, and for this purpose it was unsurpassed. But it was not built for fighting, or carrying bombs. It was a tandem aircraft fitted with dual control so that the instructor could take the pupil in the air and teach him how to fly; it had a low landing speed of about 55 miles an hour, which had saved many a pupil from crashing on landing, and its maximum speed was about 110 miles an hour. And of course it was not designed for alighting on the sea.

The use of these aircraft for harrying the U-boats was considered by the Coastal Command and apparently met with approval. The fact that the Coastal Command was forced to adopt a non-combatant aircraft of this type to help to circumvent the German submarines shows that the Coastal Command did not underrate the danger: it also gives an inkling of how gravely the Royal Air Force suffered from lack of aircraft of all kinds when war was declared.

Orders were accordingly given for the formation of several flights of Tiger Moths for use on anti-submarine patrol, each flight consisting of six pilots and nine aircraft to allow a reserve for overhauls. A veteran pilot of the last war, Flying Officer P. C. Hoyle, who was a member of the Volunteer Reserve of the Royal Air Force, was appointed to command No. 1 Coastal Patrol Flight. The first flight of Tiger Moths duly arrived at the base somewhere in Scotland.

In those days it was a small station with enough mud in inclement weather to make even the most venturesome put on gum boots before going outside, and a bleak position that might have damped the most ardent spirits. But the worst that Scotland could produce in the way of mud or weather failed to damp the spirits of those who manned that station. They were mostly members of the Auxiliary Air Force or the Volunteer Reserve, men who had taken to flying because they loved it, and they were as diverse in appearance as in their professions.

These amateur pilots who were called up to reinforce the Royal Air Force at the outbreak of war were as democratic a body as one could find. Among them on this station were a builder, a builder's merchant, a building contractor, an accountant, a salesman, a commercial traveller, an insurance broker, a cloth merchant, a banker, a brewer's agent, a doctor, a journalist, the owner of a motor transport line, a pilot of a civil air line and a games master who resigned from the squadron just before the war to go to South Africa to take up an appointment, but directly he heard over the wireless that war was declared he cabled withdrawing his resignation and caught the next boat back at his own expense in order to fly with his old squadron. His keenness was typical of that animating all the men who flew the aircraft on the Scarecrow Patrols.

The Tiger Moths themselves were camouflaged, but no attempt was made to arm them, so if they saw a U-boat they had no means of attacking it and if the U-boat attacked them, they had no means of replying. In short, the aircraft of the Scarecrow Patrol were quite defenceless. However, they were modified to carry a signal pistol and recognition cartridges, without which it would have been impossible to do the work allotted to them, and they were properly equipped with signalling lights. To ensure the safety of the pilot, or to make him believe that he stood some chance if he came down in the sea, each Tiger Moth had the inflated inner tube of a motor tyre, to which two distress signals were attached, stowed away in the aft locker. The inner tube was secured to the aircraft by a length of string which had to be broken or cut in an emergency to set the inflated tube free so that the pilot could use it to keep himself afloat.

About the middle of December, 1939, the first flight was ready to take up its duties, which embraced the whole length of the east coast of Scotland. The main object was to search for submarines and to scare them into submerging by simulating an attack on them, hence the name of scarecrow patrols. The importance of warning the base and the nearest naval unit directly the enemy was sighted was, of course, not overlooked. In addition, the patrols had to give a full report of all ships that were seen, including their names, nationalities, their estimated tonnage, their speed, the course on which they were steaming and the locality in which they were last sighted. And occasionally they were given other missions which will always remain secret.

It was quite realized that the duties would be arduous and would call for endurance as well as high courage. The Tiger Moth had open cockpits, fully exposed to the weather, and those who flew them had no protection whatsoever against wind and storm. There was no heating system in them and the pilots had simply to rely upon their own physical resistance to suffer the worst that the weather could do.

For this reason the initial patrols were kept fairly short, probably to enable the pilots to get used to the weather conditions and become hardened to them. It was a wise precaution, for only perfectly fit men who had become inured to the hardships could have stood up against them.

At the outset some of the difficulties became plain. On the seat of the front cockpit was carried a wicker basket containing two carrier pigeons which were bedded down on a layer of shavings. These pigeons were to be used in an emergency for flying messages to the base, and attached to the basket was a message pad and the usual thimbles in which messages were placed before securing them to the legs of the birds. The pilot sat in the rear cockpit which, like the front cockpit, was equipped with a windscreen.

Although protected by a windscreen, a fierce blast seemed to eddy round it and strike him in the face. Even a stoic would have found it difficult to endure for a couple of hours. The front windscreen was quickly incriminated as the cause. When the air was thrust aside by the first windscreen, it impinged on the second screen and swirled round behind in a sort of backwash. Eventually the front screens were removed and there was a welcome improvement in this respect.

This improvement was achieved only by worsening the conditions elsewhere. The removal of the front windscreen allowed the wind to blow into the front cockpit and through to the back, making a continual draught about the legs of the pilot. The discomfort was such that the pilots desired to cover in the front cockpit to make it windproof, but they were not permitted to do so and had to put up with the draught.

That was not the only thing they had to bear. The two pigeons in the basket on the front seat, although they might have saved the lives of the pilots in an emergency, were a continual source of annoyance. For one thing, little bits of the shavings along with feathers were blown through the wicker-work of the baskets into the faces of the pilots; but what they most abhorred was the fact that the frozen droppings of the birds were being continually sprayed back on them by the icy blast, getting into their noses and even penetrating to their eyes under their goggles, with the result that sore throats were very prevalent among them. They could not stop it, therefore they had to suffer it along with the recurring sore throats which the innocent pigeons inflicted on them.

Despite these drawbacks the patrols went on. At dawn a couple of Tiger Moths would head out to sea to quarter for U-boats which may have been on the surface recharging their batteries all night. The pilots always hunted in pairs within sight of each other, zig-zagging about to give any U-boat commander the impression that his presence in the vicinity was known and that the aircraft was about to attack. It was of course sheer bluff, which drove the sub-marines into crash-diving for their lives. At dusk, when the U-boats were prone to come up for a stealthy attack or a breather, the scarecrow patrols were out again, patrolling below a thousand feet and keeping a sharp look-out for the little white feather which indicated that a periscope was pushing through the sea. The periscopes were not easy to detect in broken seas, nor yet in smooth seas, even when pilots flew at the most favourable height. The leader disproved for himself the popular impression that it was easy from a considerable height to detect the shadowy form of a U-boat lurking in the depths, for he hunted them at all heights up to 5,000 feet and never once saw the slightest sign, even though he knew there was a submarine in the sea beneath him. In clearer, sunnier waters the submerged U-boats may perhaps be located easily from the air, but they are less visible in the troubled and cloudy waters around the coasts of Britain.

Day after day the leader and the five keen young pilots of No. 1 Coastal Patrol Flight took off from their aerodrome and flew far out to sea to carry on their endless search for enemy submarines. By the time they were properly dressed to withstand the weather in a Sidcot, a monkey suit, three pairs of gloves, a balaclava under their helmets, and the bright yellow "Mae West," otherwise their inflated waistcoats, bulging on their manly bosoms, with their parachute harness and their Sutton harness on top, the cockpit fitted them like a strait-jacket. They could hardly move. "It was exceptionally hard to turn one's head, let alone get at the signal pistol and flares," the flight leader once remarked. "But all this difficulty was well worth while, because the uninterrupted view from these small biplanes could not be beaten, especially as there was no semi-opaque window to have to peer through, and the aircraft could be flown slowly."

That first winter of the war was one of the worst within living memory. Countless people died of the cold in Europe. People were frozen to death. Many dropped dead in Great Britain. Roads were impassable, fuel unobtainable, with water-pipes everywhere burst and frozen, forming in some cases icicles thirty and forty feet long down the sides and backs of houses. The sea itself off the coast of Norway and Denmark was frozen for twenty-five or thirty miles from the coast; great stretches of the sea were frozen round the shores of Great Britain. Yet those brilliant pilots of the Scarecrow Patrol went out just the same in their open aircraft to continue their search.

Sometimes the temperature was below zero. The salt spray froze over their aircraft, layers of ice formed; how they managed to survive and keep going is a mystery. But they did it. There were days when the seas ran twenty feet high. A touch would have drowned them; but they did not touch. Gales assailed them, hail bombarded them, sudden flurries of snow blinded them. They endured it all. Those pilots of the Scarecrow Patrol were monuments of faith—faith in their cause, in themselves and in their aircraft. And the aircraft never failed them. From the time the first flight was formed until it was disbanded at the end of May, 1940—by which time well-armed and enclosed aircraft were available to take over the patrols—there was not one engine failure. The flight leader made over a hundred patrols without the engine faltering once.

During the latter days of the patrol when pilots were posted elsewhere for other operations the shortage of pilots caused some inconvenience. It was essential for every pilot to fly one patrol a day, which meant that no pilot ever had a free day. Chatting it over among themselves in the mess, they agreed that the pilots who did the last patrol at dusk should go out on the dawn patrol, starting at 3 o'clock in the morning and after doing their two days' work in one would take twenty-four hours off. The arrangement was eminently satisfactory to all concerned. But human nature being what it is, it was not surprising that after coming off the dusk patrol the pilots were apt to be sleepy when they turned out for the dawn patrol. This led to some incredible, well-authenticated instances of pilots actually falling asleep while they were flying, fortunately without suffering any ill-effects.

One morning, when the leader of the patrol landed and reported, the Controller inquired: "Which of you bombed that submarine?"

"Submarine?" was the reply. "What's the trouble?"

"Well, the coastguard saw a Tiger dive and drop two bombs from a low altitude and fly off," said the Controller.

"I know nothing about it," said the leader.

A few minutes later his fellow pilot returned. "Did you bomb a submarine off the point?" the leader asked.

"No," said the other pilot.

"But the coastguard saw the splashes of the bombs," was the rejoinder.

The young pilot grinned. "I think I fell asleep," he confessed. "The jolt of the wheels hitting the water woke me up and I just had time to jerk her free."

The splashes caused by the wheels were mistaken by the coastguard for bombs.

Another time the leader, looking at the other aircraft as they set course for base after their patrol, was amazed to see a great trail of seaweed streaming out for five feet behind the tail skid.

"Where did you get that weed?" asked the leader when they landed.

The young pilot stared at the seaweed in perplexity. "I don't know," he replied in a very puzzled voice. "I must have dozed off, but I've not the slightest recollection of hitting the water."

Yet there was the bunch of seawood to give indubitable proof that his skid had been in the sea and he himself standing there unharmed on the aerodrome was evidence of his instantaneous reactions when the aircraft struck. Subconsciously he must have given a lightning flick on the stick which pulled up the aircraft and saved his life. But he did not remember anything about it.

Perhaps the greatest thrill came to the leader of the Scarecrows on January 25, 1940. He was patrolling with his second pilot in the afternoon with the sun full in their eyes when they saw two destroyers which, owing to the glare off the water, appeared to be slowly steaming away from them. As the leader flew toward the destroyer inshore, he thought it was rather peculiar for a destroyer to leave a wake that was nearly three miles long. When he came up to it he found the wake was oil. He flew along toward the destroyer to signal that she had sprung an oil leak when, to his surprise, he saw that the destroyer was approaching him. In a flash it was plain that the oil trail had nothing to do with the ship. Quickly he signalled down. "Line of oil ahead."

Flying back to the other end of the line within a few feet of the water, he assured himself that the oil was coming up in bubbles and moving forward at about four knots, perhaps a bit more. When he climbed he could see nothing but oil. Not wishing to call the navy on a wild goose chase, he studied the oil from a low altitude once more and finally decided to act in the hope that it was a submarine. He felt certain that it must be, as there was nothing else which could travel under the surface, and he had heard that a submarine had been attacked in that neighbourhood the day before. Climbing to a few hundred feet, he fired a signal which meant "Submarine under me," and awaited eventualities. The pilot of the other aircraft saw it and came roaring along.

"With considerable anxiety I watched the nearest destroyer and in about a minute I saw the bow wave start to increase," he said afterwards. "I was through the last war and have seen plenty of grim scenes before, but as the destroyer dashed along, I could not help wondering what were the feelings of those wretches in the submarine below, for they must have heard the approaching engines on their hydrophones and later on their hull.

"To help the destroyer I repeatedly dived at the head of the line of oil, the last dive, in my excitement, being a race for it past the bows of the destroyer. Climbing sharply, I turned in time to watch the ship pass its whole length in front of the oil and then let fly about six depth charges in a pattern. These all exploded some seconds later with the most fearful crashes I ever want to hear or witness. The sea was illuminated deep down and appeared to jerk upwards, causing a spray over the surface. This subsided, only to be followed by giant upheavals. Apart from the usual black sort of scum caused by depth charges, more oil came up and the line ceased to go forward."

For weeks the commander of the first Scarecrow Patrol saw oil seeping up from that spot, and he even saw a destroyer make a most determined attack there with depth charges, but it throws some light on the conservative methods of the Admiralty to know that no U-boat was credited as having been destroyed there.

There was nothing spectacular about the Scarecrow Patrols, nothing to win high honours. Of the six pilots who formed the first flight, three, alas, are no more. But the amateur pilots who joyfully risked their lives without question for day after day flying far out to sea, sitting in open cockpits exposed to all the rigours of a terrible winter, until fully-armed aircraft were manufactured to take up the task, won by their quiet confidence and their physical endurance a worthy place in British history.

CHAPTER II

A SECRET FLIGHT TO AFRICA

IN the early days of June, 1940, when Great Britain, owing to the break through of the German armoured divisions across the Meuse and the capitulation of Belgium, was forced to abandon the entire equipment of the British Expeditionary Force in order to save the lives and liberties of that superb army of men by performing the miracle of Dunkirk, Britain and the British Empire were in jeopardy. The British army after a retreat which outrivalled that of Mons escaped destruction only because at that vital moment the seas abated into a flat calm and all the seafaring experience of a seafaring people crystallised into a stupendous effort which welded the Royal Navy and all the big and little ships afloat in home waters into a fleet of deliverance. Britain had an army without arms, but she had still the finest navy the world has known.

France tottered. As she was falling, the Right Hon. Winston Churchill, to save her from capitulation, made his historic offer to the French Premier M. Reynaud of a free alliance in which Britain would pool all her resources with those of France, and Frenchmen would become free citizens of Great Britain as well as of France while the British would become free citizens of France. It was an amazing offer showing the widest vision and statesmanship.

France was divided. Reynaud was prepared to fight on and remove the Government to North Africa, but the politicians who coveted power under the Nazis were too strong.

The French people and armies, unbroken in spirit, full of undying animosity against the Germans who had once more overrun their beloved country, were without leaders. To Laval, who had worked for and waited for this moment, the glory of France was past, the agony of the French people of no account so long as he could sway their destinies under the Nazi heel. He would prefer to see the French a nation of slaves under Hitler rather than a nation of free men.

Had France at that moment possessed one statesman of the stature of Churchill she could have been saved, despite her position. As it was, the capitulation was announced. Immense French armies had never fought at all, and Great Britain, standing alone in her defiance of the Nazi power and her condemnation of its foul creed, sought desperately to rally the French to carry on the struggle.

By all the rules of warfare, Great Britain at that moment was beaten, although the entire nation as usual did not realize it. Nevertheless her fate and that of the British Empire lay in the balance, with the weight of the French navy capable of swinging the scale one way or the other. If Hitler could have gained the French navy, which had taken refuge in North Africa, the position of Britain would indeed have been critical.

21

Such was roughly the position when Squadron Leader Julius Allen Cohen, D.F.C., of the Royal Australian Air Force, received orders on June 24, 1940, to fly from his home station at Mountbatten on Plymouth Sound over to Calshot, near Southampton, at dawn next day in order to pick up some important passengers.

''They will give you your destination,'' the Australian pilot was told.

Born in Sydney, Julius A. Cohen joined the Royal Australian Air Force at the age of eighteen. Passing through the usual period of training during which he learned as much about theoretical and practical flying as anyone could teach him, he in his turn qualified as a pilot. Where some men show their desire for fighters and others for bombers, his predilection was for flying-boats, and soon after the war started a Sunderland flying-boat of which he was the captain used to taxi over Plymouth Sound at dawn to go out into the wide waters to escort convoys and look for submarines, returning at dusk to settle gently upon the waters over which Sir Francis Drake used to gaze in those other great days when the glory of England began.

Many a passer-by observed with interest the lithe figure in the dark blue uniform of the Royal Australian Air Force striding through the streets. Squadron Leader Cohen was six feet tall, slim, clean-shaven, with very dark eyes that lit up sometimes with a glint of amusement, and dark brown wavy hair. He was twenty-four years old, and as resourceful as he was cool and prudent.

That day of June 24th the crew of the flying-boat busied themselves about the aircraft to make sure that everything was in perfect order; the wireless operator went over his intricate installation; the engines were adjusted and tested; the controls were examined and manipulated to see that they worked freely, the huge petrol tanks in the wings were filled; the four guns in the tail turret were checked along with the other armament; and it was seen that the full quota of ammunition was on board. The fresh water supplies were replenished and the stores, in the shape of tea and coffee and vegetables and canned and fresh fruit, taken on board, not forgetting the meat and butter and milk which were duly stored in the ice-chest—it is surprising the food a dozen healthy young men can consume in a twelve or fourteen hour day while on patrol.

It was still dark on June 25th when the crew of the flying-boat came down to the launch at the landing stage to be taken on board. Over the quiet waters the sound of the Sunderland's engines was heard, growing to a deep roar as her captain gradually opened the throttle to gather flying speed before lifting her into the air. In a few seconds he pulled the control column back and the sea streamed down from her hull and floats as she became airborne. Gaining height, he set course along the south coast to the eastward, and in less than an hour and a half alighted on Southampton Water at Calshot to pick up his mooring.

It was an hour or two later that he learned the identity of the important passengers whom he was detailed to carry. They were General Lord Gort, V.C., and the Right Hon. Mr. Duff Cooper, M.P., who at that time was the Minister of Information. They were entrusted with the important and highly secret mission of trying to arrange a conference with certain French statesmen who had crossed to French Morocco. To Lord Gort and Mr. Duff Cooper was given the supremely difficult task, in the hour when France was collapsing into chaos, of inducing the only loyal and patriotic Frenchmen within reach to carry on the struggle alongside Great Britain. So deep was the wave of despair which engulfed France that from the beginning Mr. Duff Cooper was probably realist enough to recognize that the outcome of the mission was likely to prove unfavourable. But Britain's position was so grave that her survival and the survival of civilization made it essential to do anything that promised the slightest help.

Learning that he was to proceed to Rabat in French Morocco to land his passengers and wait there for further orders, Squadron Leader Cohen went into details of the flight. Maps were consulted and the river on which the great flying-boat would have to alight was pointed out.

Lord Gort and Mr. Duff Cooper at length boarded the flying-boat and sat down in the ward-room, while the tall, dark-eyed captain of the aircraft wakened the engines to life and, calmly watching his instrument panel, deftly took her into the air about 9 o'clock. Climbing a little, he set course for the south.

Now and again they ran into a shower, but the weather on the whole was excellent, and as they could see clearly for fifteen miles the chance of being surprised by enemy aircraft was not great. Nevertheless a sharp look-out was kept, and the captain flew the flying-boat at no more than 500 feet so that if any Messerschmitts did happen to approach them unseen at a great height and dive out of the clouds, he could drop down to sea level in a second to prevent them attacking from below.

The Sunderland carried a good armament. The four guns in the tail turret alone were formidable, and there were guns to look after any enemies approaching from port or starboard, as well as guns in the front to meet a head-on attack, so the Sunderland was not defenceless, as many an enemy aircraft had learned to its cost when facing one of these flying cruisers.

Among the members of the crew, the rigger was the stand-by of a flying-boat. When anything went wrong it was his duty to put it right. He was in fact a highly skilled mechanic who looked after every part of the aircraft except the engines, and if the wing or hull were damaged he would do his best to repair it, and if a control wire were cut by a bullet he could if necessary splice it, but I need not add that all control wires were in duplicate to give a double margin of safety. He had a bench and a full kit of tools on board to enable him to carry out necessary repairs in the air. His duties were very similar to those of a ship's carpenter, with this difference—he not only looked after the aircraft, but the men as well, for he acted as cook in the galley and prepared the food.

That morning the rigger exercised all his skill at the two primus stoves in order to prepare a meal worthy of his distinguished passengers. The collapsible table was put up and laid in the ward-room, and the rigger served Lord Gort and Mr. Duff Cooper an excellent luncheon—if we hazard a guess at soup, a nicely cooked grill, a sweet, and biscuits and cheese, with a coffee to round it off, we may not be far out. Certainly many hotels have served a far less appetizing meal than the rigger served that day while the Sunderland was flying along at two miles a minute over the blue seas. However novel and remarkable it may have seemed to Lord Gort and the Minister of Information, the rigger thought little of it: he had done it so often on patrol that he regarded it as a matter of course.

For some hours Lord Gort sat in the second pilot's seat by the side of the captain with whom he chatted from time to time. He gazed out on the sea or glanced at the instrument panel and watched how the pointer of the revolution indicator maintained its steady position and the pointer of the altimeter barely moved at all from the figure 500, which was the height at which they were flying.

In the afternoon the rigger made and served the customary tea, and just before seven o'clock in the evening Rabat was sighted ahead. The pilot circled the place to examine the river on which he was supposed to come down. He did not like the look of it. In normal circumstances no captain of a Sunderland would have dared to risk his aircraft by attempting to alight there.

The river itself was barely 150 feet wide while the wing span of the flying-boat was 113 feet, which left a clearance of only 18 feet on each side of the wings if the pilot came down exactly in the centre. At first sight the problem of the pilot was difficult enough, but the difficulties were increased by a line of native boats moored down either side of the river, to reduce still further the clearance at each side of the wings, while the bends on the river prevented a straight run.

These were not normal circumstances, however. Wider issues were at stake than the safety of the aircraft; these were the safety of Britain and the Empire.

The young Australian pilot eyed the river with an appraising eye, taking it all in, noting the boats and the winding banks. Easing back the control column, he took the flying-boat up to 1,000 feet and circled the town, which lay at the mouth of the river with the build-ings grouped upon the side of a hill that rose about 300 feet above the sea. Sand and scrub stretched beyond the town, and lapping the golden shore was the Atlantic—a most intense blue. Warehouses, offices and shops and dwelling houses shone dazzlingly white in the tropic sun. Native huts sprawled about the banks of the river.

Looking down on the scene with the keenest interest, Lord Gort and the Minister of Information discussed with the pilot the difficulty of alighting there. They could see for themselves that the wings of the aircraft stretched nearly across the river, before they knew what the measurements were. They did not need the pilot to point out that there was too little room. The danger was obvious.

"Do you want to risk a landing or not?" the pilot asked Lord Gort. The ribbon of the Victoria Cross upon the General's breast was a visible sign of his courage.

"Go ahead with the landing," Lord Gort calmly replied.

It was no small responsibility that the young Australian pilot faced. Not only the lives of a distinguished British soldier and statesman, but all they hoped to accomplish depended solely upon his skill and judgment. A trifling miscalculation might well bring disaster to all on board. With the river space so constricted, even the slight cross wind of ten miles an hour might make a difference if due allowance were not made.

Coming in again over the sea, the pilot, cool and imperturbable, gave his orders to the crew to prepare to land. Losing height and speed, he glanced quickly at the banks and, handling the huge flying-boat of twenty-two tons with superb judgment, brought her safely down in the middle of the stream, but he was compelled to use his rudder to get round the bend of the river before he could bring her to a stop 300 yards further on. To alight in such conditions was a feat.

No sooner was the anchor dropped from the forward compartment than some French Air Force officers came out in a small boat to take the passengers and the pilot to the Customs wharf before going to the British Consulate.

The Australian's trained eye noted that the small concrete jetties with their steps leading down to the sea had no lifting derricks and that the river bank steepened toward the mouth where the harbour lay. Here were a few fishing boats, the largest being as big as steam trawlers, and lots of native fishing boats with their picturesque lateen sails. As he re-entered the car to go with his passengers to the Consulate, he saw that the tide was down.

The tarred road over which they drove along the waterfront was thirty feet wide, properly kerbed with concrete pavements; the side roads were just as good, if not so wide; but the roads became rougher just out of the town.

It was the French day of national mourning for the Armistice. Flags were at half mast, all shops were closed. The natives in their flowing robes and fezzes and turbans were grouped together in the streets. Many were puffing away at cigarettes. Here and there solemn black-eyed children waited while their parents talked, and the usual mongrel dogs were nosing about.

As the French Air Force car went by, the groups of natives drew back and began to chatter excitedly. Who were the strangers? What were they doing? These were some of the questions that began to flash round the little place. There was no answer to the questions.

About a mile from the Customs wharf the car stopped and Lord Gort along with the Minister of Information and Squadron Leader Cohen went into the Consulate. The Australian, who was anxious to inform the English authorities of his arrival, consulted the code book of the Consul and sent off a signal: "Landed Rabat 19.00 hours."

It must be remembered that when flying on a secret mission the strictest wireless silence was imposed, for fear the enemy picked up the signals.

Leaving Lord Gort and Mr. Duff Cooper with the Consul and some French Air Force officers of high rank, Squadron Leader Cohen returned to his aircraft, to meet further difficulties.

"The harbour master told me that I must shift my boat upstream because they were expecting fishing vessels in that night and I would have to be clear of the main Customs wharf. As it was low tide, a couple of shoals in the harbour made it dangerous to taxi, so they gave me a motor boat to tow me. The motor boat, however, was very ham-handed, so I had to cast off from it and proceed under my own power, eventually mooring up at a point suggested by the harbour master, a little Frenchman who spoke English slightly, as I spoke French," the Squadron Leader remarked later.

"At dusk a secret signal for Lord Gort was received by the wireless operator on watch. I deciphered this and decided to go ashore to deliver it to him personally, as it was a most important signal. We called for a boat from the shore—we were only twenty yards away—but we could get no reply. So I inflated one of our rubber dinghies and set off with my rigger and fitter—we were all armed with service revolvers. Before we could get ashore a police boat rounded us up and made us go back on board again."

It was plain to the Australian that they were being carefully watched and that orders had been given that they were not to go ashore. But it was essential to get the message to Lord Gort, so the captain of the flying-boat arranged with the rigger and fitter that they should try to steal ashore in the dinghy from the offside of the aircraft while the rest of them kept the police boat busy on the shore side by calling for a boat and distracting their attention as much as possible. For awhile it looked as though the ruse would be successful. The dinghy got away under the cover of the flying-boat's hull and managed to get down to the mouth of the river. Then the police boat spotted it and rushed after it to round up the rigger and fitter. Taking the dinghy in tow, the police boat brought it back to the Sunderland, whereupon the rigger and fitter had to go on board again.

In his quandary, Squadron Leader Cohen decided to make himself as much of a nuisance as possible. It was then about 9.30 and quite dark. "Let's ruin their black-out! Switch on all lights!" he ordered.

At a touch the flying-boat lit up in the darkness, her internal lights, her navigation lights, her steaming lights, her searchlights all flashed out, while one of the crew waved an Aldis signalling lamp around just to make sure that they would not be overlooked. A hubbub at once arose on the police boat, which had been circling them to confine them to the Sunderland and see that they did not escape. "Le Black-out! Le Black-out!" they cried as they circled round.

The crew of the flying-boat, who were enjoying themselves, simply shouted back: "We can't understand! We can't understand!"

"When they come alongside, pull out your revolver and follow me on board," said Squadron Leader Cohen to his second pilot, Pilot Officer D. A. Stuart of the Royal Air Force.

The police in the boat, seeing that no attempt was made to switch off the lights, drew alongside with the intention of enforcing the regulations. At once Squadron Leader Cohen jumped on board with his revolver in his hand and demanded to be put on shore. Pilot Officer Stuart was at his heels with his revolver at the ready. Both pointed their revolvers at the two chief police officers, who, completely taken by surprise, concluded that it was wiser to obey, so the police boat headed to the steps and landed the two officers. At once they were surrounded by the guard on the wharf. Squadron Leader Cohen saw an official from the British Consulate there, but they were not allowed to speak together. To circumvent the Frenchmen, the two pretended to talk to the Frenchmen in front of them, while they whispered to each other in English out of the sides of their mouths and made their plans for a rendezvous.

"The Frenchman in charge told me that if I didn't return to the aircraft at once I would have my aircraft placed under armed guard. I understood quite well what he said and meant," Squadron Leader Cohen said afterwards.

That was the last thing the captain of the aircraft desired, yet it was essential for him to go to Lord Gort. Instantaneously he saw the way out of his dilemma. In his best manner he explained that Stuart was his captain and that he was only the second pilot, but that he had to go ashore to buy rations for the crew.

This sounded plausible enough to the Frenchmen. Letting the Consular official depart, they detained Squadron Leader Cohen for a few minutes while they debated the matter and, thinking that so long as they had the captain of the aircraft safe on board there was no harm in letting his second pilot obtain rations for the crew, they let the Australian go. He hurried in the darkness up the road to the spot where he had agreed to meet the official and found him waiting there with his car. Jumping in, he was soon rushing along the road at fifty miles an hour with headlights blazing, despite the regulations. The whole way along people screamed at them about the black-out. They took no notice. Ignoring the semaphore signs of the traffic police at the roundabouts, they arrived at the Consulate to learn that Lord Gort was not there.

"He's at the hotel," the Squadron Leader was told.

"I'll take you in the car," said a lady, who drove him down to a point from which they could see the hotel. "There it is."

Going there on foot, so as not to attract attention, he was seen to enter the hotel, and he was later seen twice to come to the door of the hotel with Lord Gort, converse with the police on duty at the door and go inside again.

What exactly transpired from the time Squadron Leader Cohen entered the hotel until he left it with Lord Gort is very uncertain. It was common talk in Rabat that Lord Gort was prevented from leaving the hotel, and that the chief of police denied all knowledge of the matter and blamed a subordinate, but no English source can be found to confirm this, so if Lord Gort's appearance at the hotel door and his talk to the police before returning inside seem to lend some credence to this talk, the matter nevertheless remains in doubt.

There is, however, no uncertainty about the fact that he failed utterly to make any contact with the French statesman whom he hoped to see and that no word or message of any sort passed between them.

The third time that Lord Gort and the Squadron Leader came to the door of the hotel, they passed to the car and were driven off to pick up Mr. Duff Cooper. It was between 2 o'clock and 3 o'clock in the early morning of June 26th that the party arrived back at the Customs wharf and went on board the Sunderland.

For the rest of the night Squadron Leader Cohen kept his crew on duty with the guns fully manned. The situation seemed delicate and he had no intention of being surprised. Meanwhile the police boat kept a close watch on them.

Ten minutes before dawn, Squadron Leader Cohen gave the order to cast off and taxied quickly outside the harbour to the open sea. There was a long swell running which made the take-off risky, owing to the possibility of knocking off a float and making the landing dangerous. But Lord Gort, who was consulted, promptly gave his permission. Bounding on the top of one or two swells, the giant flying-boat rose in the air and by 8 o'clock that morning was dropping her passengers at Admiralty steps in Gibraltar Harbour.

Next morning an hour before dawn the flying-boat took wing again, and by tea-time that afternoon she settled down at Calshot on Southampton water.

One day history may relate what transpired in Rabat when General Lord Gort, V.C., and the Right Hon. Mr. Duff Cooper, M.P., were trying to rally the French to fight on. This is the appendix to that secret and unwritten history. The Distinguished Flying Cross which was awarded to Squadron Leader Cohen was a tribute not only to his brilliant qualities as a pilot when he landed in that narrow winding river in North Africa, but to his cool resource in all the emergencies which arose from a difficult situation.

CHAPTER III

THE SUBMARINE HUNTER

"THE luckiest man in the R.A.F.," was the way in which Flight Lieutenant E. R. Baker was once described, and few in the Royal Air Force or Royal Navy would disagree. Information concerning him, however, was so meagre that one morning I trudged through the deep snow of a distant city to travel all day in search of someone who knew him.

Around that city dozens of motor cars lay abandoned in the drifts, but the train gradually carried me into a belt of country that was quite balmy and spring-like, with no snow to be seen. It was an astonishing transformation. For hours I journeyed slowly through sunny valleys over which the touch of spring already seemed to hover. It was lovely country with beauty everywhere, far removed from war. But the tops of the mountains piling up around were covered with snow. Now and again the sun was reflected by fairy-like waterfalls which had solidified into icicles, and by evening I arrived at my destination.

Never in my life have I seen anything more beautiful than the scene which greeted me next morning. The snow on the peaks around was turned to a rosy pink by the sun, their bases were purple and blue, lovely clouds made a pattern in the sky and in the fore-ground were sparkling blue waters with ships falling picturesquely into place and Sunderland flying-boats at their moorings, while the buildings of the town were grouped so artistically round the waters that it was difficult to believe that this enchanted place was in the British Isles.

Gazing on the scene to take in its full beauty before the changing light banished the exquisite tones, I went on to pay a call to try to find out something about the luckiest man in the Royal Air Force.

He was, I learned, 6 feet 2 inches tall, with a spare figure, very blue eyes, a small fair moustache to set off a well-cut mouth and firm chin, and a natural wave in his fairish hair. Very modest, quiet of speech, with a sense of humour, Flight Lieutenant Ernest Reginald Baker, D.F.C., had at that time wrought more havoc among the German U-boat fleet than any other man in the fighting services. He was the captain of a Sunderland flying-boat which he regarded with as much affection and pride as any owner of a shapely yacht. His flying-boat, which he christened Queen of the Air, had her name painted over the doorway leading into the hull, and over the name were painted four white stars.

Those stars were signs of high honour, for each represented a submarine which was sunk by Flight Lieutenant Baker and his crew of the Queen of the Air. Happily the same boat and crew took part in all four triumphs.

At the beginning of 1941 Flight Lieutenant Baker had already done 1000 hours of active service flying. Before the war he was the second pilot of a Sunderland flying-boat.

"My skipper, who taught me all I know about flying-boats, was a South African—Flight Lieutenant A. S. Ainslie. He won the D.F.C. He was the grandest chap I've ever known—we used to call him Angel. Unfortunately he got shot down by a U-boat," Baker once remarked.

They were out on patrol on September 3, 1939, and when they alighted at 4 o'clock in the afternoon they had no idea that war had been declared, nor had they a gun or a bomb on board.

On September 9th, they took off on their first war patrol and were lucky enough to sight a submarine on that initial trip. They at once attacked with bombs, but to their chagrin the submarine escaped. During their second patrol on September 14th, they again sighted a submarine and let loose their load of bombs, but once more the enemy eluded them. On September 16th they went out for their third patrol and sighted their third submarine which was promptly bombed without avail.

Three submarines sighted on three trips and not one attack successful—there is no need to touch on their feelings! Hopefully they took the air again on September 19th, and generous Dame Fortune gave them another chance to sink an enemy submarine, but although their bombs crashed down without delay, the U-boat got away. Thus on four successive patrols Flight Lieutenant Ainslie and his second pilot Flight Lieutenant Baker had the unusual luck to sight four submarines and the misfortune to lose them all.

By trial and error some of the greatest discoveries have been made. As attacks had not given the results expected, it seemed that something more was needed to bring success. The question remained whether the method of attack and the weapons employed were the most suitable for the purpose. That was the problem which all those engaged on the task had to work out.

The following months increased the experience of Flight Lieutenant Baker. On those long patrols which took him hundreds of miles out into the Atlantic to watch over the convoys of ships that were conveying essentials to Great Britain, his knowledge of the tricks of the weather and the sea grew with every hour that was added to his flying time. He tasted the joy of being promoted to command a fine new flying-boat which to him and her crew was the Queen of the Air, and he suffered the loss of his friend Ainslie, who was shot down by a U-boat.

It looked as though Dame Fortune, who had given him four chances to sink enemy submarines in the first month of the war, viewed him with disfavour. Then early on August 16, 1940, he dropped into the launch at the quay to be rushed out to the Queen of the Air, and by 7 o'clock he opened the throttle, taxied over the water and took off to pick up a convoy and go on anti-submarine patrol. It was a dreadful day. The rain poured down and the base of the clouds was within 400 feet of the sea. The Sunderland thrashed through it, but the weather was so bad that her captain once said that he almost decided to go home. He changed his mind, however—which was as well.

Six hours of flying brought little improvement in the weather, but the activities going on at the primus stoves in the galley reminded the crew, whose appetites were in no way affected by weather or anything else, that lunch was ready, so they settled down to enjoy their meal and a friendly chat.

The engines roared rhythmically as the flying-boat cruised over the sea with the captain at the controls. The second pilot kept a keen watch on the seas below, though the bad weather made visibility poor. Suddenly the second pilot let out a shout of "sub!" and pointed to port. A glance revealed the U-boat to the captain, who instantly sounded the warning Klaxon which made the crew drop knives and forks and jump to action stations.

"I put my foot on everything!" was the graphic way the captain on his return explained how he unleashed all his power to get to the submarine before it could escape. "The U-boat was on the surface when we sighted it, and they must have sighted us at the same time, for they started to do a crash dive. By the time the submarine was down, I was diving low over the top of it to drop a depth charge. The result was terrific. The whole of the surface of the sea seemed to shudder for yards around and then suddenly blew up. In the middle of the boiling sea the submarine emerged with its decks awash, then sank rather like a brick. I did a steep turn and came over it again just as it was disappearing. The explosion actually blew the submarine right out of the water. There was such an enormous amount of it out of water that my rigger saw daylight under it. I turned and climbed, and as the submarine heaved on its side and sank I dropped my bombs right across it. Large air bubbles came rushing up—one was over thirty feet across. Then great gobs of oil began to spread over the surface until a wide area was covered. I waited for about an hour until there was no more air or oil coming up, then I fetched a destroyer from the convoy and signalled what had happened. After carrying out an Asdic sweep and reporting no contact, the destroyer signalled to me: 'Nice work. I hope you get your reward!' ''

From the moment the submarine was sighted until it was destroyed only ninety seconds elapsed. A submarine can crash dive in about forty seconds, and unless the first blow is struck at it within about this time, there is a good chance of it escaping, so it will be realized that the captain and crew of a flying-boat must act instantly, without a second's hesitation, if they are to sink the U-boat. Obviously much depends on the distance at which the submarine is sighted and the time that the flying-boat takes to reach the spot.

So steeply did the captain bank the Queen of the Air to bring her round with the least possible delay, that each time he turned, members of the crew were flung about, and the observer who tried to take photographs collapsed on the bottom of the boat in a heap. But it was the rear-gunner who came off worst. Sitting in the tail waiting for a chance to have a crack at something, he suddenly thought that somebody was having a crack at him, for the flying-boat was so low when she made her attack that the force of the explosion gave her tail a jolt which bounced him out of his seat hard up against the top of the turret, with the result that his souvenir of the action was a large bump on top of the head. Of course, the other members of the crew laughed—no one was in a mood to do anything else after their triumph.

But as base was informed and the Queen of the Air continued to guard her convoy, memories of the grandest chap he'd ever known crept into the mind of the blue-eyed pilot sitting so quietly at the controls. ''Well, thank God, that's one back for Angel!'' was his first reaction.

As the rigger made a cup of tea to take to the captain, he was heard to remark: ''I'll bet those fellows in the sub are drinking salt water now instead of tea!''

The Queen of the Air taxied to her moorings about 7.30 that evening, after flying for twelve and a half hours. Shortly afterwards the first white star appeared on her hull.

Less than a fortnight later, on August 29th, just before dawn, the Queen of the Air began to roar over the waters. The smoke from the adjacent city mingled with the mist to add to the difficulties of that particular base, but she got safely away and was soon heading out to sea to pick up her convoy. At dawn contact was made and thereafter for hour on hour the captain and crew of the Sunderland carried out their normal submarine patrol, circling the convoy and flying ahead to search for submarines or mines in the course of the ships.

About 11 o'clock that morning the escorting destroyer signalled: "There's a U-boat about here somewhere." The sensitive ears of the Asdic had detected the sound of the submarine moving under the sea and the naval commander had at once invoked the eyes overhead to help to find the enemy.

Diving low, the flying-boat began a creeping line ahead search, but it was about ten minutes before the keen eyes on the aircraft saw the track of the submarine's periscope. Instantly the captain attacked with a depth charge, flinging the crew about as he came round steeply to get in another attack before climbing to finish the U-boat off with bombs. He made no mistake. All that he had been taught about the distance a submarine can travel under water in a minute was in his mind as he made his three attacks along the track of the invisible enemy. Directly the Sunderland had finished attacking, the destroyer came roaring on the scene to add a few more depth charges just to make sure. The huge air bubbles which belched up to the surface and the gobs of oil which appeared and spread over the area marked the destruction of the enemy. When the destroyer carried out a sweep with the Asdic, she signalled: "No contact. Sub destroyed."

That evening the Queen of the Air landed at her base at 6 o'clock with a very happy crew. If anyone had cause for complaint it was the rear-gunner who had another large bump on the top of his head to prove how the explosion had flicked the tail and jolted him hard against the top of the turret. But he was in no mood to grouse. He was quite willing to stand any number of bumps providing they got the U-boats. So, with due ceremony, the second white star was painted on the hull of the flying-boat.

The third white star was earned on October 17th, about 300 miles away from Cape Wrath, that bleak headland in the north of Scotland, where the Atlantic pours through the Pentland Firth into the North Sea, often with such fury under the lash of the gales that the English Channel at its worst bears no comparison. Getting away in the dark about 5.30 in the morning, the crew of the flying-boat watched the dawn gradually light up the sea beneath them. For several hundred miles they cruised on their normal routine of guarding a convoy when, about 9.30, the warning Klaxon blared through the aircraft.

The front gunner sighted the submarine on the starboard side and at once signalled and opened fire. It was on the surface and travelling towards the convoy, but a smart look-out was being kept on the submarine, for it immediately did a crash dive. Quickly as it tried to escape, however, it was seconds too slow for the Sunderland, whose captain sent her diving down to attack. Round came the flying-boat, throwing her crew about, to attack again. Just before this attack, all on board felt the flying-boat stagger as a great blow hit the tail. "There was a most colossal crack on the tail plane," explained Flight Lieutenant Baker later. "It gave us a big shaking."

The rear-gunner who received his usual bump on the head when the first attack was made, got a nastier bump still the second time round, for there was a big explosion inside the submarine and he saw pieces of wreckage flying up out of the sea and felt them hitting the tail plane. "The tail plane has been damaged by wreckage from the sub," he reported to the captain.

They watched the surface of the sea belching great air bubbles, saw the oil gushing up and spreading wider and wider, and as the sea quietened down the captain turned the flying-boat for home. "Are you all right?" he inquired of the rear-gunner through the "intercom."—this is the service way of describing the inter-communication system between the members of an aircraft.

The rear-gunner felt his bumps. "There is no need for you to press the buzzer in future," he replied, "as every time I get a crack on the head I shall know you've got a sub."

They landed safely at base, to find their tail plane fabric badly cut about in dozens of places by the wreckage hurled up from the exploding submarine. In due course the third star made its appearance on the hull of the Queen of the Air.

They were a happy crew who manned the Queen of the Air; they came to know each other so well during those long and, for the most part, monotonous patrols that in an emergency they knew exactly what to do and did it automatically. If the skipper got a laugh at the bumps of the rear-gunner, the rear-gunner and the rest of the crew got many a laugh at the expense of the skipper. Often the Klaxon blared out to send them to action stations where they waited tensely to attack, only to find that the skipper had dived down on some innocent basking sharks or a whale which he had mistaken for submarines.

"They used to laugh themselves silly," the skipper once remarked.

So at his appointed times the captain of the Queen of the Air continued to take her across hundreds of miles of ocean to help to bring the tall ships, the food ships and ammunition ships and tank ships and aeroplane ships, safely to the shores of England. And throughout those long patrols, keen eyes on the flying-boat searched for a sight of submarine or periscope, while the captain was ready to let loose death and destruction upon the German outlaws of the sea.

The weeks passed uneventfully until the beginning of December. At dawn on December 6, 1940, he took the Queen of the Air off the water and flew north to shepherd a convoy. The weather was unspeakable. The cloud base was down to 300 feet and visibility was nil. It was raining and snowing hard and the temperature was at zero. They thrashed along for hour after hour, peering out and seeing nothing, wondering where their convoy was and if the rain and flurries of snow would ever hold up.

Then the miracle happened. Quite suddenly about 1 o'clock the weather broke in a perfectly straight line across the sky. "It was the most amazing thing I have ever seen in my life. We stuck the nose of the aircraft out into clear weather while the tail was still enveloped in clouds," the captain said afterwards when he came to explain this phenomenon. "It took us a few seconds to grow accustomed to this bright light after flying in gloom for so long. As the second pilot and I blinked and looked ahead, we both sighted a sub at the identical moment, turned our faces to each other, opened our mouths together and howled in unison 'Sub!' It was rather funny."

In that clear area, about a mile away, a large submarine of about 3,000 tons was travelling at ten knots on the surface. The aircraft which had been flying at cruising speed suddenly accelerated as her captain went after his quarry. He could see men on the conning tower and recognized her as an Italian submarine of the Ballilla class.

The men on the conning tower saw their doom approaching. Quick as they were to close the conning tower and open the valves to flood the tanks that would take them down to safety, they were too late.

As the Queen of the Air dived, her skipper saw part of the stern of the submarine still showing. He struck home on each side with depth charges and there was a big explosion as he climbed to renew the attack.

The rear-gunner, rubbing the usual bump on his head, looked down excitedly. "There's a sheet of metal about six feet by four just been hurled out of the sea. It was all torn and twisted," he reported to the captain.

The crew of the flying-boat, circling round, gazed on the waters. There was no doubt about the destruction of the Italian submarine. The air released from the shattered craft shot up like fountains for six feet above the surface. The oil gushed up and spread until an area of about a square mile was covered with it.

"These Italians seem to be having a hell of a fine time in this war!" commented the wireless operator. "They're getting it where the chink got the chopper."

It was indeed amazing the way the weather cleared to enable them to sight and sink the submarine; it was no less amazing the way it closed down again as soon as their task was completed. The weather in fact grew so bad that the flying-boat could not make contact with her convoy, so she was obliged to return to base, where her skipper reported his fourth success and the crew duly painted the fourth star above her name.

Thus by sinking four enemy submarines before the end of 1940, Flight Lieutenant E. R. Baker, D.F.C., made ample amends for missing those four U-boats in September, 1939, while patrolling with his friend, the late Flight Lieutenant Ainslie, D.F.C.

CHAPTER IV

THE LOSS OF H.M.S. GLORIOUS

DURING the land battle of Narvik, when the Allies were closing in on the isolated German forces in order to capture the town, from which millions of tons of Swedish iron ore a year were conveyed to Germany by sea, the information reached the Allied staff that the Germans were landing troops from flying-boats south of the port. The Germans holding the town were resisting strongly. They had made the most of the natural defences, and to overcome their resistance in the shortest time it was essential to prevent reinforcements and supplies from reaching them.

Accordingly Flight Lieutenant P. G. Jameson, a New Zealand pilot who had flown daily from a British aircraft carrier to patrol over Narvik since the battle began, was instructed with two other members of his squadron to see if they could locate the flying-boats.

Taking off in their fighters, they climbed to look round before flying to the coast. In the most systematic way they began their search.

The fiords were so winding, the declivities of many so steep, that it was not easy to sight a small object such as a camouflaged flying-boat from any great height. The top of an overhanging cliff could easily conceal from a fast-moving aircraft an enemy aircraft moored at the base.

Flight Lieutenant Jameson pushed the control column gently forward to skim the sea in order to scan both sides of the fiords. Easing it back as the fiords narrowed, he climbed to examine them to the innermost end. Fiord after fiord was searched by the three pilots, but no sign of a flying-boat met their eyes.

Eventually a glance at the clock and the fuel indicator told Flight Lieutenant Jameson that in about fifty minutes he would have to return to his base; there was not too much time left for finding the flying-boats—if they existed.

"So I thought I'd go down Romsbachs Fiord where the German headquarters were and have a look there," he stated afterwards.

They flew up the fiord, looking down on the wrecks of the German vessels in Narvik Bay which were the visible sign of the triumph of the British Navy that evening of April 13, 1940. Flying past the port into the further arm of the fiord, exactly as the British destroyers swept on to find and destroy other enemy warships that lay out of sight round the corner, Flight Lieutenant Jameson came upon two four-engined flying-boats concealed in a little cove.

Not only had the Germans chosen their hiding place with care, but they had moored the aircraft in a position which made them difficult to attack. They were tucked close in under the edge of a cliff, with a gun mounted nearby to protect them and augment their own armament. On the opposite side of the fiord the cliff was 800 feet high, and any aircraft making a direct attack could do so only by diving over the edge of the cliff and running the risk of colliding with the opposite cliff, for the fiord here was narrow.

The risks were accepted by the pilots without a second thought. Circling round, Flight Lieutenant Jameson examined the position to determine the exact spot from which to attack. Calling up his fellow pilots to tell them to concentrate on the first flying-boat and follow him in to the attack, he dived over the top of the cliff and the roar of his guns reverberated through the fiord.

Soon tongues of flame enveloped the flying-boat as the petrol tank was pierced. Looking down, Flight Lieutenant Jameson saw three men tumble into a dinghy and go ashore, just as he opened his attack on the second flying-boat. This, too, was eventually set on fire, and the pilots returned to base to report their success.

"It was my first action," Flight Lieutenant Jameson remarked later, "and I've never been so thrilled in my life. I've done a good deal of deer stalking and wild pig hunting in New Zealand, but they seem tame after that." He was born at Wellington, New Zealand, in 1912 and after joining the Royal Air Force in 1936 as a Pilot Officer he won promotion until at the time of writing he had attained the rank of Wing Commander with the honours of the D.S.O., the D.F.C. and Bar.

About 3 o'clock next morning, just as he and the other pilots were about to start on their normal patrol, they were told that enemy aircraft were over Narvik. Taking off, they arrived over the town at a height of 4,000 feet. In a few moments one of the pilots called up Flight Lieutenant Jameson. "I've sighted enemy aircraft," he said.

"Lead me on to them," replied the leader, who pulled back the stick to climb quickly after the other pilot.

"He went ahead, and shortly afterwards I sighted them and called him back to rejoin formation, but he did not hear. There were three enemy aircraft flying in line astern at 10,000 feet, with half a mile between each. The leader was a Heinkel 111 and the others were Junkers 88. He drifted out to attack the leader, and I went up to attack the rear Junkers," said Flight Lieutenant Jameson in describing the action. "I closed to 150 yards, and at my very first burst there was a terrific flash and my windscreen was obscured with oil and glycol. I broke away and circled above for a few seconds, and saw that his starboard propeller was stopping and his engine smoking. I went in again to give him another long burst, and as I was about to open fire he dropped his bombs and turned away south. I saw his starboard petrol tank between the engine and fuselage burst into flames and followed him down. Just before he crashed on top of a cliff, one of the crew baled out and alighted in the fiord—I don't know what happened to him."

Flight Lieutenant Jameson was later to learn how cruel and cold the sea can be, for he was one of the few survivors from the aircraft carrier *Glorious* which the Germans sank in those northern waters to add the culminating touch to the Norwegian tragedy. Of the twenty-seven men who originally scrambled on his float, only nine survived, among them three members of the Royal Air Force. On another float which provided about sixty men with a refuge directly the ship went down, only five men came through that terrible ordeal. One or two officers of the Fleet Air Arm who flew the Swordfish on the *Glorious* were also among the thirty-six men who were picked up, while five more men were found and imprisoned by the enemy.

The sinking of the *Glorious*, with its heavy death roll, was one of the most tragic episodes of the Norwegian campaign. Rumour was rife about it. Here so far as can be learned from sources available to the writer is an account of the end of the *Glorious* on June 8, 1940, and the experiences of some of the survivors.

In a choppy sea, with good visibility and no cloud, the aircraft carrier *Glorious* was steaming at seventeen knots when, about four o'clock in the afternoon, two enemy cruisers were sighted. At once orders were given on the *Glorious* to bring her Swordfish aircraft up to the flight deck and prepare to attack the cruisers. Unfortunately, the Swordfish were loaded with anti-submarine bombs, with a view to taking off at a moment's notice to attack any submarines that were sighted, and it was necessary to unload the bombs and reload with torpedoes which alone made possible an effective attack on the cruisers that later proved to be the *Scharnhorst* and the *Gneisenau*.

By this time all the men were at action stations. The German cruisers fired a ranging salvo, which missed. But the next salvo was dead on the target. The shells burst in the top hangar and set all the aircraft alight. Petrol and oil blazed up and made it impossible to get out the torpedoes with which to load the Swordfish for their attack on the cruisers. Then salvo followed salvo, hitting the ship all the while and adding to the destruction.

The destroyer *Acusta*, acting as one of the escorts of the *Glorious*, sped toward the enemy battle-cruisers to deliver a torpedo attack. It was a most gallant action, ranking with the finest deeds of the Royal Navy, for the commander knew that he stood little chance in the face of such impossible odds. The guns of the cruisers ranged on the destroyer rushing toward them. A salvo crashed home and she blew up and went down with her ensign flying. Without hesitation Commander C. E. Glassfurd sacrificed the *Acusta* and himself in his attempt to save the *Glorious*.

While this tragedy was happening, the other destroyer, *Ardent*, steamed at speed to lay a smoke screen round the *Glorious* to hide her from the enemy cruisers and obscure their target. Even as the smoke screen was being laid, orders were given on the *Glorious* to take up stations and prepare to abandon ship. The aircraft carrier was still moving at high speed. The laying of the smoke screen brought a lull in the firing, and the captain, no doubt thinking there might still be a chance of escaping, ordered the men back to action stations.

"The thing which struck me most was the way the ordinary seamen carried out orders—absolutely no sign of panic or anything," a survivor remarked.

Then salvoes of six-inch and eight-inch shells started again, hitting all the time. They shattered the bridge, wrecked the forward part of the ship, started up fires everywhere. The German cruisers had the *Glorious* at their mercy and it was impossible for her to escape.

Once more orders were given to prepare to abandon ship. This time she was burning so fiercely that those on board knew she could not last. Without the slightest fuss and without waste of time they began to prepare to save themselves.

Carley floats and rafts and planks were got up on the quarter-deck and thrown over to support survivors until they were picked up. The only boat that got away was a little dinghy which was pushed over the stern from the quarter-deck. Men quickly jumped over and clambered into it.

The life-jacket of Flight Lieutenant Jameson was in his cabin down below along with his log book, which contained the notes of all his flying operations and flying times. A pilot's log book is his most precious possession, as it is to the captain of a ship. At that moment of jeopardy he was apparently determined to save his log book, if he lost everything else.

He was seen to go down to his cabin, while his Commanding Officer and two other members of his squadron were on the quarter-deck. Moving rapidly, he attempted to reach his cabin, only to find that he was shut off from it by a water-tight door. Running up to the quarter-deck again, he found that his companions had all disappeared over the side.

He took off his flying boots and was just about to jump over when he saw a raft, which was being towed by the *Glorious*, strike a rating, who was swimming in the water, a terrific blow on the head and lay open his brow. He moved along to avoid a similar danger and then jumped over. For a quarter of a mile he swam to a Carley float on which he saw his Commanding Officer.

"Hallo, sir, can I come on your raft?" asked the New Zealand pilot. There was still one destroyer floating and they were not worrying at all. They thought they would be picked up either by the destroyer or the Germans. A couple of ratings soon reached down and helped him on the raft.

By that time there were about twenty-seven on it. But there were no oars. A rating pointed to one floating about ten yards away and the young New Zealand pilot promptly dived in and recovered it. That oar helped quite a lot, for they were able to rig it with a sail made out of a pull-over and a shirt. Then the man who was injured by the raft swam along hanging to a plank. He must have been as tough as nails, for it was a great feat of his to get to the Carley float.

Lots of men were floating in their life-jackets; many were hanging to planks of wood; the sea was dotted with them. The German cruisers came to within a mile and a half of them, still firing at the remaining destroyer, which fired back as hard as it could. It continued firing right up to the time it sank. The men on the float saw it disappear; they were watching it very intently, hoping when the Germans went that it would pick them up.

So the destroyer *Ardent* went down with colours-flying, firing to the end, and crippling the *Scharnhorst* with a torpedo before she sank. The Royal Navy on that black day lived up to its finest traditions.

By now the *Glorious* was stopped. She was absolutely obscured by smoke. From the Carley float they could see no portion of the ship at all, only those great clouds of smoke on the surface of the sea, so they did not actually see her sink. Amid that shroud of smoke from her burning debris, she vanished beneath the waters, unseen by any human eye.

In those northern latitudes it was light all night. The Carley float was crowded, and the waves continually washed right over the men. So cold was the sea that within four hours men started to die from exposure. The strongest among them did what they could to help and comfort the others. They held the heads of the dying men out of the water, and when they died the bodies were committed to the sea. Some of the survivors had on so few clothes that it was necessary to remove some of the clothes from the dead to clothe the living in order to keep the spark of life in their frozen bodies.

When the men first got on the Carley float some of them started to sing cheery and popular songs. As the hours went by, they sang a hymn or two. Then as the cold gripped them they fell into silence. They were drenched to the skin, and lacked water and food.

By next morning ten men were left on the float, among them three members of the Royal Air Force, Flight Lieutenant Jameson, his Commanding Officer and an aircraftman. Eighteen died that first night.

In the afternoon of the next day it became calm and one survivor remarked that it would have been quite pleasant if they had possessed something to eat and drink and a few more clothes. One man went to sleep and fell overboard, but they were too weak to pull him back. Two others died from exposure. The others spoke very little and there were no complaints at all.

They just endured and hoped. On the second day the Commanding Officer made a suggestion which did much to aid their ultimate survival. "If we cut the bottom out of the float and put it across the top, we may be able to get a little sleep," he said.

Without delay they set about this task, and they found that it was a big improvement. It not only enabled them to snatch a little sleep, but to a certain extent it kept their legs out of the water.

"One of the things which got us down was the fact that we saw a British cruiser squadron of three or four ships searching for us. They put up an aircraft and we saw it taking off and landing, but it did not come in our direction," one of the survivors stated. "We saw several of our own aircraft as well as those of the enemy, but they never spotted us." Who can plumb their agony of mind as they saw those searching ships turn and vanish from sight?

The rating with the injured head clung grimly to life. He grew weaker under the exposure, but he was still alive next day, although he began to wander in his mind. No one could help him. Some were weaker than others, but all were suffering from the exposure and strain.

Then a corporal of marines dropped asleep, lost his balance and fell over into the sea. Weak as they were, they managed to grab him before he floated away, and after a big struggle dragged him out of the sea to safety.

A couple of hours afterwards one of the ratings sighted a trawler. "There's a ship!" he said.

"We'd been seeing ships before," said one of the survivors. "We looked round and saw the ship about two miles away. It was coming towards us. We could see the masts in line. When it got to within one mile of us it turned off—it was an awful moment—but the trawler only stopped to pick up people off another Carley float, then it came on towards us. By this time one of the officers was waving his yellow Mae West and we all shouted as much as we could. They soon came alongside and one of the Norwegians got down the ladder on to the float and made a loop of rope in which he hoisted the worst cases up on board. Those who were not so weak were helped up the ladder.

"No one could have been kinder to us than those Norwegians—their kindness was beyond praise! They gave up their bunks for the worst cases—there were thirty-six survivors in all. They gave us cigarettes, shared out their only half bottle of whisky among us, and made tea and coffee for us. Then they pointed out the best and warmest places in which to sleep, while they slept on deck or anywhere else they could find."

After picking up the survivors of the *Glorious*, the fishermen set their course for the Faroes, while the cook in the galley made some Scotch broth for them which was the finest food they had ever tasted in their lives. It was rather sad that the injured seaman who had clung so desperately to life should die after being taken on board.

The trawler was not equipped with wireless, so her skipper could not inform the British authorities that he had picked up the survivors of the *Glorious*, thus for nearly a week it was feared that there were no survivors at all. So the trawler plugged along in fairly heavy seas at about eight knots, while the Norwegian fishermen lavished all the care and attention in their power upon the men they had rescued, nursing them and feeding them and making them as comfortable as they could in the circumstances.

After a rough passage lasting three days, the trawler arrived at the Faroe Islands, where British army officers met the survivors and notified the British authorities of their rescue.

CHAPTER V

WING COMMANDER D. R. S. BADER, D.S.O. AND BAR, D.F.C. AND BAR

THE fascination exercised by the sea over sailors is well-known, and there is no doubt that the air exercises a similar fascination over many airmen who have fought and trounced the German legions in the skies. Just as the born sailor feels in his element when he is at sea, so did Wing Commander Bader feel in his element in the air, for his eagerness to fly at all times was always impossible to conceal.

Born in London in the neighbourhood of Regent's Park in 1910, Douglas Robert Stewart Bader went to St. Edward's School at Oxford to receive his education. By the time he was eighteen years old he had thoroughly made up his mind that he wanted to be a pilot in the Royal Air Force. Accordingly he went from school at Oxford to the Royal Air Force College at Cranwell as a cadet to receive a thorough grounding in the theory and practice of flight and in 1930 he received with pride his commission as a Pilot Officer in the Royal Air Force.

The very keenness and mastery of the air which he displayed almost led to his undoing. Taking off in a Sopwith Bulldog on the morning of December 14, 1931, he flew around and, diving low, started to stunt about ten feet from the ground. A slight misjudgment, a touch of the aircraft on the grass, and Pilot Officer Bader who had been stunting so joyously a second earlier lay mangled among the wreckage.

He was shockingly injured. His right leg was nearly severed above the knee, his left terribly smashed below, with broken ribs and an injured lung to make his recovery seem almost impossible. The extraordinary thing is that he remained conscious all the time. His body was shattered, but his mind remained clear. It was a significant fact which showed the beginning of that strength of mind which was later to become manifest to the world.

Tenderly he was extricated from the wreckage and rushed by ambulance to the Royal Berkshire Hospital at Reading where his clothes were cut from him and he was put upon the operating table and under an anaesthetic without delay. With the right leg practically off, there was nothing to be done except amputate it. Deftly the surgeon tied up the blood vessels and applied the dressings. The left leg was carefully examined, the fractured bones set, in the hope of preserving it.

Somehow his wonderful vitality enabled him to survive the shock, but it became increasingly evident that his left leg could not be saved, so it was amputated a week after the accident. During the following fortnight death hovered very near, his black hair making more pronounced his pallid face, which was as white as the pillow. The lamp of life burned very dimly indeed in his body throughout those three weeks.

Then a most pronounced change took place. He started to improve and, once on the way to recovery, made rapid progress. His well-developed, sturdy body gathered strength, the stumps of his legs healed. The day came when a wooden peg was strapped to his leg and he took a pair of crutches and began to get about again. It felt strange to a young man who had been used to playing games, whose whole temperament was keyed up to rapid movement. Without legs, condemned to getting about on crutches—the disability must have been very bitter. Yet, strangely enough, he was not depressed. The kindness all about him in the hospital helped him more than he knew.

Directly after the accident the main concern of the doctors was to save his life. They were compelled to do the best they could with his maimed limbs in order not to add to the shock, which would otherwise have killed him, although it was plain that his limbs would need further attention later on. In three months when he was fit and strong again, he was wheeled once more to the operating theatre where the stumps of his legs were re-amputated for permanent healing. His physical condition at that time was so good that in a fortnight he had his wooden peg on his leg again and was moving about on crutches. He spent two more months in the hospital at Reading, amid the kindness of doctors and nurses that will ever remain in his memory.

It seemed rather ironical that while he was lying in bed without legs his promotion to Flying Officer should have been gazetted, yet so it was. Not a man in his place but what would have been convinced beyond all doubt that his flying career was at an end. Flying Officer Bader was the one young man in the world who was not convinced. On the contrary there was in his mind the idea that somehow at sometime he would once more climb into the clouds and be as free as the birds on the wing.

Five months after his accident, he went off to Roehampton to be fitted with his two duralumin legs. That was his testing time, when the strength of his mind alone triumphed over the disabilities of his body. He was determined, no matter what happened, that once his legs were fitted he would never make use of a stick to help him to walk.

He never did. The first time his legs were fitted, he rose upon them unsteadily and walked a step or two. He strove to walk again, just like a baby, falling down sometimes, but rising with his determination to succeed growing stronger than ever. Occasionally he would take the arm of another patient for support, but always there was the inflexible mind to drive his body to do his bidding. Time and again he tried, learning how to balance his body upon his metal legs.

Only he knows the difficulties he surmounted. Sometimes he was depressed beyond words. No one could help him. He had to fight the fight alone and win the victory in his mind, to abolish all doubts, to feel sure beyond peradventure that he could stand as firmly upon his artificial legs as he once stood upon his own. Orderlies and the boys in the hospital watched him fighting his battle. They lent what aid they could, and he was filled with gratitude; but they could not know the depths he plumbed, he who had been so active.

It took him three weeks to learn to walk, three of the most depressing weeks of his life. By then he had largely mastered the technique, the art of balancing, all the little movements of walking and sitting and rising from a chair. By then he began to feel that the seemingly insuperable difficulty had been overcome and that the rest would follow . . . it was just a matter of time and practice.

Following that month in hospital at Roehampton, he was granted two months leave, part of which was spent at his home in Yorkshire. Then he went off to spend some of his holiday with his friend Sir Philip Sassoon. While there he experienced the greatest thrill of his life. An aircraft stood before him—it was an Avro No. 504 K—and he climbed in, not with the old agility, perhaps, but with considerably greater ease than most people exercise the first time they clamber into an aircraft. He settled himself into place, had a good look round the cockpit, waggled the stick, fingered the throttle and swung the rudder from side to side with his artificial legs just to get the feel of it.

He was going to fly again. He felt sure he could do it. There was no doubt about it. Perhaps, far, far back in his mind there lurked the merest shadow of uncertainty, so slight as to be almost unnoticed. So he took off, as he had done hundreds of times before, to enjoy the ecstasy of flight, landing perfectly to demonstrate to the world that a man, given the will and skill, can fly as well with artificial legs as with his own. He had no trouble at all. That day he proved to himself that the so-called impossible was possible.

In September, 1932, he went back to duty at Uxbridge. Later he was posted to the Central Flying School where he was permitted by the medical board to fly in dual controlled aircraft. It soon became obvious that he flew as competently and confidently with his artificial legs as any pilot could fly with his own legs. The accident had not affected his nerve. He could do all the aerobatics with the same joy and abandon as of old. The result was that he flew all the normal service types of aircraft without any difficulty and went off from the Central Flying School with a letter written to the Air Ministry saying he was 100 per cent competent as a pilot.

Fortified by his recent flying experience, with such a letter to back him, he went up for his final medical examination before the Central Medical Board, thinking it would be merely a formality and that he would at once be passed as fit. Physically he was as fit as any man alive.

To his consternation the Board refused to pass him. He could hardly believe his ears.

"I'm sorry we cannot pass you fit, because there is nothing in the King's Regulations which covers your case," said the President.

It was true. There was nothing in the King's Regulations to cover the case of the one man in the world who was genius enough to fly as well with artificial legs as the ordinary pilot flies with his own legs.

The iron will which had sustained the brilliant young pilot through all those dark days and had enabled him to accomplish a miracle broke down before that verdict. He lost his temper. The injustice of deluding him by letting him go back to fly and then rejecting him when he had proved himself fit was too much for him to suffer in silence.

His protests, however, made no difference. A few weeks later he received a letter from the Air Ministry asking him to resign on the grounds of ill-health. In the circumstances there was nothing he could do, so Flying Officer Bader was forced to relinquish the career he loved, the one which he had chosen above all others, the one in which he had sacrificed his limbs and nearly his life and for which he had learned to do what no other man had ever done.

Sadly the young pilot gave up his career in the Royal Air Force and in May, 1933, joined the staff of the Asiatic Petroleum Company, donning a hard hat and the clothes of a city man in place of the Air Force blue, reaching the office at 9 o'clock in the morning and leaving for home at 5 o'clock.

But if his artificial feet were anchored to the earth, his heart was still in the sky. Now and again in the course of his duties on the aviation side of the business he flew in a passenger liner to the continent. Then the urge to fly must have welled up in him stronger than ever. At very rare intervals he took up an aircraft for a short time to taste again the joys of flying.

Determined in 1935 to get back to the Royal Air Force, he had an interview with Air Vice-Marshal Sir Frederick Bowhill, who was then Air Member for Personnel, and later became the Chief of the Coastal Command. Sir Frederick Bowhill received him most sympathetically, but the earlier ruling seemed to preclude all possibility of the pilot rejoining the Royal Air Force.

Bader bowed to the decision, but in his heart he did not accept it. Meanwhile he continued to live the life of a city man and go to his office regularly.

The tense atmosphere of Munich in 1938 drove him once again to try to get back to the Royal Air Force. Air Chief-Marshal Sir Charles Portal, who became Chief of Air Staff, was then Air Member for Personnel and to him Bader wrote a letter asking if he could be taken back on the reserve in order to be in flying practice if war broke out. The reply he received from Sir Charles Portal set his mind at rest. Although it pointed out that the Medical Board would not hear of it, Sir Charles added that he could rest assured that in the event of war they would accept his services. The young city man, who longed to don the Royal Air Force blue again, was content.

For a year he continued to go to the office, while the European skies grew darker under the menace of German might. In the six years since he had left the Royal Air Force he had flown for perhaps five hours, no more. But he had no doubt about his ability to fly.

At the outbreak of war his application to rejoin the R.A.F. was answered by an appointment to see Air Vice-Marshal F. C. Halahan, C.M.G., of the Royal Air Force Volunteer Reserve Selection Board. Fortunately for Bader and for his country, this officer was his Commanding Officer while he was at Cranwell and was therefore well aware of his outstanding abilities and the miracle he had accomplished in learning to fly with artificial legs. This time the Medical Board were instructed to see if he was organically sound, apart from the loss of his legs, and as he was in perfect health he was passed as fit. Off to the Central Flying School he went for a test, which gave him no trouble at all, and on November 26, 1939, he took out his uniform and donned it once more as Flying Officer D. R. S. Bader.

Since his resignation from the service six years earlier, aircraft had made big strides; Spitfires and Hurricanes were coming into production, so he went to the Central Flying School for a refresher course on modern aircraft, and flew like a bird—his artificial legs caused him no difficulty.

Posted as Flying Officer in February, 1940, to the Spitfire Squadron No. 19, he was promoted to Flight Lieutenant two months later and posted to Squadron No. 222, with which squadron of Spitfires he fought and patrolled over Dunkirk. During patrols over Dunkirk he proved his ability by shooting down a Messerschmitt 109 and 110; but strangely enough although patrolling with the rest of his flight twice a day looking for the enemy, they did not often make contact, while other squadrons at different times of the day ran into flocks of German aircraft.

From high in the sky he saw Dunkirk ablaze. He stated afterwards that one of the most remarkable things was the sight of a great column of solid black smoke from the oil tanks pushing through a blanket of cloud over which he was flying at 10,000 feet. There was the great white level sea of cloud, with a dense peak of black smoke thrusting through the surface. It was an unusual sight that he will not soon forget. His graphic description of the evacuation from Dunkirk calls up the whole picture in a few words: "The sea from Dover to Dunkirk was like the Great West Road on a Bank Holiday. It was covered with shipping of all descriptions."

His dash and leadership over Dunkirk brought him further promotion on June 24, 1940, when he took command as Squadron Leader of the famous Canadian Squadron No. 242. These were the fighters whom he led so brilliantly throughout the Battle of Britain. Their Hurricanes tore through the German masses and wrought terrible havoc. So cleverly were they led, so fiercely did they fight that their losses were trifling compared with the losses they inflicted.

The German air offensive began to flare up in earnest on August 30th, when the Canadian fighters shot down 12 of the enemy without loss to themselves. On September 7th they shot down 11 Germans and lost 1 pilot; on September 9th they chased the enemy bombers over London and came up with them over the Thames at Hammersmith—I happened to be in a train packed solid with passengers when bombs were dropped and that fight was going on overhead, but people were so interested in the air battle that they completely ignored their own danger—that day the Canadians knocked down 11 of the enemy aircraft, driving them towards Enfield around which they all crashed, while only 1 pilot of Squadron 242 was lost; on September 14th the Canadian squadron destroyed 12 and on the 18th they shot down 11 without any losses to themselves and on September 27th the Canadians shot down 6 for a loss of 1 pilot. In all, during the Battle of London, Squadron Leader Bader's Canadians destroyed 63 aircraft and lost only 3 of their own pilots. It was a magnificent record.

While those battles were raging, Squadron Leader Bader himself shot down 10 of the enemy aircraft. Two of them were fighters, Messerschmitt 109s, but the remainder were all bombers, twin-engined aircraft, Junkers 88, Dornier 17 or Messerschmitt 110. Once he was leading 8 pilots of his squadron when they ran into 100 of the enemy at about 15,000 feet. The Hurricanes promptly sailed in to such good effect that the 9 fighters between them shot down 12 of the enemy, completely breaking up the formations and sending the survivors fleeing for their lives. From that battle the Canadians emerged unscathed.

Once a friend asked him if he was ever bored. "I'm never bored except by lack of fighting," he replied.

During the mass attacks on London, he saw one German bomber

shot down and crash right into the heart of a fiery furnace. There was another day when his eagerness to get at the enemy might easily have ended his life if the little god of chance had not been watching over him.

Notification of an impending attack reached him a little late and he and his squadron were unable to take off in time to reach the required altitude. In his anxiety to come to grips with the enemy he gave his Hurricane full boost and shot ahead so rapidly that he left the rest of his formation, with the exception of one pilot who kept up with him, trailing out behind him.

Approaching him over the Thames Estuary were 36 bombers, with attendant Messerschmitt fighters above. Without hesitation he and the pilot who followed him made a beam attack. As he swept past the formation, he turned in behind the bombers. At once the German bombers opened up with all their guns upon the two Hurricanes. In the concentrated gunfire of the 36 bombers their destruction appeared to be certain. The squadron leader said afterwards that he could see the tracers streaming past him like hail. To make his position more deadly some Messerschmitt 109s dived down and started to fire on the Hurricanes from behind, so the two British fighters were fairly caught between two fires.

Instantly Squadron Leader Bader did the sensible thing and broke off the attack. In turning away, a Messerschmitt 110 came right into his sights and he immediately shot it down. As his companion swerved to avoid colliding with another German bomber he gave it a burst which sent it crashing, so they took their toll in the very act of escaping.

When the two Hurricanes landed they were simply riddled with bullet holes—they were in fact unfit to fly, although the two pilots managed to fly them safely home. The other pilot got a bullet right through his reflector sight, yet it did not touch him; Squadron Leader Bader got an explosive bullet in the cockpit which missed him by just two inches. Anyone seeing those two aircraft would have sworn it was impossible for the pilots to escape, yet neither was touched. The little god of chance was certainly looking after them that day.

To see the Canadians lounging in their chairs at the dispersal point, with the yellow dope on their Mae Wests almost rubbed away by continual usage and to watch the way they were galvanized into life by the entrance of their squadron leader and his terse: "Come on!" was to witness a living example of leadership. He was the captain of their team and they would have followed him anywhere, as they did. They flew into the fury of the fight undismayed by any odds. It was a sad blow to them and to him when his promotion to the rank of Wing Commander in March, 1941, compelled him to relinquish his command and go elsewhere.

Plate 2.—WING COMMANDER, D. R. S. BADER, D.S.O. and Bar, D.F.C., who lost both legs while stunting in the Royal Air Force in December, 1931. Indomitable will-power enabled him to surmount his physical disabilities and become one of the most brilliant fighter pilots in the Royal Air Force and an inspiration to the whole world.

Plate 3.—AIRCRAFTMAN C. R. DRIVER, D.F.M., who fought against over-whelming odds in the great air battle over Heliogoland Bight until the floor and front of his cockpit were blasted away and both his gun barrels were sheered off by the cannon shell of the Messerschmitts. His superb courage won the second Distinguished Flying Medal to be awarded during the war (see page 50).

A worse blow came on August 9, 1941, when he led his fighters against a formation of Messerschmitts over France. "Come on, boys, there are plenty for all, pick one each," he called to them over the radio-telephone and dived after a Messerschmitt which he shot down in flames. In turning away as the enemy crashed he knocked off the tail of his own aircraft by colliding with another Messerschmitt which also crashed. As his aircraft went down, he had a terrific struggle to bale out, for as he humorously wrote home, his right leg wished to stay inside the cockpit while he wanted to get out. How he managed to undo his leg as he plunged to earth in his tailless aircraft while fully clothed in his flying kit remains a mystery. But he did it and came down safely, leaving his leg behind. His astonishing escape gave point to his favourite jest, that he was better off than the ordinary pilot, because if one of his "tin" legs were shot away, all he had to do was to get a new one.

In due course a message came through the Red Cross asking for another leg to be sent to him, and this was dropped over France on August 19, 1941, by a bomber captain who flew round and round the parachute, despite the heavy gunfire, until the leg reached the ground. It was undamaged, and Bader's acknowledgment ran: "Leg arrived. Thankfully received." Later two new legs were dropped in the same way.

Even in captivity his dauntless spirit shone out, for he made several attempts to escape, only to be recaptured after various spells of liberty; but the Germans were so afraid that he might succeed that they imprisoned him in a castle, from which he was released at last in the final phase of the war on April 17, 1945, having, in the words of his wife, "come through it remarkably well".

Honours and promotion came to Wing Commander D. R. S. Bader, D.S.O. and Bar, D.F.C. and Bar, for his fearless leadership and the many victories he won in the air. But his greatest triumph of all was won when, deprived of his legs, he determined to prove that if the will be strong and the spirit right, the gravest physical disabilities of man can be overcome.

He proved it to the world, and most relentlessly of all to twenty-two Germans whom he sent flaming out of the skies down to the earth they defiled.

CHAPTER VI

THE COURAGE OF AIRCRAFTMAN DRIVER

ALL the diatribes about the slackness and softness of the younger generation were soon falsified by the war in the air. Churchill was right when he said: "Never in the field of human conflict was so much owed by so many to so few." Youth preserved the civilization of the world and slender boys performed deeds which grown men have seldom equalled and never surpassed, as the gallantry of Charles Ronald Driver, who was born in 1921, goes to prove.

The eugenist will note that he sprang from two of the hardiest races in the British Isles, his mother being a Scotswoman and his father a Yorkshireman. For a time the boy, after leaving school, helped in the office of his father, who was a wool buyer, but in November, 1938, he joined the Royal Air Force and before a year had passed he could write the words "1st Class" after his title of Aircraftman.

Returning to the aerodrome after time off on the night of Sunday, December 17, 1939, he learned that the bomber crews had to report to the crew room, which he did without delay. He was delighted and excited, as were all the other members of the crews present, to hear there was a chance of finding the German Fleet in Heligoland Bight and that they would all be on operations next day.

At 4.30 the following morning, December 18, 1939, they were roused, and after breakfast went to the crew room where they stood by until 8.27 a.m. when the order came through to take off. They crowded out to find their great Wellington bombers all bombed up and ready to depart.

These were the aircraft in which the lightness and strength of the geodetic principle of construction had made it possible to carry such a heavy load of bombs. One of the most impressive sights I have ever seen was when the belly of a Wellington suddenly opened and hung down like five long fins to expose the rows of bombs ready for dropping. In appearance the aircraft were not of the long, thin type such as the Hampden or Dornier "flying pencil," but rather dumpy, resembling more a carp than a mackerel in shape. There was not only a camp bed in the fuselage, and room for more, but it was possible for a man standing upright to walk down the catwalk to the turret in the tail, where the rudder, or tail fin, rose so high in the air that a man seemed a pigmy beside it.

Into one of the Wellingtons mounted Aircraftman Driver, to make his way to the twin guns in the front cockpit which, with doors closed and the canvas door drawn at the back, was entirely separated from the rest of the aircraft by an inch or two of space. The captain was Sergeant J. R. Ramshaw, who was 35 years old, and his second pilot and navigator was Sergeant Hewitt, while Driver's great friend

Leading Aircraftman W. Lilley, was the rear-gunner, Leading Aircraftman J. Conolly being the wireless operator.

By 8.35 a.m. they got away. They were all in the best of spirits, laughing and joking, and no doubt wondering what they would do on their leave which was due next day. Their aircraft was one of a formation of bombers detailed for the raid. It was a fine day, with a good deal of cloud, when they started, and these conditions persisted as they climbed steadily while crossing the North Sea. About ten miles from the German coast, however, the cloud cleared, and the sun shone in a clear sky which gave them no cover whatsoever. It was unfortunate for them that just where clouds would have been welcome they vanished from the heavens and left them very vulnerable to attack.

As they flew over the centre of Heligoland Bight they saw below them about eight German destroyers which quickly put about and made for port. But the bombers, being after bigger game, carried on over Wilhelmshaven, taking photographs which later proved of great value. The first Messerschmitt 109 which came up to intercept them over Wilhelmshaven met with a burst from one of the aircraft which sent him down.

For about fifteen minutes the Wellingtons went inland, flying in close formation at 18,000 feet. Then they ran into a terrific barrage. Without a wisp of cloud to veil them, they made a perfect target for the German gunners. Just as they were wheeling on the instructions of the Squadron Commander, a piece of shell scored the first hit on the bomber in which Aircraftman Driver flew.

As they were completing the turn they saw the enemy fighters coming up at them. There were droves of them—at least 200— taking off in the distance and climbing to intercept. Most of them were Messerschmitt 110s. That was the beginning of a terrific air battle.

The enemy fighters, climbing to about 500 feet above the British bombers, came in to the attack on the outskirts of Wilhelmshaven. In that turning movement of the bombers, six of the Wellingtons were compelled to break formation in order to run up on the others and resume their places. Upon these the fighters pounced and gave them no chance at all. One after the other went down, after taking their toll of the enemy.

The air was filled with the thunder of machine guns. Messerschmitts whirled about. Driver in the front turret kept gazing all around him, getting in bursts whenever a fighter came within his sights. Sergeant Ramshaw, the pilot, carried on imperturbably as though he were flying over Hyde Park instead of taking part in an air battle over Wilhelmshaven.

Ten minutes after the battle began, Lilley, the rear-gunner, got his first Messerschmitt 110 full in the sights and sent it down. The attack intensified, and a few seconds later the aircraft was hit by a cannon shell which put the wireless out of action, whereupon the wireless operator, Conolly, strove in the most methodical manner to get the set to function again.

It is a striking commentary on his coolness to know that in the midst of that fierce air battle, which started at mid-day and did not terminate until after 1 o'clock, the wireless operator calmly examined his leads to try to find out what was wrong. He managed to fix the generator to give some power, although it was barely turning over.

While he was doing this, a constant stream of fighters kept diving on the tail of the aircraft in an attempt to shoot it down, but Lilley kept them at bay. Another Me 110 came right in his sights and he promptly destroyed it. Barely had he shouted the news over the "intercom" when a third Messerschmitt came too close and was met by a burst of fire.

By now the Wellington was becoming separated from the other bombers. The enemy fighters, determined to destroy it, kept diving to the attack.

Waiting his opportunity, the rear-gunner blazed at a fourth Me 110 and saw it dive away. A little later the intercommunication system was smashed. Then his guns jammed.

Leading Aircraftman Lilley made no attempt to leave his exposed position in the tail where he was a target for every enemy aircraft that came along. Instead he strove to get his guns working again.

If he had abandoned his damaged guns and gone forward after putting up such a valiant fight, all would have praised him and none could have criticised him. But he preferred to sit in that exposed post and struggle to put his guns right, knowing that by so doing he was giving his friends in front a chance to survive. Seeing his duty, he did it, and while grappling with his guns the enemy fighters, who failed to drive him from his turret, simply riddled him. So died a young hero.

Meanwhile the Messerschmitts were making a fierce attack on the front turret in an effort to silence its guns. Aircraftman Driver, seeing one enemy aircraft firing at him from the starboard, gave him a burst which sent him smoking down to the sea. Immediately another Messerschmitt 110 appeared overhead and claimed the gunner's attention. Driver barely had time to see it go into a three-quarter turn when he found himself under the fire of another fighter on which he had to swing his guns. While he was fighting with this aircraft, the Messerschmitt which went into the turn came up beneath him and simply blew out the bottom and the side of the turret with cannon shell.

"The first thing I knew," said Aircraftman Driver afterwards, "was that I felt pretty cold around my feet and legs. I looked down and saw water below me."

He sat there in the top of the turret with his legs dangling over the North Sea and nothing between him and the sea but the little seat on which he sat. The air was full of fighters with others climbing to attack.

"The next thing I knew," he continued, "was that my guns refused to fire. I looked to see what was the matter and saw they'd been blown in halves at the barrels."

The cannon shell had cut through the barrels half way down and sheared both of them clean off.

"Then a hail of cannon shell passed in front of me and blew the perspex off," he went on.

The perspex is the artificial glass front of the turret or nose of the aircraft. He sat there quite in the open, exposed to the full blast of the bomber flying at top speed, and the bitterness of the blast on that December day can be imagined. His guns were useless. There was nothing more he could do, so he decided that the time had come to retreat.

As he swung on his seat, he saw that the turret was on fire behind him, where some of the woodwork had been ignited by the cannon shell or tracer. Whipping the glove off his right hand—he wore silk gloves under his thick flying gloves to keep his hands warm—he began to beat at the flames with it. Soon he was beating as hard as he could go with both hands as the few remaining rounds exploded. To such good purpose did he lay about him that in a few minutes he had completely smothered the fire which threatened to endanger the whole aircraft. Then he climbed out of the shattered turret to join the rest of the crew.

That Wellington bomber personified the unbeatable spirit of the Royal Air Force. When Driver appeared, his captain, Sergeant Ramshaw, sat at the controls whistling and looking perfectly happy. The front of the aircraft was shot off, the rear-gunner was dead, the middle turret knocked out, the intercommunication system wrecked, and the wireless damaged; enemy fighters were attacking from all directions, bursts of bullets were passing in front of him into the control board, but Sergeant Ramshaw went on whistling.

That one man sitting there during that air battle over Wilhelmshaven and the North Sea was a symbol of Britain's ultimate victory. In the midst of death and destruction he calmly whistled.

"Are you O.K.?" he said to Driver.

Aircraftman Driver put up his thumbs. His guns had been shattered, his turret blown to bits, he had fought the Germans and fought a fire successfully and he was still unconquered and unconquerable.

Directly the second pilot saw him, he put his arms round the front-gunner, being under the impression that when his guns ceased firing he had been shot. Without speaking a word the second pilot gave a jerk with his thumb over his shoulder and a nod of his head, and Aircraftman Driver knew that he had lost his best friend.

As they made their way aft, Aircraftman Driver heard how
Lilley's guns had jammed and how he had stayed there trying to put
them right in order to give the others a chance. Extricating the dead
gunner with difficulty from the cockpit, they laid him on the floor of
the fuselage and covered him.

At that moment the second pilot was shot in the arm. "It doesn't
hurt," he said, and went forward to help the captain.

Aircraftman Driver went to the astrodome and gazed around. "As
I looked out I saw all the fabric flapping on the wings," he said later.
"The insides were all exposed and you could see the way they were
built up. It was as though someone had taken a great knife and
carved all along the leading edge of the wings. The nose of the
aircraft was sheared away, but I had closed the bulkhead doors to
exclude the blast from the other part of the fuselage. The engines
themselves looked as though someone had used a sledge hammer and
chisel on them, the metal was all ripped away. We wouldn't have got
back but for the pilot. He was cheerful all the way, looking after us
like a father, he was marvellous."

As he stood there and surveyed the damage, the last enemy fighter
finished off his attack and turned away, to run into the guns of
another Wellington which shot him down. In the distance were
Messerschmitts at varying heights flying toward the land, but how
many reached there will never be known.

As if the Wellington were not damaged enough already, it was then
discovered that the petrol tanks had been holed. No winged duck
ever flew more gamely than that shattered Wellington.

"We are running out of petrol," said Sergeant Ramshaw, at last.

They possessed an emergency supply which it was necessary to
pump by hand. The pump handle was placed at the foot of the camp
bed in the fuselage. To this Aircraftman Driver went and began to
pump the petrol to keep the aircraft in the air. For half an hour he
pumped, until their petrol reserves were exhausted.

"We can't make it," said Sergeant Ramshaw. "We'll have to land
in the sea."

They were then limping along at 10,000 feet. As the petrol failed,
the engines cut out and the captain told the crew to get ready to
abandon the aircraft on hitting the water.

The wireless operator tried desperately to send out an S O S and
did not cease trying until the bomber came down.

Toward the end of their glide, as they were bracing themselves
against the impact, the pilot said very off-handedly: "I've seen a
ship and I'll try to make it."

He succeeded. By careful manœuvring he came down about 400
yards away from a Grimsby trawler.

The shock as an aircraft hits the water is always great, and
fatalities often occur, so if the crew escape injury they may count

themselves lucky. In this case Sergeant Ramshaw, who handed the controls so skilfully and who was later awarded the D.F.M., received a heavy blow on the head which left him very dazed; but although they were all shaken up, Aircraftman Driver got off lightly.

The latter at once concentrated on releasing the rubber dinghy which was stored in a small compartment in the port wing. He got it launched at last and helped the others in, after the wounded second pilot had done what he could.

Aircraftman Driver and the wireless operator made their escape from the sinking bomber by the astrodome, while the second pilot and Sergeant Ramshaw struggled out of the escape hatch in the top of the pilot's cabin.

Unfortunately the captain was so badly shaken by the shock that in climbing out he fell into the sea. But for the prompt assistance of Aircraftman Driver he might easily have been drowned, for the seas were rough and the shattered bomber was low in the water and in imminent danger of foundering. Driver, with the help of the others, managed to haul him into the dinghy just as the bomber put her nose straight down and sank.

For fifteen minutes they tossed about in the heavy seas, then they were picked up and transferred to the trawler. The skipper and crew did all they could for them, providing them with dry clothes and hot coffee. The seas, however, were too much for Aircraftman Driver, who was seasick all the way back to Grimsby, where they landed about 10 o'clock next morning amid the cheers of the crowds on the docks.

The heavy losses suffered by the British bombers in that battle over Wilhelmshaven caused many a sad heart; but Mrs. Driver in Stockton-on-Tees was filled with joy and pride when, on December 21st, she showed her son, who was home on leave, a telegram announcing that Aircraftman Charles Ronald Driver had been granted the immediate award of the Distinguished Flying Medal. It was the second to be awarded in the war.

The boy was then nineteen years old, tall, of fine physique, with black, wavy hair, dark eyes and an open countenance. How he escaped that hail of cannon shell which cut off the barrels of his guns and shot away the greater part of his turret is a mystery.

In fighting for all that is good in the world, he won high honour. His best friend willingly gave his life.

Many a mother has welcomed her son back with rejoicing; many another has received a dreaded telegram to tell her that nevermore will she see her son or hear the sound of his laughter, among them Lady MacRobert, who suffered the loss of her three sons in the air. All three were flying enthusiasts who took their pilot's certificates long before the war. Her first son, Sir Alasdair MacRobert, Bart., was the Chairman of the British India Corporation, founded by his father in

1920 to manufacture woollens and cottons and leather goods. Sir Alasdair not only founded an Indian aviation company, but he flew his own aircraft on business journeys, just as other men go by train. With all the ripe experience of nearly a thousand hours of flying, he flew home to England in 1938, and within a few days of his return his aircraft crashed at Luton. He was only 26.

Her second son Roderic, who succeeded to the title, joined the Royal Air Force in 1937 and gained his commission as a pilot officer in May, 1938, shortly after his brother died. Going out to Egypt to complete his training, he went to Palestine to join an Army Co-operation Squadron. He was so popular that all his colleagues called him ''Mac'' and he saw service in Aden before joining a Hurricane squadron to help to quell the rebellion in Iraq. On May 22, 1941, he flew off with another pilot to attack Mosul aerodrome and destroy the aircraft which the rebels had seized. Diving down with his guns blazing, he exploded two lorries laden with petrol before sweeping the hangars and grounded aircraft with his fire and putting several aircraft out of action. Climbing steeply, he dived to make another attack and was just turning away from the aerodrome when the other pilot lost sight of him. He never reached base, for he was flying over the desert about twenty miles from Mosul when some of the rebels shot him down. He, too, was only 26.

Thus the title passed to Lady MacRobert's sole surviving son Iain, who was as keen on rugger and cricket and other sports as on flying. Directly war was declared he joined up in the ranks of the Royal Air Force as an aircraftman, and by November, 1940, had won his commission as a pilot officer. During the ensuing months he did fine work for Coastal Command, piloting his Blenheim across the North Sea to reconnoitre the coasts of Denmark and Norway, searching the seas for U-boats as he shepherded the convoys along the east coast. He loved the work. Nothing shook him. Whether he was fighting a raging gale or enemy aircraft he remained quite calm.

It happened that a Hampden bomber was forced down in the North Sea and the airmen were obliged to take to their dinghy. At 7 o'clock on the morning of June 30, 1941, Pilot Officer Sir Iain MacRobert took off in his Blenheim to try to locate and rescue the drifting men. He was never seen again. In seeking to save the lives of others, he sacrificed his own.

In that dark hour the inspiring spirit of Lady MacRobert was manifest. Bereft of all her sons, she strove to help the great cause of Humanity by presenting a Stirling bomber to the nation.

''I have no more sons to wear the Badge or carry it in the fight. My eldest son, Sir Alasdair, was killed when his own 'plane crashed soon after he had flown home from India in 1938. Sir Roderic was the third Baronet and joined the Royal Air Force in 1937. Iain, my youngest, had just become the fourth Baronet. None of them ever looked for the easy way. If I had ten sons, I know they would all have followed that line of duty," she wrote to the Secretary of State for Air.

"It is with a mother's pride that I enclose a cheque for £25,000 and with it goes my sympathy to those mothers who have also lost their sons and gratitude to all other mothers whose sons so gallantly carry on the fight."

The following month of September, 1942, Lady MacRobert gave a flight of four Hurricane fighters to the squadron with which Sir Roderic was operating when he was killed, and during the presentation in the Middle East on September 19, 1942, Air Vice-Marshal W. A. McClaughry, C.B., D.S.O., spoke to the squadron and paid her the following tribute.

"While we have mothers like this one, there is little fear that the British people will fail to win through, no matter what the difficulties. This is an example, a woman's example, of what we should all strive to be and to achieve. How many of us can claim to have the spirit and courage like hers, which willingly gives all and then only regrets that she cannot do more in the service of her country?"

CHAPTER VII

THE BALLOON BARRAGE

AT the outbreak of war the Germans were rather contemptuous of balloons and balloon barrages. Whether this was due to the fact that Goering had come to believe his own assertions that no enemy aeroplanes would ever be able to fly over the Reich or whether the German war lords were so intent on creating an offensive force that they had no inclination, time, money or materials to devote to balloon defences I do not know. They may, of course, have misled themselves into concluding that balloons were of no value, in which case they soon revised their opinion, for the much-criticised early leaflet raids not only proved to the German people that the Royal Air Force could fly over Germany, but they started the war lords constructing balloons for defensive purposes with all the application and celerity of which the Germans were capable.

Their attitude to balloons, whatever its reason, was not easy to understand. Hitler and his fell associates for years used every artifice and weapon by which to create fear among the nations. They made fear their strongest weapon. Yet these adepts who played on the fears of nations in order to scare them into surrendering their rights and liberties seem to have overlooked the value of balloons in creating fear among the men who fly.

The barrage balloon, with its grotesque elephantine ears and trunk, was the bogey of the sky. Like Hitler, it was a perpetual threat and a great part of its value consisted not so much in what it did as in what it threatened to do. It floated aloft in the sky and menaced the life of the airmen. If a pilot was flying in the dark at balloon height in a defended area, he never knew when he was going to collide with a balloon cable. The threat was always there to wreak havoc with his nerves and implant fear in his mind. It was the uncertainty which told upon him, and the British balloon barrages most certainly helped to undermine the morale of the German air force.

One pilot of a British bomber had an experience with a balloon which he was not anxious to repeat. Tall, slender and young, with a mass of dark wavy hair and a charming manner which made him popular everywhere, he went so far as to admit that it was rather a near thing—as I have no memory for names I will call him Barry.

One night Barry climbed into the pilot's seat of his Beaufort—it was a pleasure to see how proud he was of his aircraft—and set off from one of the Coastal Command stations to help to smash up the German submarines in the French port of Lorient. For that trip he had a new navigator who had never before been on active service in a night operation. They managed to locate Lorient all right and the Beaufort duly dropped its load where it was likely to do the most damage.

While circling over their target to pick out their objective, they met with a good deal of anti-aircraft fire which recorded one or two hits, upsetting the wireless and making the controls rather difficult. To avoid the fire, Barry swung the Beaufort about quite a lot, and after taking violent evasive action a pilot often found it difficult to learn exactly where he was unless he had some well-defined landmark to go by. He was rather like a man playing blindman's-buff who had been spun round four or five times.

Barry, who wanted to set his course for home, asked the navigator for his position and course. The stars were obscured, the night was dark, there were no landmarks, but only the sea below them, and the Beaufort had made such rapid changes of course that the navigator had to confess that he did not know where they were.

Barry was displeased, but his natural courtesy prevented him from administering anything more than a polite rebuke. He felt the responsibility. The lives of his crew were in his keeping and there he was cruising over the sea in his Beaufort without having any idea where he was flying, whether he was heading out to the illimitable ocean or toward land.

The navigator himself was far from happy. He had started out in high hope on his first night operation, and despite all his hard work and his theory and practice he had lost himself the first time. His feelings can be imagined.

In the circumstances the pilot was obliged to trust to his own sense of direction and hope that it would lead to a happy landing. Eventually Barry detected land ahead and felt sure it was England. The navigator, however, was still uncertain. He did not know where they were and said so. The polite pilot became a little more displeased, in fact, he grew rather ruffled.

Flying along the coast, he at last came to a harbour which he recognized at once as Plymouth. "*Now* do you know where we are?" he asked rather heatedly.

"No, I don't!" was the emphatic rejoinder of the navigator.

There was a jolt in the aircraft, which started to spin round and round and to go down. The navigator, under the impression that the pilot was just displaying his anger, did not like it at all. "Don't do that!" he pleaded.

Actually the Beaufort had crashed into a balloon cable which cut through the leading edge of the wing right back to the main spar. Then, as the aircraft started to spin and go down, the cable cut its way along the edge of the main spar toward the tip of the wing for a distance of fourteen inches, so the cut in the wing was shaped like the letter "L" and it seemed impossible that the aircraft could ever escape.

The Beaufort spun round from a height of 2,000 feet down to 200 feet, and just when it seemed absolutely certain to crash, Barry felt it suddenly fly free. By some inexplicable chance the movements of the aircraft had managed to work the cable back again along the edge of the main spar and out of the straight cut in the wing. It was the chance in a million which came off.

Not until the Beaufort landed did Barry and his crew realize how near they had been to crashing and how lucky had been their escape. They were not anxious to repeat their experience of flying into a balloon cable.

One man in the Royal Air Force, however, flew slap into balloon cables so often and got so used to it that he would calmly take off and fly into a cable again without turning a single hair. He was Squadron Leader John Alexander Kent, a six-foot tall, dark-haired, lean-faced, blue-eyed Canadian, who was born in Winnipeg in 1914, and displayed on his tunic the ribbons of the Distinguished Flying Cross, the Air Force Cross, and the Vertuti Militari or the Polish V.C. More than once he risked his life by flying into balloon cables to see what would happen to the aircraft, while an escorting aeroplane filmed the impact to obtain a scientific record in order to make the British balloon barrage as deadly as possible to any German pilot who got caught.

When Squadron Leader Kent began to fly he was only sixteen years old. By the time he was seventeen he had taken out his pilot's licence, so while still young in years he was old in experience. Arriving in England in February, 1935, he joined the Royal Air Force the following month and after receiving his training was posted to Farnborough as a test pilot.

He was an all-round pilot, not one who tested a particular type of aircraft. To him all types were alike, fast fighters, slow trainers, heavy, light or medium bombers, he was the master of them all. He flew and tested ninety-two types of aircraft, taking them up in the air for the first time to see what they could do, learning their faults and advantages, whether they were heavy or light on the controls, their rate of climb, their speed at various altitudes, their oil and petrol consumption—all the essential facts were plainly recorded on his writing pad when he landed.

His task as a test pilot necessarily demanded great skill and judgment, as well as courage, and only a man possessing these attributes could have carried out with success the many experiments he made. He once confessed that when he was asked to fly straight into a cable to see what would happen, he did not like it very much. He was used to taking risks with new aircraft, but this was something specifically designed to bring disaster to any aircraft that did it. No wonder he did not like it. Yet he did it just the same.

Special precautions were devised by the technical experts to protect him, so far as they could, and for the first experiment a light cable was used. Then one day he got into a Fairey aircraft, climbed to the specified height and flew straight at the cable. He said afterwards that he did not know he had flown into it—he just went straight on. That was the beginning of dozens of experiments with cables of increasing weight during which he flew all types of British bombers and cut many a wing to ribbons. The weather had to be fair and visibility good for these experiments so that he could judge the position of the cable accurately and the cine-camera in the other aircraft could obtain a clear record.

Although every precaution was taken to eliminate risks—so far as they could be foreseen—no one knew what would happen at each experiment, and on several occasions many a competent pilot would have crashed to his death whereas Squadron Leader Kent was saved solely by his superb skill and presence of mind. Once he had three feet of his wing sheared off at the end and landed the bomber without much trouble. The real danger came when the cable whipped round the bomber. If it smashed an aileron, the control became difficult, if it destroyed the elevator as well as the aileron the pilot needed all his skill to get down safely, because there was so little control.

There was a day when he flew straight at a cable which carried away and wrapped itself round the elevator and tail plane. When he came to push forward the control column to go down, he found it was jammed. With difficulty and by using all his strength he managed to ease it an inch or two and gain a very slight amount of control as he lost height approaching the aerodrome, then it seized up completely and the bomber just dropped with a crash on to the aerodrome.

Another time he carried away a cable weighing some tons wedged in his wing. This sudden accession of weight which completely upset the balance of the bomber would have sent most pilots crashing, but Squadron Leader Kent managed to keep control.

Losing height, he was just about to land when the dangling cable caught round some high-tension electricity wires. The bomber, slewing round on one wing just as a straining dog circles on the end of its chain, stalled. Even as it did so, Squadron Leader Kent opened the throttle wide and by using full engine power managed to pull the bomber round level.

Had he not acted instantaneously, that experiment would have ended in disaster. Directly he pulled the bomber level, it simply fell down on the aerodrome. By the greatest good fortune the cable drew clear of the high-tension wires before the aircraft touched, otherwise it would probably have gone up in flames.

In one of his most remarkable exploits on active service, he was trapped in the middle of a formation of forty Messerschmitt 109s and managed by his coolness and courage and superb skill as a pilot to drive them off and escape. He was flying with the famous Polish squadron who were ordered to attack German bomber formations and leave the Canadian squadron working with them to deal with the fighters.

They were patrolling at about 24,000 feet when Squadron Leader Kent saw below him a formation of aircraft which he thought were bombers. Diving down to the attack, he found in front of him a number of Messerschmitt 109s on one of which he promptly directed his guns. As he fired, he saw streams of tracer bullets rushing past him. Whipping round, he found he was quite alone among the enemy.

At once he went into a tight turn, circling in the smallest possible radius, chasing his own tail like a cat in order to prevent the enemy from getting on it and shooting him to pieces. The Messerschmitts milled round about a thousand feet above him at 20,000 feet, waiting and watching for their opportunity to pounce. With clouds nearly a mile and a half below him at 12,000 feet, he had no chance of beating them to cover. They would have been on him before he could get there.

"I knew I could not get away by diving, because they would have fixed me; so I sat and watched, and waited to see what would happen," he remarked afterwards.

While he was circling in those tense conditions with forty-one Messerschmitts just above him looking for an opening, he heard the voice of his Controller over the radio-telephone saying: "Have you engaged the enemy yet?"

"No, but I think the enemy are waiting to engage me at any minute!" replied the cool Canadian.

"Then they came down on me one after the other," he said later. "I went into the tightest turn possible and kept going while a whole lot of tracer kept streaming past. I waited until the tracer died down and then whipped out of my turn. About eight Me 109s passed in front of me, so I fired at the first which turned on his back and went down smoking. Then the rest dived down on me, so I went into a tight turn again until the tracer died down, when I repeated my tactics and saw one about 200 yards away. I gave him a good long burst and he caught fire and went down. Two dived down on my tail, so I whipped round head on and rolled on to my back and rolled up and gave one a burst as he went past. After that they decided to go home and formed up and went off. I was so mad that I flew after them 2,000 feet below them in case one was so misguided as to attack. I had plenty of time to count them—there were thirty-eight. Then I half rolled and went down and away and found another Me 109 in the clouds. I squirted, but nothing happened, so I climbed up again and met another bunch of twenty-seven Me 109s. They were 4,000 feet above me, but they paid no attention, and as I could not get up to them, I went home.''

Such was the restrained, simple account of the fight of a single fighter pilot against at least forty of the enemy. A false move and he knew he would pay the penalty with his life. Their numbers were no match for his skill, and after shooting down three he drove the remaining thirty-eight to retreat. It was a triumph.

''I was so mad that I flew after them,'' said the Canadian pilot who later attained the rank of Wing Commander.

There spoke the spirit of the British Empire. Wing Commander J. A. Kent, D.F.C. and Bar, A.F.C., V.M., did great work in the defence of Britain and the Empire by shooting down more than thirteen German aircraft.

The courage and skill of the modest Canadian pilot was tempered by a pretty sense of humour, as he proved one day when he nodded towards a collection of medicine bottles in the mess belonging to pilots on the sick list. ''That shows you how fit we are in the R.A.F.!'' he said, with a smile.

They proved themselves to be quite fit enough for the Germans.

CHAPTER VIII

THE COPPER DINGO

THEY called them the Dingo Flight, and Squadron Leader D. C. F. Good was their leader.

The Dingoes were proud of their name and fame, and up in the office of Squadron Leader Good was a black board with rows of dingoes, cut out of sheet copper and nicely engraved, all running for their lives. Each copper dingo represented a decoration won by the Dingo Flight which was largely made up of Australians. The dingoes, of course, are the wild dogs of Australia, but what the Dingoes did to Germany when they dropped their bombs must have made Hitler and Goering and Goebbels wilder than any wild dog, must in fact have worried the Germans far more than any dingo ever worried the sheep farmers of the Commonwealth.

A whole book could be written about those little copper dingoes on that black board, but I shall confine myself to telling how the copper dingo came to be added by Squadron Leader Good, who was born in Adelaide in South Australia in 1916 and received his commission in the R.A.F. in 1937.

Quiet, unassuming, Squadron Leader Good sat on one of the bomb trolleys by his Hampden waiting while the ground staff completed their preparations for the night's operations. It was just after 7 p.m. on Saturday, May 4, 1940. The sky was red and the Squadron Leader felt decidedly uneasy. He had been briefed to mine the port of Oslo, and it was a long sea crossing from England to Norway and back again.

The crew got aboard, Sergeant Smith, the rear-gunner sitting in the "tin," with an angle of fire below the tail to deal with attackers who came up from below, Wallace the wireless operator sitting in the turret above him with an angle of fire over the tail to cope with attacks from above, while Pilot Officer W. G. Gardiner—"nothing could shake Gardiner," Good once remarked—was the navigator and bomb-aimer seated in the front cockpit.

Taking off about 8 o'clock, the pilot set course for Norway to help to make Oslo as dangerous as possible for the German supply ships using the port. Throughout the long journey across the North Sea he remained uneasy, looking round for fighters all the time. It was as though he had a foreboding.

About 11.30 p.m. the Norwegian coast came into sight. The pilot was by no means sure of his position after the long crossing. Flying at 8,000 feet, he saw above him a layer of strato-cumulus clouds at 10,000 or 12,000 feet; below him the mountains of Norway were covered with snow.

Changing course, he flew inland across Norway in search of his target. The crew of the bomber were quite undisturbed. No searchlights sought them, not a gun fired at them. Squadron Leader Good scanned the land below him all the time to try to pick up Oslo Fiord.

"Finally, about fifty miles away, I saw a whole packet of search-lights and flak go up and decided that was the place, so I went across to have a look," the Squadron Leader said afterwards. The Hampden was then about twenty miles away. Maintaining the same course, the pilot started to lose height until he was down to 2,000 feet. The tongue of land running up to Oslo and dividing the fiord into two was plainly visible. He decided to use that tongue of land to mask his approach to the port, dart from its cover at top speed, deposit his mine and do a steep turn away to head for home.

With the plan firmly fixed in his mind, he took the Hampden down until it was just below the level of the spit of land. Everything remained quiet, and the pilot was convinced that the enemy had no idea of his approach or that the port was likely to be attacked. Boosting the speed, the pilot flew out from the cover of the point into the open fiord with bomb doors open. As he did so a searchlight from the opposite cliff caught the pilot and navigator and nearly blinded them. At once the defences came into action. "The ack ack was the heaviest I've ever seen. You would not think an aircraft could fly through it without being cut to pieces. There were a lot of light guns as well as machine-guns firing tracer," Pilot Officer Gardiner stated after his return.

Squadron Leader Good saw streams of pink shells like fireworks spraying out from the opposite sides of the fiord ahead. He observed the two streams of fire crossing each other in the centre and, knowing that no aircraft could possibly run that gauntlet of fire, decided on the instant to drop down almost to water level in order to run under the fiery arch of shells and tracer.

Moving the stick forward, he dived under the barrage of fire. The masts of ships rushed past just above the level of his wing tips. Ahead was the spot where he was to lay his mine. Just as he was about to shout to Pilot Officer Gardiner to drop it, there was a crash like the breaking of windows, an enormous flash of light which blinded him so that he could not see what he was doing, and an acrid, sulphurous, burning smell.

He knew he had been hit. The aircraft started to run away from him. Yet even at that moment the task he had come so far to perform overshadowed everything else. "Let it go—I'm hit!" he shouted to advise Pilot Officer Gardiner to deposit the mine and tell him that he was wounded. "I'm hit! I'm hit!" he repeated.

But no one could hear him. The wires of the intercommunication system were severed by the explosion.

The Hampden ran on past the island where the mine was to be dropped and did a steep turn. The senses of the pilot were so clouded that he could never afterwards recall anything that happened from just after he was hit until he came out of the turn. He must have been flying the aircraft subconsciously according to the plan so firmly fixed in his mind.

Coming out of the turn, he sought to climb, but when he tried to pull the stick back he discovered that his arms were powerless. Wounds in the left wrist and right elbow rendered both arms useless.

The Hampden's nose dropped and pointed straight toward the sea. Unable to use his arms to pull back the stick, in that desperate emergency he thought of the trimming wheel at the right hand side of his seat.

The trimming wheel is a device which acts upon the tail plane in order to take the physical strain off the pilot. Directly he has found the correct amount of control required to hold the aircraft on her course at the desired height, by turning the trimming wheel he can hold the rudder and tail planes in position without having to endure the strain all the time on his arms and legs.

Unable to use his arms, which hung down helplessly, he finally hooked one of his fingers in the trimming wheel and, by swaying his body, gradually moved it round and gained a little height. A gigantic effort was required to do this, but he managed it. Then he started to kick on the rudder, thinking that the noise made by the escape of the compressed air would attract the attention of other members of the crew.

All this time the searchlights were flashing and the guns were doing their best to blow the Hampden out of the sky.

He looked at the altimeter and saw that they were climbing. He knew something was wrong with his face. Dimly he saw the blood dripping out of his cuffs. Although so sorely wounded, he still remained conscious. It must have been through sheer will-power that he clung to his senses. He kicked again on the rudder, but the crew merely thought that he was taking the usual evasive action.

Less than a minute earlier as the Hampden made its run up under the cover of the spit of land, Pilot Officer Gardiner saw the ships slipping by. They were moored close inshore parallel with the cliffs, no doubt to protect them from air attack. How he regretted that they had no bombs with which to attack them, for there was no one on board and the ships were quite undefended. Dazzled by the search-lights as they ran out into the open fiord, amazed by the heaviness of the gunfire which greeted them, he waited patiently for the island to turn up where he had to drop his mine.

"I think it was a Bofors gun which hit us," he stated later. "It was the last shell of a burst of five—they fire in clips of about five. I could see them—bang! bang! bang!—and the last got us. They must have had our range nicely. I thought it had hit the outer fuselage and did not worry very much."

The Hampden ran on its course as he expected. Although he received no order, he automatically dropped the mine on the right spot and reported that it was away. Then the bomber banked in a right-hand turn and began to sway and dive. Pilot Officer Gardiner remained there quite cool, thinking the captain was just doing his best to dodge the shells. Not until the wing nearly hit the mast of a ship did he suddenly wonder if all was well. Quickly he switched on the light in his cockpit to have a look round. To his surprise there was a pool of blood in the tunnel under the pilot's seat and he saw the blood steadily dripping down.

Instantly he realized that the pilot was wounded, realized also that he would have to pilot the Hampden back to its base. He had already worked out the two courses to take them back to Britain. Knowing these would be essential to him, he rapidly noted them on a piece of paper—it shows how cool he was, how calmly his brain was working— then he crawled through the tunnel and stood up behind the pilot.

A glance revealed the serious face wounds of his captain, then his eye caught sight of the altimeter. Swiftly he thrust his arm past the wounded pilot, caught hold of the stick and pulled it back. The aircraft was so low that he anticipated hitting the edge of the cliff at any moment.

As soon as he pulled the stick back, the bomber started to climb, but not until he had taken the aircraft to a safe height and knew it was no longer in danger of hitting anything could he attend to the pilot. With difficulty he unbuckled the captain's parachute harness; then he undid the straps which held him in his seat, after which he was able to pull down the back of the seat—for the back cannot be let down with the pilot strapped into his seat and his feet in the pedals.

Wriggling over the wounded man, the navigator grabbed the stick to take the Hampden to a higher level. Eventually he attracted the attention of Sergeant Wallace, the wireless operator, who had no idea that anything was wrong. He heard the bang, as did Sergeant Smith, the rear-gunner, who was also a trained navigator, but they were so busy firing at the searchlights and guns on the ground that they paid little attention to it.

In the pilot's cockpit blood was everywhere.

"Pull him out from under me," Pilot Officer Gardiner said.

With considerable difficulty, Sergeant Wallace succeeded in drawing the wounded man backwards until his head lay on the padded top of the main spar, on which the back of the pilot's seat rests when it is pulled down. After further efforts, he manipulated him so that the back of the pilot's seat could be raised again.

The remarkable thing is that Squadron Leader Good had made his crew practise this exact manœuvre in case something like this ever came to pass, in which event they would know exactly what to do. It almost looks as though he had a sense of prevision.

Somehow Sergeant Wallace and Sergeant Smith managed between them to lower Squadron Leader Good down the well leading to the front cockpit. The wounded man was bleeding badly from one arm, and it had to be stopped quickly to give him a chance. Obtaining the bandages and dressings from the first-aid kit, Sergeant Smith improvised a tourniquet with a small bottle and succeeded in checking the loss of blood. Then he gave him an injection of morphia in the calf of the leg, and covered him up with fur coats to make him as comfortable as possible.

The extraordinary thing was that in spite of the morphia and the loss of blood, the wounded man did not lose consciousness. He was very weak, and in a sorry condition. He had a hole in his cheek, his tongue itself was torn, and part of his nose was nearly off; he swallowed a tooth or two that was knocked out and a lot of blood, yet he still knew what was going on.

Meanwhile Pilot Officer Gardiner had taken the bomber up to 8,000 feet to fly across the country to Stavangar. Asking the wireless operator to see if the tanks were holed, he was thankful to learn that they were intact.

Leaving Stavangar behind, the bomber sped homeward across the North Sea. The wounded man lay with his back against the bulkhead listening to the hum of the engines. A sudden flapping disturbed him. "It's all right," shouted the pilot down to him. "We're on our way home."

And they were. Advising the base that they were returning with a casualty on board, the wireless operator got a fix by which they checked their course, and they duly touched down and taxied right up to the tarmac where an ambulance was waiting to take Squadron Leader Good to hospital. Before he knew what was happening they were cutting his uniform off him—his Royal Australian Air Force uniform which was something he prized beyond anything.

No words could express his gratitude to the surgeons whose skill left him almost unscarred. In ten days he was out of hospital.

That is how he and Pilot Officer Walter George Gardiner won the D.F.C., and incidentally how another copper dingo won a place on that black board.

It was an amazing adventure which shows how skill and courage and fortitude can save an aircraft from disaster when all seems lost.

Lucky as they were to survive then, their survival from a previous trip savours of the miraculous. They were making one of the last daylight bombing raids upon the Norwegian coast at Christiansand and a dozen Hampdens in sections of three went in to attack a German anti-aircraft ship. The British bombers were met by an enormous barrage as well as nine Messerschmitt 109s which dived to attack. One of the enemy made a bad mistake by flying right over the top of the aircraft piloted by Squadron Leader Good, presenting a nice blue belly as a perfect target for Sergeant Smith and Sergeant Wallace who promptly shot it down, amid much jubilation.

More than one Hampden went down under that attack. They closed their ranks, and another nine Messerschmitt 109s attacked and continued to attack until the British aircraft were sixty miles out at sea. The British bombers fought back furiously, but how many of the enemy failed to return remains unknown. Of that dozen Hampdens, only six got back.

When Squadron Leader Good landed, his aircraft was very much shot about. But the unbelievable thing was that the petrol tank had been pierced and the petrol had caught fire. The tank itself was all blistered, and there was an area of the wing some five feet long by four feet wide all burned.

Somehow, in some way the blazing petrol was put out. How it happened nobody knows. It was the first known instance of a petrol tank catching fire and going out again.

Everyone was amazed. It was one of those things which the experts considered to be impossible.

That day it was surely a miracle which saved Squadron Leader Good and his crew.

CHAPTER IX

NIGHT FIGHTER TRIUMPHS

A GERMAN bomber at any particular second may be flying in any direction at any height from ground level up to its ceiling at a speed of say five miles a minute. The pilot can dive, climb, switchback, weave about and change his height and direction all the time he is flying. He is never still for one fraction of a second in one particular spot in the air. Always he is moving, and if he is flying on a straight course he travels 130 yards in one second. He cannot climb 390 feet in a second, but he can dive more than 390 feet in a second, so he can alter his height, direction and position at the average rate of 130 yards a second.

A shell must burst within twenty-five yards of a bomber to bring it down, so a bomber can never be within range of a bursting shell for more than one-fifth of a second. It is a very short time. A gunner who aimed directly at a bomber, assuming that he could see it flying and knew its exact height, would never hit it. By the time the shell had reached the exact spot at which the gunner had seen the bomber flying, that bomber would be far away out of danger. Therefore the gunner all the time is compelled to try to anticipate or predict the exact spot where the bomber will be when the shell bursts. The wonder is not that he misses, but that he scores so many hits. Even in daylight when the gunner can see the aircraft he finds it is no easy task, despite the most wonderful automatic aids devised by science. In the darkness it is infinitely more difficult.

The night fighter has no simpler problem to solve. He has to mount into illimitable space and intercept an aircraft that is free to move in any direction at any height and variation of speed between the maximum and the minimum that the pilot chooses. At one second the enemy aircraft may be six miles high and forty-five seconds later it may have dived down to 500 feet. Despite the scientific wonders performed by the sound locators in detecting the course and height of the enemy and the quiet voice which reaches up from the ground to whisper into the ears of the night fighter pilot to help and guide him in his task, the difficulties are immense. The night fighter must be able to see the enemy before he can destroy him, and for this reason the chances of success are so much greater on bright moonlight nights than on dark moonless nights.

These were some of the difficulties confronting the first night fighters when a few enthusiastic pilots were risking their lives to prove that night fighting was possible and the specialists of the Royal Air Force were striving in secret to formulate the best methods of training. It is my privilege to describe a few outstanding night-fighting feats, including the triumphs of the first three men to accomplish the feat of shooting down two enemy aircraft in one night.

"In June, 1940, during a night attack by enemy aircraft, he shot down two Heinkel 111s. His magnificent leadership, skill and courage have been largely responsible for the many successes obtained by his squadrons," was a part of the citation announcing the award of a Bar to the Distinguished Flying Cross of Flight Lieutenant Adolph Gysbert Malan, who eventually attained the rank of Group Captain and was awarded the D.S.O. and Bar.

Born at Wellington in South Africa in 1910, Adolph Gysbert Malan in earlier years showed definite leanings toward the sea, for after leaving Wellington Public School, he entered the South African training ship General Botha and became an officer in the Royal Naval Reserve. From the sea, however, his attention turned to the air, and in 1936 he gained a commission in the Royal Air Force. The war brought out his abilities, and under his leadership No. 74 Fighter Squadron, which was the first squadron to knock down 600 enemy aircraft, outrivalled the deeds and reputation of the old No. 74 Squadron of the last war.

It was on the night of June 18, 1940, a clear sparkling night with everything illuminated brightly by a moon almost at the full, when the enemy sent about thirty bombers at intervals up the Thames estuary. They began to drop their bombs, and dozens of searchlights swept the skies and held them tenaciously in their beams as the guns started to boom out.

At the time Mrs. Malan was in a nursing home expecting a baby and her husband must have been rather concerned about her, particularly as she was right in the area which was being attacked. The bombing continued and for some time the pilots on his station watched the searchlights picking up and holding the Germans. As they watched the enemy bombers coming over, they chafed to get into their Spitfires to attack, but the area was so heavily defended by guns that it was considered inadvisable for any pilots to fly there. Conditions were so ideal for attacking the raiders from the air, however, and the pilots were so insistent, that permission was granted to send up one aircraft, and Flight Lieutenant Malan was at length permitted to fly.

According to an eyewitness, he called for his fitter and rigger, who happened to have turned in for the night. Without waiting to dress, they pushed their feet into gum boots, slung their rifles over their shoulders, put on their tin hats and reported for duty in their striped pyjamas. No one seemed to take much notice of their incongruous appearance. More vital things claimed their attention.

Along with the pilot, they were rushed out in a car to the aircraft dispersal post.

While the rigger and fitter worked swiftly to start up the Spitfire, the pilot methodically buckled on the harness of the parachute. By the time he had got his gear on, the engine had started, so he climbed into the cockpit and strapped himself in, before opening up the throttle to warm the engine up a bit.

Meanwhile he looked up and tried to pick out a target ahead, and saw a Heinkel 111 at 6,000 feet being held by the searchlights. It was making a straight run directly across him.

A second glance at the approaching bomber made him decide that discretion was the better part of valour and that the engine was quite capable of warming itself up. Leaping out of the cockpit with his parachute on, he made a dive for a little trench close at hand.

The last time he saw the trench it was only about eighteen inches deep. But unknown to him the men had continued to dig until it was about five feet deep. He dived in just as the bomber arrived slap overhead, and landed on his face in the mud at the bottom.

When the Heinkel had passed over, he got into his Spitfire and cracked off and made straight for the same Heinkel, which was obviously blinded by the searchlights. Heading for the coast and climbing quickly, he intercepted it just as it was on a slow climb crossing the coast.

The beams of the searchlights made things very deceptive. The first thing he knew he was about fifty yards from it. One moment it looked like a moth in a candle flame, the next the wings suddenly took shape and he realized he was very close.

He gave signs to the guns to stop firing directly he was in a position to attack and they at once stopped firing—the whole thing worked like a charm—and in he went. He pressed the trigger, but after a three second burst he had to jam his stick forward to avoid colliding with the enemy. In this short time his screen was covered with oil from the bomber, which spiralled out of the searchlights and soon crashed on the beach, half in and half out of the water.

As the South African pilot returned to his base, he looked back and saw another Heinkel 111 held by the searchlights. Climbing in a spiral below the enemy he signalled the guns to hold off. Then he moved in to attack at 16,000 feet. This time he was a lot more cautious and determined not to overrun the enemy, so he opened fire at 200 yards and closed to 100 yards. As he passed, the Heinkel burst into flames, and a parachute became entangled near the tail. Then the enemy aircraft went down in a steep spiral well on fire. The pilot of the Spitfire saw it crash in a vicar's garden near Chelmsford with a terrific sheet of flame that was seen all the way from Southend.

So the South African pilot in twenty minutes shot down two of the enemy bombers out of the seven destroyed by British fighters that night. The following night three more of the enemy bombers were shot down by British fighters, and directly the German bombers learned that the fighters were up they began to turn off to sea. The losses suffered by the Germans on these occasions curtailed their night attacks for some time.

Less than a week earlier, on the evening of June 12th, a Hampden bomber took off from its base in England to obstruct the German advance into France by bombing some cross roads at Rheims. It was a very dark night, with no moon, and cumulus clouds massed up to 10,000 and 12,000 feet. The captain of the aircraft, Squadron Leader R. S. Allen, climbed to about 5,000 feet, picked up the French coast and set course for Rheims. The weather was very bad.

As the Hampden flew along in the intense darkness, Squadron Leader Allen suddenly noticed some lights moving along a course parallel to his own. They were the navigation lights of an aircraft, but he could not make out what it was, so he asked his wireless operator and gunner, Sergeant William Richard Williams, if he could identify it.

The wireless operator, standing up in the turret by his guns, looked across and saw the navigation lights in the murky night, but it was so dark that he could not be sure of it.

Very skilfully Squadron Leader Allen dropped his aircraft and swung underneath the stranger to try to get him in silhouette against the sky, then swung up on the other side of him. Aided by the navigation lights on the other aircraft, the captain of the Hampden saw without doubt that it was a Heinkel 111, a fact which was confirmed by Sergeant Williams.

The British aircraft had barely started to swing up on the other side before the Heinkel switched off the lights.

At once the captain of the Hampden decided to attack. Dropping down again, and manœuvring his aircraft with uncanny skill, he brought it slowly right up under the bomber until he reached a position where he was no longer able to see the enemy, who was directly overhead.

The wireless operator was in a much better position. The dome of his turret gave him a clear view right overhead and around, as he stood tensely by his twin guns which pointed upwards towards the tail.   Flying blindly on the instructions of the wireless operator, Squadron Leader Allen piloted his machine gently ahead until Sergeant Williams saw the Heinkel above the tail of the Hampden at no more than twenty yards range.   It took four or five minutes to accomplish this feat, so the Hampden must have flown sixteen or twenty miles while working into position.

"Then I opened fire with my two guns," Sergeant Williams reported. "I was standing up and firing right up above my head. All I saw was an immense silhouette and two tongues of flame flowing from each engine. We were then between 3,000 and 4,000 feet. I did not have to use my sights at all, and my tracer bullets were lighting him up all over the place. You could see the light greenish-blue colour which they use on the German aircraft as well as the black crosses on the wings. I kept my triggers pressed until all the hundred rounds in each pan had gone, a total of two hundred rounds. Just before I'd finished he started to dive over our port side. The tracer still lit him up and queer lights came from him as smoke poured out of him. He disintegrated in the air and that was the last I saw of him as he went down over our port side."

We can imagine the scene in the aircraft.

Sergeant Williams, naturally very excited, shouting: "He's going down! He's going down!"

The navigator, Sergeant Cadman, in the nose of the aircraft, no less elated, calling out: "Good old Bill!"

Squadron Leader Allen asking Sergeant Stratton, the rear gunner, "Did you see him going down?"

And the cheery reply: "Yes, he was going down all right. He was full of smoke and breaking up!"

"Then I sat back on my seat feeling very happy, and I just said to myself, 'I've won the D.F.M.' It was always my ambition to get one," remarked Sergeant Williams afterwards.

And so he did.

By one of those incredible strokes of luck which cannot be explained, Squadron Leader Allen was looking out into the blackness a minute or two later when he saw another aircraft flying along with navigation lights burning, and recognized it as a Junkers 87.

"There's a Junkers 87 over there. I think I'll have a go at this with the front gun," he said to Sergeant Williams.

"I wouldn't do that," was the reply of Sergeant Williams. "Two guns are better than one! Besides," he added jokingly, "you might miss!"

The squadron leader laughed. They were all very happy on board that night.

Once more, with very great skill, Squadron Leader Allen employed the same tactics, dropping down to draw gradually underneath the enemy. But it was not quite so easy this time. The Junkers now and again kept popping down and the pilot of the Hampden had to move smartly to get out of his way, but each time he worked carefully back again until the Junkers was within point-blank range at twenty yards and slightly to the starboard of the Hampden.

In the interval Sergeant Williams reloaded, and as he saw the great shape above him he fired with both guns at the pilot's cockpit. The tracer bullets from the British bomber lit the belly of the Junkers and showed up the black crosses. It seemed to hesitate in its flight, then it dived under the starboard side of the Hampden and Squadron Leader Allen, who saw it blazing, followed it down to see it crash.

Climbing again to have another look round, and failing to see any more German aircraft about, the captain of the Hampden, after this thrilling interlude of ten minutes, decided to carry on with his job, which was to bomb those cross roads. But in the darkness and the excitement of stalking the two enemy bombers he did not know exactly where he was, so he turned round to pick up his position on the French coast, before going on to Rheims, where two of his bombs made a mess of the cross roads.

It was daybreak when they touched down at their base, and the ground crew, seeing Sergeant Williams patting his guns and holding up two fingers, knew at once what had happened. The news is said to have flashed round the station and reached the Intelligence Department before the captain and crew of the aircraft could get there to report.

Congratulations were showered upon Squadron Leader Allen, who received the D.S.O. The sergeants duly celebrated the event in a glass of ale, by which time they were ready to enjoy the breakfast of ham and eggs that was prepared for them. Then they turned in to sleep, after the most exciting night of their lives.

Next day saw Sergeant Williams on leave at his home in Merseyside, his dark eyes sparkling and his wavy black hair sprucely brushed, while his mother and father and sister crowded round him, on that happy Saturday. On the Sunday morning a telegram arrived to say that Sergeant William Richard Williams had been awarded the Distinguished Flying Medal.

One of the noteworthy things about the first year of the air war was that the British bombers shot down more enemy aircraft at night than did the British fighters. This was largely due to the fact that the Germans did not start mass raids over Britain at night until June, so in these months the British fighters lacked the opportunity to destroy the enemy night flyers, while the British bombers flying over Germany at night were now and again fortunate enough to come upon the enemy, generally as they were flying over their own aerodromes or about to land on them, and were able to get in attacks and shoot them down.

About thirty enemy aircraft were destroyed at night by British bombers in the first twelve months of the war.

It was not the member of a bombing crew, however, but the fighter pilot of a Hurricane, Pilot Officer R. P. Stevens, D.F.C., who bagged the third brace of bombers in one night. His strong face and blue eyes were well-known on the air-route between Croydon and Paris before the war. Night flying was no new thing to him, for he had long experience as a pilot of commercial aircraft, and often flew English newspapers over to the French capital in the dark hours, so his log indicated about 400 hours of night flying.

The night of January 15-16, 1941, when he achieved his first double success, was almost ideal for the purpose. There was bright moonlight, and the earth was covered with a layer of snow against which an enemy bomber stood out to the night fighter pilot flying above it, while the snow reflected the moonlight to make the night even brighter. Listening posts all over the country were busy with their sound locators to catch the sound of the raiders so that the course and height could be plotted and warning could be given to the towns and cities which the raiders threatened to attack.

Pilot Officer Stevens and other night fighting pilots on his station awaited orders. They were ready to take off at any moment and their Hurricanes were serviced, with ground crews standing by. Reports of enemy aircraft making for London began to come in, and just before 1 o'clock Pilot Officer Stevens climbed into the cockpit, strapped himself in, had a look round to assure himself that everything was all right, closed the hood, signalled to the crew to pull the chocks from under the wheels and roared off into the moonlit sky. His clock on the instrument panel showed that it was 12.56.

Climbing steadily, he flew south, keeping in touch with his base by wireless. It was cold enough on the ground, but it was much worse in the air. The higher he climbed, the lower the temperature fell. It dropped to the zero mark and continued to drop as he rose. Despite his warm clothing and the enclosed cockpit he began to feel a little cold. He kept a sharp look-out, weaving about at times to try to find the enemy, but he flew for half an hour without seeing anything at all. He was now over three miles high and feeling almost frozen.

A minute or two later he saw the flashes of bombs exploding ahead of him. The magic voice whispered directions in his ears and he made a slight alteration of course.

When he got near London the anti-aircraft shells bursting above him told him that the enemy was at a still higher altitude. Climbing another 500 feet, he began to weave up and down and sideways, as the magic voice told him that the enemy was somewhere near.

He looked around, but saw no signs, so he decided to follow the line taken by the bursting shells. It was then 1.30 a.m. A few seconds later he caught sight of the raider crossing his path. It was a Dornier "flying pencil" turning and climbing very fast about 400 yards ahead.

At once the fighter pilot gave the Hurricane full boost to attain the highest possible speed in order to overtake the enemy, but after that momentary glimpse the Dornier vanished. Flying at top speed the fighter pilot sought his quarry. "I picked him up again," Pilot Officer Stevens remarked afterwards, "climbing at 20,000 feet. He had dropped his bombs and was light. I climbed after him and chased him up to 30,000 feet. Throttling back to cruising speed as I closed, I swung out to make my attack between fifty and twenty-five yards. I saw my ammunition going home and striking him. Bits flew off and hit my aircraft. Oil came back on my windscreen and he just reared straight up. I thought I was going to crash into him, so I turned to one side to get away and only just managed to avoid him. As I did so he went straight down.

"Thinking he was trying to fox me, I went down after him flat out from 30,000 to 3,000 feet in a steep spiral. I've never travelled so fast before—you've no idea of speed when you are looking for a Jerry, you just notice when the ground is coming too close and then pull out. I saw him shooting away in a steep climbing turn, so I pulled everything back and did a gentle black-out. Owing to my excess speed I went well outside him and lost him again for a moment. Then I saw him still climbing and quickly closed on him. I gave him a burst from my eight guns and saw little blue flames dancing about his wings and fuselage. At the top of his climb, as he started to stall, I gave him another burst. Flames streamed from him as he went down and crashed at 1.35 a.m. among some trees which he set on fire. Circling round, I climbed to 15,000 feet and went home."

The gentle black-out he referred to was caused by turning at such a high speed that centrifugal force drove the blood away from the blood vessels behind the eyes and caused him momentarily to go blind, although he remained fully conscious of what he was doing. This phenomenon was first suffered by Air Commodore A. H. Orlebar in training for the Schneider Trophy race and he very courageously experimented and subjected himself to a complete black-out in order to see what happened. He found the senses were not otherwise affected, although he could see nothing at all. Medical researches proved the cause and found that the effects were in no wise dangerous or permanent, so this was something else which the Schneider Trophy races taught the world.

So fast did Pilot Officer Stevens travel during his dive that the bottom of his aircraft cracked under the tremendous air pressure. Although the pilot did not know it at the time, he himself suffered in his zeal to overtake the enemy. At 30,000 feet the air pressure is about $4\frac{1}{2}$ lbs. per square inch, while at ground level it is 15 lbs. to the square inch. He dived so rapidly that the pressure inside his body could not adjust itself quickly enough to the increasing pressure outside his body, with the result that some fluid formed in one of his ear drums. Luckily it soon came right.

We can imagine how the news of further raiders broke up the discussion in the mess and sent Pilot Officer Stevens and the other night fighters to fresh Hurricanes to take up the hunt once more. Pilot Officer Stevens, with his mind full of the unforgettable impression of the greatest city in the world dwarfed to microscopic proportions as he viewed it in the moonlight from a height of six miles, and what appeared to be a torch, but was actually a fairly large fire, blazing amid the tiny buildings, sped away in the direction of the capital and climbed to about 17,000 feet. Alert ears listened at innumerable posts below to pass on information with which the voice on the radio-telephone helped him. For a time his search was fruitless. Suddenly he glanced round and saw a Heinkel 111 coming up on his tail. Opening his throttle wide, the night fighter made a steep turn to get round on the tail of the enemy and attack. As he approached to within a quarter of a mile, the enemy aircraft opened fire, but did not hit the night fighter.

Closing up, Pilot Officer Stevens squeezed the button on his control column to set his eight guns blazing away at the enemy. He saw his tracer going home, but this was a bigger, heavier aircraft that could take more punishment than the Dornier. Observing little result, he attacked again, and saw the lines of tracer flying past him as the enemy fired back. Suddenly he noticed a parachute rip open almost on his wing. In a few seconds another parachute cracked open and floated away with the moon illuminating it and making it look quite beautiful.

Attacking again, Pilot Officer Stevens saw the Heinkel begin to lose height, but all the time a German gunner was firing back. Turning away, the night fighter closed and sent in another sharp burst as the Heinkel went down. Again the Hurricane turned away and coming in from another angle blazed away at the enemy. One engine of the Heinkel began to give out white smoke. Pilot Officer Stevens stuck grimly to his prey, following one attack by another from different angles as the Heinkel went smoking down.

"He continued to lose height, with both motors smoking," the pilot said afterwards in describing the end. "I ran out of ammunition and followed him down to 1,500 feet and then down to 1,000. A little later I lost him over a dark patch of water, so I did not actually see him land."

But immediate confirmation was forthcoming that the Heinkel had crashed, and Pilot Officer Stevens joined that very select band of pilots who had shot down two enemy aircraft in a night, and the even more select band who have been awarded an honour on the field in England, for it is said that within ten minutes of his victory, he was decorated with the Distinguished Flying Cross.

In the days of April, 1941, when the full moon fell on Good Friday, conditions were extremely favourable for intercepting the German bombers. Then for a few nights the British night fighters struck heavily at the raiders and scored numerous successes, one pilot making history by being the first to shoot down three enemy aircraft in one night.

Pilot Officer R. P. Stevens, D.F.C., also made night-flying history. He was up hunting in the moonlit skies on the night of April 8th, when his keen blue eyes detected first one and then another German raider, each of which he shot down and destroyed.

Forty-eight hours later, on the night of April 10th, his lucky star was again in the ascendant as he climbed high to stalk the enemy by the light of the moon, for he was once more able to make contact with the foe and bring two of the raiders within reach of his avenging guns. Thus on three occasions he shot down two enemy raiders in a single night—a remarkable record which not only won for him the Bar to his D.F.C., but also a warm commendation for his great determination to attack the enemy and to fly in the most difficult weather conditions. "His courage, determination, thoroughness and skill have set an excellent example to his unit," ran the official citation—which Pilot Officer Stevens fully justified by excelling his own record and shooting down two more of the enemy on the night of May 7, 1941.

After he scored his first double success in January, he was rather peeved because the medical officer said he could not fly again until the fluid in his ear was absorbed, as it might disturb his sense of balance. "I could fly on my side," laughed the fair-haired pilot with the strong face. That was the spirit of England.

On Friday, December 12, 1941, came the news that Flight Lieutenant R. P. Stevens had been awarded the D.S.O. for shooting down 14 enemy aircraft in night combats since January 1941—a record which stamped him as a master of night fighting, for he always hunted and fought alone. Some five weeks later while engaged in developing intruder patrols he set out to hunt for the second night over an enemy aerodrome in occupied territory and was never seen again.

Another pilot who made his mark as a night fighter was Wing Commander John Cunningham, D.S.O. and Bar, D.F.C. A year after Lieutenant Stevens started to make night-flying history by his lone patrols, Cunningham began to hunt the night skies in a Beaufighter with Pilot Officer C. F. Rawnsley, D.F.C., D.F.M., as his observer. They proved a perfect team and between them they shot down 14 enemy raiders during the hours of darkness. In one night in May, 1941, during a raid on the Midlands, they scored a triple success by shooting down three bombers; but the night they will remember as long as they live was the night their Station Commander presented them to the King and they flew off and shot down two German raiders within half an hour while His Majesty was in the Control Room following operations.

Now and again, if conditions be right and luck be good, something exceptional may happen, as it did on January 17, 1943, when Wing Commander C. M. Wight-Boycott and his observer, Flying Officer E. A. Sanders, shot down four enemy raiders in a night. Interested in flying since his university days, Wing Commander Wight-Boycott flew before the war with the Cambridge University Air Squadron, and like many other amateur pilots joined the Volunteer Reserve of the Royal Air Force. When the war came he was one of the officials in the Criminal Investigation Department of Scotland Yard and was at once called up by the Royal Air Force.

For months he went up in his Beaufighter and failed to make contact with a single raider. Then on the night of January 17th-18th it seemed that he could do no wrong, for in three sorties, lasting six hours, four raiders fell to him and his observer.

Let Wing Commander Boycott, who was 32 years old, record the details of his extraordinary feat in his own words. "I had been waiting for this for eighteen months," he said. "Our first Hun, a Dornier 217, exploded somewhere in the middle of the fuselage when I began firing. It went down in a steep dive and we saw it blazing on the ground, where the bombs appeared to explode. We didn't meet a thing on our second patrol, but shortly before 4 a.m. we took off again and, after about half an hour's flying, we saw another Dornier 217, which was jinking violently. The pilot was obviously scared of night fighters. I got in a fairly long burst and he went down in flames. We could see him burning on the ground.

"By this time I was getting rather tired, but when we saw another Dornier 217 I got in a long burst amidships. There was an explosion and the Hun went down. I found, by the way, that my tiredness was due to the fact that I had turned off my oxygen by mistake. As soon as I switched on again I felt fine.

"Our fourth Hun of the night was a Junkers 88 which caught fire in both engines. The fire spread along the wings and back along the fuselage. It lit up the whole sky so clearly that we could see the black crosses on the aircraft. We watched four members of the crew bale out, one after another. The aircraft then went down, exploding with a brilliant flash.

"It was a grand night for night-fighting, for the moon and cloud made the conditions almost ideal."

The late Squadron Leader Archie McKellar performed the unique feat of destroying three German bombers in one burst during the Battle of Britain; but that was in daylight. The record for the quickest destruction of three bombers at night was made by Flight Sergeant A. M. O. Pring and Warrant Officer C. T. Phillips who shot down three Japanese raiders in four minutes just before midnight on January 15, 1943, thus defeating a Japanese attack on Calcutta.

Pring, who was slightly built, about six feet tall, with brown hair and brown eyes, looked younger than his 21 years. Joining the Royal Air Force in 1940, he eventually teamed up with Phillips. They viewed the Pyramids by moonlight and shot down a German bomber in the desert. They flew from the embattled isle of Malta many times to meet the air assaults of the Germans and Italians, shooting two of the enemy into the sea. And they had been in India but a short time when they took off in their Beaufighter that night and wiped out the entire raiding force of Japanese bombers.

In the brilliant moonlight they sighted three bombers that were travelling very fast. Then for a few moments they lost track of them. But the moon was so very bright that they soon picked them up again. "I drew very close to one bomber and my first burst set his starboard engine aflame and I saw him break in half and go down," said Pring. "I then picked up the other two bombers and administered the same treatment to the nearer one, while some return fire came from the third bomber. As I saw the second raider afire and going down, I attacked the third and gave him a hearty burst. Flames shot from the fuselage and I saw him crash. I could see all three Japanese aircraft burning below."

So both men won immediate awards for a night-fighting feat of outstanding merit, Pring gaining the D.F.M. and Phillips the D.F.C.

CHAPTER X

MISSING

OF all the adventures and escapes which took place in France in the days of May, 1940, few were more thrilling than that of Pilot Officer B. J. Wicks. Very tall, very modest, with blue eyes, a wave of fair hair and the temperamental spirit of a good fighter, Pilot Officer Wicks, who was posted as missing for twelve days, turned up at Dunkirk in such strange garb that, lacking anything by which he could prove his identity, he was arrested by the British army authorities under suspicion of being a spy.

The army officer was not to blame. Anyone looking less like an officer of the Royal Air Force would have been difficult to find. Accordingly the young man who called himself Pilot Officer Wicks, but who was more like a Belgian refugee, was conveyed across the Channel under open arrest in charge of the naval commander of a torpedo boat who did not let him out of his sight until he had delivered him to the Air Ministry.

Even after the missing pilot spoke from the Air Ministry to the adjutant of his unit by telephone, telling him he had returned, that officer diplomatically suggested that the Air Ministry had better send an officer along with him to his unit to make sure that he was not stopped on the way—apparently the adjutant, prudently and rightly, was taking no chances of letting a German spy loose in the country, so Pilot Officer Wicks was provided with an escort until his identity was proved beyond doubt.

That was the happy ending to twelve exciting days which started on the afternoon of Wednesday, May 23, 1940, when Pilot Officer Wicks flew off with Squadron No. 56 from his station in England to patrol Arras and prevent enemy reconnaissance or bombing aircraft from approaching the town. As General Lord Gort was making the town his headquarters and spent at least one exciting night there while the place was being bombed to pieces by the enemy, it is now possible to realise why this fighter squadron of Hurricanes guarded the spires of Arras.

Soon after the Hurricanes arrived they saw several Henschel reconnaissance aircraft which were attacked and dispersed without delay. Pilot Officer Wicks, fastening on one, sent it crashing, the pilot baling out. Then the Hurricane pilot went after another German who was too wily for him. Playing hide-and-seek amid the intermittent cumulus clouds, the Henschel pilot at length dived to lead the Hurricane to and fro within a hundred feet of the ground over a little town that was well fortified by the Germans with anti-aircraft machine-guns. Not until Pilot Officer Wicks saw the tracer and heard some ominous clanging sounds in his aircraft did he realise that the German had tricked him into trouble.

Leaving two Hurricanes to finish off the enemy, which they did, he turned away to check the damage. Petrol was gushing out of a bullet hole in his front tank at a rapid rate, while petrol pouring back into the cockpit from the reserve tank was already soaking his clothes and drenching everything there. With petrol supplies running away, menaced by the risk of the aircraft suddenly going up in flames, the pilot flew off to the south-west to land in France well out of the way of the German invaders. By now he was saturated with petrol and a spark would have turned him into a living torch.

Thinking he was over unoccupied France, he saw a large field which offered a possible landing ground. There were strips of growing corn a few inches high and strips of ploughed ground, so he put his undercarriage down and made a clever landing.

Lacking maps, not knowing where he was, he climbed out of the aircraft. To the south was a small village with a church spire showing among the trees, to the west, half way across the field, ran a road; another road lay to the east, while to the north was a great stretch of marsh, full of stagnant pools with a river winding into the distance. Not a human being was in sight.

Calling up his flight commander on the radio-telephone, he explained his predicament, but failed to make contact. Then he put his parachute pack on the ground with his helmet on top and set forth to find help.

Plate 4.—SQUADRON LEADER B. J. WICKS, D.F.C., who made such an amazing escape from behind the enemy lines in the guise of a Belgian refugee after being posted as missing for twelve days.

Plates 5, 6.—SERGEANT JOHN HANNAH, V.C., who extinguished the fire in the burning bomber, with the late PILOT OFFICER C. A. CONNOR, D.F.C., who flew the aircraft so calmly when disaster seemed imminent. The lower photograph shows how the fire destroyed the rear cockpit (see page 94).

The fumes from his petrol-soaked clothes made his eyes smart and affected his lungs and there is no doubt that if he had struck a match or approached a fire he would have been burned to death.

He had gone but a short distance when a column of transport began to pass along the west road toward the north and he came to the conclusion that it was French. Then the crack of rifle fire rolled out to the east and he realized with a start that he was the target. As he was soaked with petrol, it would have been throwing his life away to attempt to fire his aircraft. The only available cover was a dip in the ground to the west, for which he ran under continuous fire until he gained its shelter. Directly he had dropped down the shoulder of the hill beyond observation from the east, he changed direction and wormed his way forward over marshy ground to the north.

Lying under cover about 200 yards from the west road, he watched the passing transport. Groups of French soldiers marching between ambulances and staff cars convinced him that the convoy was French and that he was quite safe, so he got up and walking to the fringe of the road stood under the hedge for five minutes while cars and ambulances went by.

"Verboten" he read on the side of an ambulance.

He could hardly believe his eyes. They were Germans. Dropping back through the hedge, he lay low till the convoy had passed, rather shaken by his blunder and thankful to escape.

Proceeding with the utmost caution—for the Germans were too close to be pleasant—he came at last on a humble dwelling and ventured to make inquiries. One of the peasants spoke English. "The Germans are here. Throw away your revolver or you will be shot," he said.

"Which way shall I go?" he asked.

They pointed out the way, which he took until beyond their sight, then he hid his revolver and doubled back toward the coast. Knowing that the Germans were bound to make inquiries for him, he thought it safer to leave the peasants in ignorance of the real way he had gone.

The roads offered the only passage through the marshes, but they were far too dangerous, and instead of leading to freedom they were more likely to lead to a German prison camp. Anything was preferable to that, so he plunged into the marshes, walking where he could, wading where necessary and made slowly toward the coast, after discarding his Sidcot flying suit.

Very wet and with the mud of the marshes clinging to him, he came at nightfall upon a small cottage where two kindly countrymen took compassion on him. Making him welcome at their fire—which dried his clothes—they provided him with a meal of radishes, bread and butter and cheese. Never was a meal more welcome. From the tin of coffee stewing perpetually on the grate they poured some in a cup, which they promptly filled with brandy. As soon as he had taken a drink, they insisted on filling the cup again with cognac, and as the

F—6

fighter pilot considered that the cognac spoiled the coffee, he made his
excuses and drank very little. The risks of being surprised by the
enemy were too great to allow him to sleep in the cottage, so his hosts
provided him with a big down quilt in which he rolled himself up and
slept in a corner of the barn.

Next day, a gloomy, wet day, his simple, kindly hosts provided him
with some coffee before he started about 6 o'clock in the morning to
try to reach the coast where he hoped to find a boat that would take
him to the south, or alternatively make his way into the Allied lines.
Passing a farm about four hundred yards along the road, he was
stopped by some Belgian refugees who, recognizing his uniform, at
once wanted to help him. Taking him into a barn, they gave him a pair
of dungarees to put over his trousers. Although so short that his
uniform trousers projected below the bottom of them, they served as a
disguise in conjunction with the raincoat which was provided for him.

A Peugot saloon car stood in the farmyard. "You can have it,"
they said.

"But how am I to return it to you?" he inquired.

"We don't want it," was the reply. "We've tried to get out with it
and can't. To-morrow we are going to try by bicycle, so you can take
the car."

He was rather staggered at being presented with a car in this way,
but they insisted that it was useless to them and that he must take it
to help him to get away. The tanks of the car were full of petrol, so
expressing his gratitude for their kindness he started on his adventures.
Less than two miles along the road he was hailed and stopped by more
refugees.

"Where did you get the car?" they asked.

He told them. Directly they learned he belonged to the Royal Air
Force they were as anxious as the others to help him. Taking him in,
they prepared a good meal for him, and while he was eating it he told
them of a project he had of swimming the Somme.

"Two tried to escape across the Somme last night, and one was shot
in the spine, and the other in the thigh. The German line runs along
there and you can't get past the sentries," he was told. In the circumstances he decided to search the coast to see if he could escape by boat,
and if he failed in that to try northward in the direction of Calais
where the position was very fluid and there was a much greater chance
of getting through. Supplying him with some hard-boiled eggs to stay
his hunger later in the day, the kindly Belgians sent him on his way,
wishing him luck. "You won't get across the Somme, but you may get
north if you keep inland," they assured him.

For five or six hours in the pouring rain, he explored miles of coast
for a boat, leaving the car now and again in a deserted farmyard and
going on foot. Not a boat was to be found, so he took a chance on the
inland road to the north. A refugee gave him a map issued for

advertising purposes by a motor firm, and although many roads and villages were not marked it proved of great service; another sympathetic refugee gave him a cheap French-English dictionary to help him if he were lost for a word. Amid all the hardships and sufferings of war, it was astonishing how many hands were held out to aid him, people who had lost everything and did not know themselves what they were going to do were anxious to do anything they could to enable him to escape.

Every road, every turning was a problem to him. Becoming confused by the roads, he turned down one that developed into nothing more than a cart track in which he got stuck. He was not pleased at having to turn back, but it was a bit of a blessing, for at the cross roads two young refugees accosted him and asked him for a lift. His French was so poor that they mistook him for a German. Inquiry revealed that they were Belgian university students who spoke fluent German and English and he offered to help them by giving them a lift if they would help him to get through by acting as spokesmen should they be stopped by Germans or anyone else.

"But what about your uniform?" asked one.

"I'll get rid of that later," Pilot Officer Wicks replied.

One of the Belgians was no more than eighteen years old, the other about twenty. As they were arrayed against a common enemy, they agreed to stand together. The two Belgians had the advantage over the pilot inasmuch as they had papers to show if challenged, whereas he lacked papers and had his air force uniform to give him away if the Germans came along. In common prudence he kept his raincoat carefully buttoned.

Coming to some cross roads, they were about to turn into a road leading to a town a few kilometres distant when a German appeared on a motor cycle and waved them back in order to let through a big enemy transport column which was following him. Seizing their opportunity to test out their plan on the enemy, one of the Belgians got down and started to talk to him in German.

"How far north can we go?" asked the young Belgian at last. "Can we go through to St. Omer?"

"Oh, yes, you can go as far as St. Omer, but no further," was the reply of the German, who seemed quite friendly and in no way suspicious.

The natural reaction of most men would be to get out of the way of those Germans as quickly as possible; but when the German started up and rejoined the convoy, Pilot Officer Wicks calmly followed him and also joined up with the enemy convoy. It was the height of audacity.

There was something more than audacity, a display of sound reason and logic without which Pilot Officer Wicks would never have escaped. Comment on his audacity brought forth the reply: "It was the obvious thing to do. We'd gained his confidence and if any question arose I thought he'd look after us."

So for several kilometres the officer of the Royal Air Force drove steadily along in the midst of his enemies without turning a hair. The peculiar thing was that throughout those twelve desperate days he faced all the risks without the slightest fear. But directly he was back in England he could not sleep for several nights owing to what he had been through.

On the outskirts of the town the German convoy turned off to go round it, so the Peugot car pulled out of the convoy and went into the town, at the entrance of which wrecked French lorries were lying along the roadsides. The Peugot had barely arrived before it was stopped by some German officers who announced that it was to be taken over. They demanded the papers so that they could register the owner of the car, implying that compensation would be paid, but this of course was just a farce to cover the usual German highway robbery. They also demanded the papers of the occupants of the car.

As Pilot Officer Wicks had no papers of his own and no papers for the car, he was in a fix. Had he opened his raincoat to go to his pockets, the enemy would at once have seen his uniform underneath. And there were those blue trousers showing below his overalls. The position was very dangerous, so he sat silently in the seat while the two Belgians got out and engaged the Germans in conversation and fiddled about with their own papers.

Meantime the German driver came up and started to question the fighter pilot about how to drive the car.

"Accelerateur?" asked the German.

Pilot Officer Wicks pointed to it, and got out of the car while the German got in. The enemy inquired about the petrol and was making inquiries about the non-existent key of the car when his attention was distracted by his officers and the Belgians, which gave the fighter pilot a chance of fading out of the picture. Thus the car which was given to him in the morning was stolen from him by the Germans at night. He probably would have been captured by the Germans on that occasion if they had not been so intent on their loot.

Fully alive to the dangers around him and to the necessity of discarding his uniform as quickly as possible if he was to play the part of a refugee successfully, he managed to acquire for exactly thirty francs a pullover with a zip fastener. This enabled him to get rid of his tunic in a wood.

When the Belgian refugees rejoined him, they told him that all refugees had to remain in the town for two days in order to register, and then they had to pass through the control at Arras back to Belgium. The net seemed to be closing in on him, and he decided to get away from the town that night. Tramping with his friends through the town until they hit on a small inn, they turned in for refreshment and rest.

Making tentative inquiries about staying a day or two in order to allay any suspicions of the proprietor and establish friendly relations, they went into a little room in which were about forty people who slept there at night. As soon as they settled down to their drink, the two young Belgians joined in the conversation, but Pilot Officer Wicks prudently said nothing.

A Frenchman eyed him suspiciously from time to time and at last said to the Belgians: "That chap's in the R.A.F."

"No, he's not," said the young Belgians.

"Look at his trousers!" said the Frenchman, pointing to the trousers showing below the overalls.

"He's been with us for days!" protested the Belgians, boldly standing up for their companion, while the eyes of the other occupants in the room began to glance curiously at the silent man in the raincoat.

"But look at his moustache—no Frenchman wears a moustache like that!" the Frenchman insisted.

The situation was becoming too delicate for Pilot Officer Wicks, who considered it time to retreat. Getting up in a surly manner and grunting ill-naturedly to his companions, he went out and promptly clipped off his toothbrush moustache with a pair of nail scissors as he walked along. It had nearly given him away once, and he was determined that it would not give him away a second time.

About midnight he arrived at a wayside estaminet where he got a drink of water and a simple meal from the friendly Frenchman before hiding away in the barn to sleep. After eighteen hours on the road the fighter pilot was very tired and even the rats failed to keep him awake.

It was about 6 o'clock next morning when he opened the barn door and cautiously peeped out, only to be waved back by the proprietor from whom he learned that a number of German officers and men had called there for a wash and a shave and a meal. He heard them cluttering about in the yard as he lay in hiding in the barn, and it was about 9.30 a.m. before the last German departed and he could emerge in safety. After taking a simple breakfast of boiled potatoes and milk, he started off again.

All sorts of rumours were rife, and although the peasants told him what they had heard from the German soldiers, nobody knew what was happening or where the Allied lines really were. The result was that he had frequently to change direction and retrace his steps to avoid places where the Germans were reported to be. That afternoon, very tired and with large blisters on his feet, he came on two more Belgian refugees who were as kind as they could be when they learned he belonged to the Royal Air Force.

That night he slept in the stable, and next day, as the Germans were moving about, the Belgians advised him to go into the woods until the evening. Remaining in hiding all day, he ventured back towards dusk for some food, but it was too dangerous for him to remain that night, so he took his departure and found a deserted barn in which he slept.

Making his way over the fields next day towards a little town which lay on his route, he came out on a road along which German transport poured. There were heavy tanks, light tanks, heavy lorries with enormous pontoons, troop carriers, motor cyclists with machine-guns all travelling towards the town where he proposed to go. There seemed to be no end to them. He stood at the roadside watching them pass and at length moved off until he arrived at a cottage where he was able to obtain some milk and ham sandwiches. While he sat in the cottage a long line of German ambulances stopped outside, whereupon he took refuge in the attic until they went on again.

It became obvious to him that he must get rid of his Air Force trousers without delay if he wished to win free. Fortunately he was able to beg a pair of pin stripe trousers from a woman whose husband was in the army, so he made his uniform trousers up in a bundle and watched some French peasants put them in the fire to destroy them. With a coat and waistcoat and cap provided by a generous French farmer, he now looked a typical refugee, with nothing about him to prove that he was anything else—except his slight knowledge of French. As the majority of Germans did not speak French any better than he did himself, he stood a good chance of carrying things off if it came to the pinch.

Next day he arrived at a village which was filling with German troops and transport. As he walked down the road in the direction of a farm, a German officer in a staff car focused his field glasses on him and watched him carefully all the way. Pilot Officer Wicks did not like it at all. Something had undoubtedly aroused the enemy's suspicions. Directly the flying officer came to the farmhouse, he turned in as though he belonged there and explained the position. Those kindly French folk with the utmost generosity gave him the meal they were about to eat themselves. Finding later that the way forward appeared to be barred, he made a detour in the direction from which he had come and spent the night in a stable amid the scuffling and squeaks of rats.

A refugee of whom he started to make inquiries next day said at once: "You are English! My husband would love to meet you."

Accompanying her to a farm, he met her husband, who had escaped from Holland. The fighter pilot rested in the stable there for two days. The French farmer, who was taken into his confidence, had very little food, but he shared what he had. Throughout the day sounds of a big battle were heard in the distance and the village doctor eventually came trotting up on his pony to say that the British had made a big push, but it proved to be false.

The following morning, as all was quiet, the English pilot decided to try to get through to the north again. His escape was made more difficult by the German order which compelled all refugees to travel to the southward to register and then go back to Belgium through

Arras, consequently he was compelled to travel in the opposite direction to the refugees, which was so suspicious that any alert German was likely to pounce upon him at any time. Fortunately none did.

That day he had a bad moment when he knocked at the door of a mansion for a drink of water, for the door was opened by two German soldiers. Apparently quite unconcerned, although the sight of them was a bit of a shock, Pilot Officer Wicks simply ignored them. Seeing in the background the lady of the house, he walked up to her without hesitation and asked for a drink of water, which was brought for him and he was allowed to depart unmolested.

He stayed the night in the stable of the mayor of a small village who, knowing he was English, told everyone that he was a Belgian refugee. The mayor was kindness itself and gave him all the information he possessed about the canals which the Germans were guarding ahead and which the Englishman had to cross in order to escape.

Throughout twelve days of hardship and anxiety, there was only one man to whom he appealed in vain for help. That was a French farmer who must have been one of the fifth-column Frenchmen in league with the Germans, for when the British pilot asked for permission to sleep in his barn, he agreed quite affably, and told the young man in the raincoat to follow him. Not anticipating any treachery, the pilot did so. He was very surprised to arrive at an anti-aircraft post where the farmer handed him over with a smile to the Germans manning it.

"You are English," they said. He denied it and swore he was a Belgian. The more they swore he was English, the more fiercely he denied it and expostulated with them. They made a most thorough search of his pockets and of course found nothing at all to prove his nationality or to give him away. Eventually he protested so violently at being detained, that they let him go; thus by sheer bluff he escaped out of the hands of the Germans.

He did not linger longer than he could help in that neighbourhood, but walked some distance until he came to another farm, where he slept in the barn. During the night he heard German soldiers draw up outside, and waited tensely in the dark, expecting every minute to hear the door of the barn being thrown open and gruff voices demanding his surrender; but luckily the Germans drove away and left him undisturbed on his bed of straw.

Approaching a canal the following day, under the impression that it was one of the main canals in his path, he found a punt on the banks and drew himself over by hauling on a chain put there for the purpose. To his disappointment he discovered this was a subsidiary canal and the main one lay in front of him. French barges were passing along, but no bargee would put him across because of the Germans who were patrolling up and down the canal in a motor boat.

"There's a bridge to the south," he was told.

Following the canal to the south, he came on the bridge at last and found, as he expected, that it was well guarded by the Germans. Numerous farm carts and refugees seemed to be crossing over and he went off to a farm a little further along to inquire how they managed it. His satisfaction can be imagined when he learned that Belgian refugees were being allowed to cross it.

Retracing his steps, he joined up with a party of poor refugees who had a cart containing all their belongings drawn by a horse whose ribs were his most prominent feature. The whole family got out at the bridge and started to push the cart up the incline. He pushed with the rest, just to give them a hand. As he walked down the other side behind the cart, the German soldiers stared at him, but no one stopped him, and in a little while he was able to breathe freely, knowing he had crossed one of the canals which barred his way to freedom.

The contradictory information he received from the peasantry was amazing and often swung him to and fro like a pendulum for many a weary mile in order to evade the Germans whose convoys were moving all the time along the roads. He met with kindness and a helping hand even in the poorest cottage, and by June 1st estimated that he had about ten miles to go before reaching the German front line. Obviously he had a greater chance of getting through in the darkness than in the daylight, so he planned to arrive in the neighbourhood in the afternoon and lie low until nightfall before making his attempt.

Starting out early in the morning, he was perplexed to find himself about 9 o'clock within a mile of the German lines. Enemy patrols were active all round, but he managed to evade them and spent the rest o the day finding out where the enemy posts were and acquiring information from the cottagers who, over a cup of coffee, were happy to pass on any news.

From one or two vantage points in the afternoon he surveyed the water ahead and selected what he considered was the best place for crossing the canal. Then he fell in with a friendly farmer and burrowed into a haystack in one of his outbuildings to have a rest. It was well that he took the precaution of concealing himself, for later on the Germans called at the farm to demand papers, and they went round the outbuildings to see if anyone was there. He heard them calling out as they poked their heads in, but he did not stir. The utter silence satisfied them, and he was glad to hear them depart.

Just as darkness was falling he set forth on his attempt to get through. To his disappointment he discovered that the water which he regarded as the canal was in reality nothing but a marsh in which he became hopelessly bogged. Finding it impossible to go forward, he was obliged to return, while a nearby German mortar and a French gun ahead carried out a duel in which they lobbed their shells over his head. The French shells were exploding far too close to please him as he made his way back to the farm and burrowed into the haystack to sleep for the night. That haystack was in the direct line of fire, but it was not hit.

At 6 o'clock on the morning of June 2nd, he started out again. Groups of German posts armed with anti-tank guns, machine-guns and rifles were stretched in a zigzag across the country at intervals of about 400 yards. In front of them was a stretch of open country about a mile and a half wide to the banks of the canal. A partially destroyed village and a small group of houses screened by trees provided the only shelter in the neighbourhood and his one chance of getting through was to reach this shelter.

"I passed the first line of sentries without difficulty," he said, "and whilst I was resting a large number of dive bombers flew overhead with their fighter escort. These were attacked by Hurricanes and a grand dog fight ensued. Assuming that this spectacle would hold the attention of the sentries, I set out for the houses.

"Throughout this crossing, carried out on my stomach, I could see the German soldiers, but they did not observe me. By the time I had gained the shelter of the trees I was thoroughly soaked and coated with mud, and I must have looked a very suspicious object to all who saw me. Reaching the cover of the trees, I made my way through the shelled village to the edge of the canal, where I attracted the attention of the French soldiers on the other side. They pulled me over in a boat and took me to a French officer."

It was a stroke of good fortune that the Hurricanes overhead were able at the critical moment to create a diversion which enabled the missing Hurricane pilot on the ground to make his escape from the enemy. When the Frenchmen came to search him they found a sausage slung round his neck by a piece of string. They did not know what to make of it. Rather apprehensively they examined it and found that amid the packing of meat inside the sausage skin was a wrist watch.

The fighter pilot, thinking he might have to swim the canal, and not wanting to ruin his watch, had adopted this unusual method of preserving the watch from possible harm!

The French officers passed him from one to another until he was brought before a General who passed him on to the British Intelligence Staff and so at last to Dunkirk.

The evacuation of the army was going on ceaselessly. He had no papers and bore a greater resemblance to a Belgian refugee than to an officer of the Royal Air Force, although he was able to answer all questions satisfactorily. He was accordingly allowed to take his place on the jetty among the soldiers who were waiting for a boat to take them back to England. That was on June 3rd. All the time they were subject to attack. German dive bombers dropped bombs. German batteries at the other side of the town shelled the beaches continuously.

Having been missing for twelve days, he had no idea what had occurred in the interval. Naturally he started to ask questions of the Tommies about him. As he was already under suspicion, the expected happened.

"You can't ask questions," said a staff officer, and had him searched and put under arrest. He was duly handed over to the special care of Commander Banks who delivered him safely to the Air Ministry, with the happy results already known.

Step by step promotion came to him until Squadron Leader Bryan John Wicks became the proud leader of as keen a band of fighter pilots as any to be found in the Royal Air Force.

CHAPTER XI

TRAPPED UNDER THE SEA

APRIL 3, 1940, was not a good day so far as the weather was concerned. The clouds were down to within 300 feet of the sea and it was impossible to see anything much more than half a mile away. Yet on this day a footnote to history was made, for it marked the loss of the very first Spitfire that fell before the guns of the German Luftwaffe.

The weather, in fact, was so unpleasant that there was a good deal of talk in the operations room of an aerodrome toward the north of England as to whether the patrols should be sent out at all. Then the news came through that a Heinkel was attacking some trawlers about a dozen miles off Whitby and the Controller gave permission for one fighter to see about it.

Forthwith Flight Lieutenant Edgar Norman Ryder climbed into his Spitfire and took off with the intention of putting an end to the murderous Germans who were shooting innocent fishermen. Crossing the coast near Redcar, he flew over the trawlers which had been sorely knocked about by the Heinkel. The fishermen, however, had not taken their punishment lying down; they had hit back to such good effect that when the Spitfire pilot located the Heinkel it was flying along about 200 feet above the surface of the sea with one engine disabled.

As the enemy aircraft staggered along, Flight Lieutenant Ryder throttled down and circled it in order to decrease his speed. Then he went in to attack on a left-hand turn. Concentrating his fire on the other engine, he squeezed the button on his control column for four seconds while his eight guns spat death and destruction at the enemy. At the same time he noticed a couple of bangs under his own engine, but he was so intent on his attack that he paid no attention to them.

Giving the rear-gunner of the Heinkel a short burst to keep him quiet, Flight Lieutenant Ryder marked with satisfaction the flames and smoke beginning to spurt from the top and bottom of the main plane of the enemy. Then he turned away to run in to renew his attack. It was quite unnecessary. As he came about, the Heinkel was pancaking on the sea completely disabled.

Circling awhile, the fighter pilot watched the crew of five climb out upon the top of the main plane and passed the information back to his control. The Germans, after doing their best to murder the fishermen, disclosed their abnormal mentality by approaching as close as possible to a trawler, knowing that they would be rescued and treated well instead of being left to the fate which they fully deserved.

By now the pilot of the Spitfire, having cleverly intercepted and destroyed the raider according to plan, concluded it was time to return. As he set his course he realized that the cockpit was beginning to get rather hot. A glance at his instrument board revealed that his oil temperature was rising rapidly.

Calling up control, he advised them that he was in trouble and from then on gave them a running commentary of what was happening. Oil fumes began to fill the cockpit which grew hotter and hotter. Making out a small trawler ahead, he circled it while the fumes grew thicker and the heat more intolerable. The clouds were so low that it would have been suicide to attempt a parachute jump, so he told the Controller that he was going to land in the sea as near the trawler as possible.

While he was opening the hood of the cockpit, the engine seized up and failed completely.

"I'm about fifty feet off the sea now," he told the Controller, and switched off.

The sea was much rougher than he thought. Waves were running six and seven feet high as he sped at about eighty miles an hour toward the trawler, which was still half a mile away.

Then the Spitfire hit a wave with a crash. There was a great noise which the pilot afterwards remembered perfectly, before he was knocked out and rendered unconscious.

As the Spitfire dived below the surface, the sea surging over him brought him back to consciousness and his recollection of what occurred while he was trapped in the cockpit is so remarkable that it is worth placing on record: "I remember sitting in the cockpit and everything was a bright green. I was very fascinated by the stillness of it all—it was amazing, and I recall watching a lot of bubbles running up the windscreen before my nose and parting as they got to the front. I sat there fascinated by the sight and not a bit afraid. The calm was so restful after the noise. The green colour about me was lovely, but it turned to blackness before I got out.

"I started to get out by undoing my straps. I stood on my seat and just when I thought I was clear I found my parachute had caught under the sliding hood, and I could not move."

Owing to the nose of the aircraft being down, the front of the hood when open was above him and, as he rose, it pressed against his back, sliding down between his body and the packed parachute. Any attempt that he made to force his way upward while the hood was caught under the parachute was doomed to fail and would only have wedged him the more securely and led to his death.

In his efforts he swallowed a deal of water, yet his mind in that crisis worked so clearly and calmly that he at once knew what he was caught upon and did the only thing which would enable him to escape.

"I got partially into the cockpit again and at this point noticed it was getting very much darker as the aircraft sank. I was again nearly hooked up by my parachute, but I wriggled and got clear. By now it was very black and I just saw the silhouette of the tail plane pass my face. I still had on my parachute which hampered my movements, but I managed to dog paddle my way upwards."

These vivid words describe not only the most remarkable escape of a pilot during this war, but one hitherto unique in the history of aviation.

His struggle for life was by no means over when he reached the surface. The fact that his parachute had caused him so much trouble made him decide to get rid of it as quickly as possible. His thick flying clothes, being saturated with water, weighed him down; he had not blown up his Mae West, which would have supported him on the surface, but he felt quite sure that he would get along much better without being cumbered by the weight of his parachute. Although able to take breath now and again, he was so heavy in the water that instead of being able to surmount the six-foot and seven-foot waves, they rolled over him and submerged him each time.

His efforts to escape from the sunken cockpit had naturally used up much of his strength. Now, buffeted and swamped by the waves, he fought to undo the straps of his parachute harness. It was no easy task, yet he managed it.

Instead of gaining relief, he discovered that he was in a far worse position, for without his parachute he could not keep above the surface at all. As he started to sink, he managed to grab his parachute pack, which floated on the surface, and hang on to it grimly with his left arm. The waves kept washing over him. He was so exhausted that he could barely retain his hold of the life-saving parachute.

It began to dawn on him as he weakened under the buffeting of the seas that he would not be able to hang on much longer. It was as much as he could do to get his breath between each wave. As a big wave passed he saw the trawler approaching. He heard men shouting words of encouragement. The waves kept rolling over him. Then something touched him and, weak as he was, he remembered grabbing a boathook and being lifted out of the sea by numerous strong hands.

The fishermen took him back to their trawler—it was quite small, no more than forty feet long—and laid him down on the deck until he had partially recovered from his exhaustion, then they carried him below and placed him in a bunk. He was frightfully seasick owing to the rough seas. The little craft pitched and rolled so badly that once he was flung right out of his bunk on to the floor.

When rescued, he was about fifteen miles from Hartlepool, a distance which he had flown in three minutes, but it took the fishing boat six hours to reach port. While on the way he heard the wireless report that he was missing. The skipper of the smack notified a destroyer that the missing fighter pilot was safe, but that skipper was loath to give him up—having made the rescue, he wanted to finish the job himself and put the fighter pilot safely ashore.

"Not likely!" remarked the skipper as he got a signal from a destroyer. "I'll stove in my plates if I go near them."

Consequently he plugged along to port, with the sea-sick pilot down below.

It is not surprising that the young fighter pilot who showed such calmness and courage and resource in escaping from the cockpit of his Spitfire as it sank ever deeper into the sea was recognized by the award of the Distinguished Flying Cross.

Not until Dunkirk did he and the rest of his squadron have their first experience of meeting the famous Messerschmitt 109s—that was in a dog fight at 20,000 feet. One Spitfire pilot never returned from the sortie, but the squadron had the satisfaction of putting down two or three of the Me 109s.

Throughout those days of the Dunkirk evacuation, the Spitfires suffered the gunfire of all the belligerents; the anti-aircraft guns of the Germans, of the French and of the English all did their best to shoot them out of the sky, which, to say the least, was rather disconcerting.

Once when glancing down on a naval craft in the Channel, he saw a sudden spume of spray completely cover it and as the spray subsided the ship vanished under his eyes, probably from the direct hit of a bomb. He gazed down on the beaches black with men who seemed to be moving about like ants. Wrecked aircraft were scattered over the sands, the funnels and hulls of wrecked ships stuck up all over the shallows, while the destroyers and tugs and yachts and every conceivable kind of craft were ferrying to and fro carrying off their precious cargoes of human lives. The burning oil tanks fouled the heavens with their black smoke which plainly marked the position of Dunkirk to all aircraft. Far below him as the evacuation reached its zenith the Channel was crowded with craft of all kinds. Among them he particularly noted a tug towing lots of little boats so crowded with men that they were nearly swamped—"It was an awful sight," he remarked, when it was all over.

His main impression of the Battle of London was of masses of German bombers flying in perfect formation to attack the city, with the sky full of Messerschmitts.

Day after day he went off with Squadron No. 41 to counter the German air offensive over London and from first to last 100 of the enemy aircraft fell to the squadron's guns. They had sad losses as well as victories to count, but the fearless young pilots who went down helped to win a great triumph.

Ryder afterwards won a Bar to his D.F.C. and attained the rank of Wing Commander.

Many a pilot, like himself, abandoned his aircraft high in the sky and was saved by his parachute; but he was the only pilot to be saved by his parachute after abandoning his aircraft down in the dark depths of the sea.

On that dull day of April 3, 1940, when the Germans in shooting down his aircraft were able to claim their first Spitfire, they provided the world with an incredible but perfect paradox.

CHAPTER XII

SERGEANT JOHN HANNAH, V.C.

CLIMBING into their Hampden bomber on the evening of September 15, 1940, Pilot Officer Connor and his crew prepared to go to Antwerp to bomb Hitler's invasion barges. The Hampden was flown by a crew of four, the pilot and navigator, who faced forward, being completely cut off by an aluminium door from the wireless operator and the rear gunner, who faced the tail.

Behind the pilot amidships was a well in which the collapsible dinghy, fire extinguishers and other things were stored; then came the door, behind which sat the wireless operator whose dials and instruments were conveniently disposed to hand, while in front of him were two guns, pointing aft, with a sliding cupola overhead. There was a step down of perhaps two feet into the tail section of the aircraft, and the vertical of this step was cushioned to form a back rest for the rear-gunner, who sat on another cushion on the floor with his legs stretched straight out in a turret or cockpit which was known in the service as "the tin." Obviously there was not much room for the crew to move about.

In the front cockpit the navigator emptied his canvas bag of its maps and rules and pencils and compasses and the various books and dozen and one things which enabled him to fix his course and find his position. These he placed in their appointed places on his little table.

The propellers were ticking over, the engines roaring, the whole aircraft pulsating, ready to take off.

Adjusting their earphones, the crew plugged in to the "intercom" and pulled the chamois-covered mouthpieces up to their lips to settle them in place. The captain made the routine inquiries to learn if they were ready, then he got his signal to depart. After a short run he was in the air flying the usual circuit of the aerodrome to make sure that everything was working all right before climbing up on his course.

Their flight to Antwerp was uneventful. They picked up the docks and circled round to locate the barges as the searchlights groped for them in the sky.

"We started to make our bombing run, but found that we were not in line to make a good attack, so we turned, circled round and got into a better position," reported Pilot Officer Connor. "As soon as we arrived we noticed that the anti-aircraft gunfire was fairly heavy, but during that first run none of it came very close to us. It wasn't long, however, before they got our range and as we came round for the second attack we met a terrific barrage which we determined was not going to stop us. We were hit in the wing several times on the way down and the aircraft shook so much that it was not an easy matter to control it. However, we released our bombs and it was then that I saw flames reflected in my perspex windscreen. I soon realized that something had happened, but I was so busy taking violent evasive action that I did not at first give it any serious thought."

As the Hampden was diving, one of the German gunners got a direct hit with a shell which probably burst in the bomb compartment under the fuselage.

Instantly the rear-gunner's cockpit took fire. Flames flared up in the cockpit of Sergeant John Hannah, who wore his oxygen mask as usual. In a second or two both cockpits were alight.

"The aircraft is ablaze," announced Hannah to his captain over the intercommunication system.

"Is it very bad?" asked the pilot.

"Bad—but not too bad," was the reply.

The pilot saw the reflections of the flames in his windscreen getting brighter. "You had better prepare to abandon the aircraft!" he ordered.

The rear-gunner, unable to stand the heat, and feeling sure that the aircraft was doomed, opened his escape hatch and baled out.

Not so Sergeant Hannah. From the very first moment his one idea was to fight the fire and try to put it out. To him it was the natural thing to do. The thought of his personal safety did not enter his mind.

Instantly he began to beat at the flames with his gloved hands, but as he beat them out in one spot they took hold elsewhere. Seeing that they were increasing, he snatched up his log book and began to use that, finding it much more effective than his hands.

As the flames reached the pans of ammunition, cartridges started to explode and bullets flew all about him. He did not see the rear-gunner escape from "the tin," did not at that moment know he had gone. All his faculties were concentrated on fighting the fire.

The draught caused by the open escape hatch fanned the flames. The bomb compartment under his feet was all holed where the shell had struck it, and as the Hampden flew along, the air rushing through these holes acted as a forced draught, increasing the intensity of the fire. But the deadliest danger threatened from the port and starboard petrol tanks, which were both pierced. Had the petrol caught fire human courage would have been of no avail—only a miracle could have saved the aircraft.

Of these things he was ignorant. All he thought about now, as he flung down his log book, were the fire extinguishers at the other side of the door behind his back. The flames flared up about him as he swung round to get them. He tried to open the door, as he had opened it dozens of times before. It would not budge. He tried again and again to move it, pushing at it with all his strength. It remained firmly fixed.

What had happened was that the fire had already distorted the floor so badly that the door was jammed almost immovably: the bottom of the door would not pass over the part which had been warped by the fire in the bomb compartment below it.

The young Scot, when he found that his efforts to open the door in the normal way were useless, turned his back and charged with his whole weight at it. As it flew open under his impact, he sat down heavily on the floor amid the flames.

Picking himself up, he backed through the doorway, reached behind the door for the extinguishers and turned one on to the flames which were licking all around him, meanwhile doing his best to stamp them out with his feet. Such exertions in that heat forced him to pull off his oxygen mask, but the fumes and heat made it so difficult for him to breathe that he was obliged to put it on again. As he put out the fire in one part with the extinguisher, it blazed up more fiercely elsewhere. Nearly stifled inside his mask, he whipped it off again and sought relief by breathing the oxygen straight from the tube at the side of the aircraft.

The flames licked about his face, they singed off his eyebrows, but he was fighting so desperately that he did not notice it. Under his feet, the aluminium flooring began to melt and run. His right foot went through on to one of the cross bearers. He dragged it up, flung aside the empty extinguisher and turned on the other.

Pushing back the cupola of the cockpit, he grabbed the exploding drums of ammunition and started to throw them over the side. The reports from the exploding bullets were continuous.

Nearly suffocated by the heat, he pushed his head out of the cockpit to get a little air which revived him and braced him to continue his task. Seizing all the blazing stuff he could lay his hands on, he heaved it out of the hatch.

Working swiftly, but methodically, he pulled away the flaming woodwork and pitched it overboard. His thick gloves happily shielded his hands from harm. When he was at his last gasp he bobbed up and leaned out of the cockpit to get more air, and the arm he rested on the side was nearly wrenched from his body by the force of the slipstream. Bobbing down again, he made another effort and cast out the last of the flaming material.

Bits of timber still glowed evilly. Little tongues of fire started to lick up here and there, so seizing his log book again he attacked the burning embers until he had beaten them all out.

All this time, while the blazing bomber was flying through the sky, it made a first-class target for every gun within range. The shells came up continuously as the enemy gunners tried to complete their task, and the pilot now and again felt one ripping through the fuselage, others seemed to bounce off, while tracer made a good imitation of a firework display around them.

"It seems to me that most of the credit ought to go to Pilot Officer Connor," Sergeant Hannah said afterwards.

"People don't fully realize that while I was doing my best with the fire he was sitting up aloft as cool as a cucumber taking no notice of the flames, which were only two or three feet away from him, or the sound of bullets which were either whizzing close to his head or hitting the armoured plating just above. He was pretty calm, and if it hadn't been for him I should not have got back."

Pilot Officer Connor simply carried on as if nothing were wrong at all. It was a fine exhibition of skill and courage. When the fire was at its height he could feel the heat increasing on the back of his neck, then he noticed that the heat and the reflections gradually died away.

"How are things going?" he inquired of Hannah.

"The fire is out, sir," was the cheery reply.

"How are the others getting on?" asked the pilot.

"I'll find out," said Sergeant Hannah, who went to the rear cockpit and found it empty with the escape hatch open. "Nobody here, sir!" he called in astonishment.

"Go through and see about the navigator," said the pilot.

Sergeant Hannah dropped down the opening behind the pilot's seat and crawled through the tunnel underneath it into the front cockpit, to find that the navigator also had baled out. "We are all alone, sir!" he exclaimed in amazement.

"I knew then that if we did not have a navigator we would need a fix by wireless," he remarked later.

Crawling back through the tunnel, he went through to his wireless panel and, as is to be expected, found it all burned out, so it was impossible for him to send or receive any signals by which to fix their position.

"By this time my eyes were all swollen and I could hardly see," he said. Going forward, he secured the navigator's maps, and stood behind the pilot peering at the map and watching carefully to see where they made their landfall on the English coast. During this time he had no idea that his face was so badly injured.

Directly they struck the coast, he fixed the position, whereupon the pilot followed the coastline and landed safely at his base.

Even when they landed Hannah did not feel any pain. At that moment if anyone had asked him how he was, he would probably have replied that he was quite all right, yet parts of his face that were not protected by his helmet were badly burned, his helmet and goggles were all burned, there was a great burned patch on the seat of his flying suit which was scorched about the arms and legs. Indeed, it is doubtful if he could have survived that terrible experience in the burning cockpit if he had not been so thickly clad; it was the thick clothing which saved him, coupled with his quick thinking which drove him when almost suffocated to breathe the oxygen direct from the tap and afterwards to put his head outside the open cockpit until he revived.

So, after they landed, Pilot Officer Connor got out of his seat to examine the aircraft. He was astonished at the damage. The wireless cabin was a charred ruin with the aluminium flooring melted away; the rear cockpit was burned out; there was a hole in the fuselage through which it was possible to crawl, and numerous holes in the wings to prove what the aircraft had endured; but not until he looked at the holes in the petrol tanks did he realize to the full their extraordinary escape and Sergeant Hannah's outstanding courage. It seemed impossible that an aircraft could survive so fierce a fire, yet the young Scottish lad, unaided and undismayed, had fought it and put it out, thinking so little of his own safety that he allowed the flames to destroy his parachute and rob him of his only means of escape.

"I consider that this is one of the clearest examples of most conspicuous bravery and extreme devotion to duty in the presence of the enemy under the most harassing conditions that I have ever come across," stated the Air Officer Commanding the Hampden Bomber Group of which Sergeant John Hannah was a member.

Sergeant Hannah was not long in climbing down from the bomber. "Directly the guard came up and flashed his torch on us, I went blind straight away," Hannah remarked later.

It was then that the pilot saw the full extent of Hannah's injuries and had him taken off to hospital.

Sergeant Hannah's sense of humour peeps out in the following quotations from a letter written to his mother while he was in hospital. "Apparently it was the first time that a fire has been put out in the air. My pilot got the D.F.C., so I expect that I will be getting something too. But if you feel the way I do, you will be quite thankful that I am alive, without worrying what I am getting or am going to look like.

"Well, if you could see me now I'm sure you would burst out laughing. They have my face all covered with a black plastic stuff and my hair is still black from the smoke, so I look like a nigger. The nurses won't believe I've got fair hair. If what they tell me is true, my face should be practically clear when the stuff comes off. It is a new pattern stuff, and if it works I should be as good as new. They were worrying about shock when I came in, but I seem to be O.K. The only snag is that I cannot eat. My skin is all frizzled up. You won't likely know me when you see me. If they have changed my face, I hope I don't get lost looking for my home."

The nurses prophesied truly. Not a scar or blemish eventually marred the face of Sergeant John Hannah, V.C., to tell of the ordeal through which he had passed.

It throws light on his superb courage and strength of purpose to know that the two homing pigeons which they carried in the aircraft in case they came down in the sea were roasted alive.

CHAPTER XIII

RESCUE AT CALAIS MARCK

IN those crowded days of May, 1940, when the Germans were thrusting to Calais and Boulogne while the British army was fighting and retreating night and day to reach Dunkirk and freedom, the fighter pilots and bomber crews of the Royal Air Force made superhuman efforts to stem the German advance and to hold the German fighters and bombers at bay. In the most fearless manner the British bomber crews dropped their bombs on bridges and roads and ammunition dumps and enemy transport parks and columns, while the Spitfires and Hurricanes swept the skies and fought desperately against the overwhelming masses of Messerschmitts and Heinkels and Dorniers and Junkers.

Some of the fighter squadrons made four and five sorties a day, flying and fighting until they were utterly exhausted, dropping down on the straw in hangars and sleeping like dead men, to get up perhaps at 3 o'clock in the morning, shave in cold water and fly across the Channel to carry on the fight at dawn. Not in years will the full tale of those days be told, the thrills, the endurance, the gallant adventures when life and death depended upon a quick eye and the flick of a finger. Many a courageous pilot who could have told of adventures almost beyond belief, flew into the skies and vanished forever from mortal ken, the only certain thing about his end being that he went down fighting.

But the rescue at Calais Marck aerodrome was an adventure with a happier ending, one which exemplified the coolness and resource of the men in the Royal Air Force, and the stock from which they sprang, even when nations and cities and civilizations were palpably disintegrating before their eyes.

By dawn on the morning of May 23, 1940, the pilots of the famous Squadron No. 74 made their preparations, and shortly after daybreak they were in the air and on patrol between Dunkirk and Boulogne. Flying alone at 1,500 or 2,000 feet, they swept the coast between the two ports. A layer of cloud provided excellent cover for friend and foe alike, and presently an aircraft moved across some of the thin patches—but rather too quickly to be recognized.

Other aircraft flying in Vic formation—the Royal Air Force's way of describing what is commonly known as Vee formation—were sighted, and there followed a game of hide-and-seek in the clouds in which the squadron was broken up, one flight going above the clouds and another flight searching below. It was not long before the flights of Spitfires became split up still more and there were loose aircraft flying about all over the place, appearing and disappearing in and out of the clouds in all directions.

Eventually Squadron Leader F. L. White saw in the distance an aircraft that was a mere speck moving at a low altitude, so he called off the other two pilots of his section and, thinking it was the aircraft which they had seen previously, went to investigate.

Approaching it in the region of St. Omer, they still could not make it out owing to the clouds, so they closed right in to identify it, taking up a position to attack in case it happened to be an enemy aircraft.

It proved to be a Henschel 126. There was the rattle of machine-guns as the antagonists flew in and out of the clouds and a minute or two later they saw the enemy aircraft crash, but not before he had put a bullet through the radiator of the Squadron Leader's Spitfire. At once glycol, the fluid used for cooling the engine, began to pour out. The pilot, under the urgent necessity of finding a spot in which to make a forced landing, turned to the coast. Gazing down, and noting what appeared to be a large field, he steered towards it, with glycol streaming all over the place, and landed in what was actually Calais Marck aerodrome, which was some miles from Calais. Other pilots of his squadron saw him land, and reported his whereabouts to their base.

The first decision of the Squadron Leader was to hide his Spitfire from enemy aircraft. It was a new Spitfire which he did not want to lose. Seeing that the only damage was to the radiator, he knew that if he could get a new radiator she would be faultless, and he could fly her away. This is what he was most anxious to do.

Requesting aid from the men on the aerodrome, he got them to tow the Spitfire across the landing ground to conceal it in the hedge. The Germans, who were closing in all round Calais, had already paid considerable attention to the aerodrome, as was indicated by the bomb craters and battered buildings. No one knew exactly where they were or when they were likely to appear. For aught the pilot knew, enemy armoured cars might roll up or dive bombers appear out of the clouds at any minute.

Amid these uncertainties, the one certain thing in the pilot's mind was that he must get to Calais. Once there he could tackle the problem of securing a new radiator.

The rest of the world was not yet awake—it was only 5.20 in the morning—as he started off. Presently an army lorry parked beside the road seemed to offer him welcome transport, so he awakened the driver who was still sound asleep, and induced him to try to reach the port. After driving some distance, they came on a balloon section, with which they joined up and at last managed to enter Calais. Everything in the town was disorganized. Among the refugees and retreating troops crowding the streets, he picked up another pilot of his squadron, who had been shot down previously and was trying to make his way to England.

The Squadron Leader sought someone in authority who could help him, and after much trouble ran to earth the Railway Transport Officer, or the R.T.O., as he is known.

That officer promptly demanded proofs of the identity of the

Squadron Leader. He knew that the Germans were masquerading in all sorts of disguises and was taking no chances. The pilot, not knowing where he would be forced to land, had taken no chances either, with the result that it was impossible at the moment for him to prove his identity. So he found himself under arrest. It looked as if the very man whom the Squadron Leader expected to help him would be anything but helpful; but the R.T.O. in taking precautions was sensible, and he soon proved to be helpful as well, for during the course of the morning he managed to secure for the Squadron Leader the use of the only telephone line that was still operating to England.

Thus Squadron Leader White, amid all the confusion of war, with the German hordes blasting everything to pieces and countless French refugees frantically fleeing for their lives to some place of security, managed to get a call through to his headquarters where a voice he knew well answered him. Calmly he explained his position, told where he had left his Spitfire and asked for a new radiator. There were a few swift inquiries about spare radiators at the English end of the line, then the voice told the Squadron Leader that they could manage it and would have one sent over—as though it were someone ordering a spare part for a motor car in peace time!

He also learned that Flight Lieutenant Leathart was going to fly over a Miles Master trainer with an escort, in order to pick him up at Calais Marck, but what probably pleased him more than anything else was to learn that his own squadron were also planning to cross, directly they had refuelled, and fly him to safety.

Meanwhile, as the pilots of Squadron No. 54 sat lunching in their mess in England, Flight Lieutenant Leathart mentioned to Pilot Officer A. C. Deere that he was flying a Miles Master over to Calais Marck aerodrome to pick up Squadron Leader White who had been shot down there that morning. "Would you like to act as escort?" he queried.

Pilot Officer Alan Christopher Deere jumped at the chance. He was one of those young New Zealanders who afterwards did much to add to the renown of the Royal Air Force. The extraordinary thing is that during fourteen patrols over the French and Belgian coasts in the previous seven days, lasting roughly twenty-eight hours, he had only once seen a German aircraft which escaped in the clouds after the whole flight had raced each other to be the first to get a shot at the enemy.

About 12.30 p.m. Flight Lieutenant Leathart took off in the Miles Master, a two-seater training aircraft, followed by Pilot Officer Deere and Pilot Officer John Allen to protect him in case of attack. It was a lovely day, with a good deal of cloud at about 5,000 feet, and in about fifteen minutes they arrived over Calais Marck aerodrome. Flying down and noting the position of the bomb craters, the pilot of the Miles Master made a successful landing between them.

Pilot Officer Deere sent his friend Allen above the clouds to keep watch there while he himself circled the aerodrome at a little less than a thousand feet. He saw his flight commander draw up and speak to some workmen—they were filling in the craters caused by the bombs. Then he saw the Miles Master taxi over to the other side of the aerodrome where the pilot parked it while he made inquiries about the missing Squadron Leader.

Pilot Officer Deere, who had detected the Spitfire tucked away under the hedge, was chatting with his fellow pilot above and asking what it was like.

"All clear up here, Al," came the reply over the radio-telephone.

Just as Pilot Officer Deere saw the Miles Master taxi out and take off, the voice of Allen shouted in his earphones: "Twelve Messerschmitt 109s approaching at six thousand feet."

The Miles Master was quite defenceless. In the circumstances it was much safer on the ground than in the air. Knowing this, Pilot Officer Deere drew close to the other aircraft until he was flying level with it and not more than five spans away. He waved frantically upward to attract the attention of his flight commander and then pointed down to indicate that he must land.

"The jolly things are on my tail," shouted the voice of Allen.

Pilot Officer Deere started to weave about in order to keep a look-out all round. When Flight Lieutenant Leathart, realising his peril, put his nose down, a Messerschmitt dived fast out of the clouds and fired a burst of cannon shell at the training aircraft, starting from about 600 yards and finishing at 200 yards. Not a shot hit.

While Pilot Officer Deere turned to port to attack, the Messerschmitt, breaking away from the Miles Master, flew right across his sights as it started to climb. Instantly Pilot Officer Deere squeezed the button which set his eight guns blazing. He saw the enemy aircraft continue to climb, hang for a moment, turn over on its back and dive straight into the water a few yards from the shore—its tail was sticking up there for three months afterwards.

Squadron Leader White, who had been making his way to the aerodrome to await his rescuers, arrived just as Flight Lieutenant Leathart was taking off. The Squadron Leader shouted and waved and set the men around shouting and waving, too, in efforts to attract Flight Lieutenant Leathart's attention, but it was too late; the Miles Master gathered speed and rose into the air. By the time that Squadron Leader White had started across the aerodrome, the Miles Master was landing again. It came to rest about twenty yards from a ditch in which some of the aerodrome staff as well as Squadron Leader White and Flight Lieutenant Leathart were very glad to shelter.

The air seemed suddenly to be filled with Spitfires and Messerschmitt 109s diving in and out of the clouds and performing all sorts of crazy evolutions. The roar of all the machine-guns blazing away was like thunder in the ears of the men crouching in the ditch. They saw a Messerschmitt dive into the sea, watched another go down in flames over Calais, expecting each moment that the enemy aircraft would dive down on the ditch to spray them with machine-gun bullets. The Germans, however, were kept far too busy by the Spitfires to be able to turn their attention to the men on the ground.

Directly Pilot Officer Deere shot down his first Messerschmitt 109 he swung round to protect the training aircraft while it landed. A split second afterwards he saw another Messerschmitt diving on his tail. He dodged by doing a quick loop, which sent the enemy aircraft flashing by underneath him, so fast was it diving.

Rolling off the top of his loop, Pilot Officer Deere caught sight of five Messerschmitt 109s chasing his friend Allen through the clouds. Climbing at top speed he started to chase the enemy, who were so intent on the Spitfire in front that they did not notice the Spitfire coming up behind. Creeping up to within 150 yards of the rear Messerschmitt, the New Zealander squeezed the button and fired for seven seconds. It was enough. He saw the aircraft burst into flames and dive towards Calais town—this was the enemy aircraft seen to crash in Calais by those sheltering on the ground.

This unexpected attack from the rear at once relieved the pressure on the other Spitfire pilot and diverted the attackers.

Pilot Officer Allen conducted himself like a veteran in that mêlée. He shot down one enemy aircraft and saw it crash, then he took on another and observed his tracer going home, but before he could see what happened he had to break away to escape an enemy coming up behind.

Looping, diving, rolling, climbing, doing all the aerobatics which he had learned so well for just such an emergency, he evaded and fought the Messerschmitt 109s, getting another in his sights and giving it a good burst, before he had to break away without having the satisfaction of seeing it crash.

No sooner had Pilot Officer Deere shot down his second enemy than another began attacking him from the starboard. It was nearly half a mile away. Noticing the German tracer passing under his wings, Pilot Officer Deere pulled round in a steep turn and saw the Messerschmitt hurtle past. Immediately the Spitfire got on its tail and the New Zealand pilot put in a burst. As soon as the enemy was well in the sights again, he fired another burst. They were travelling fast and for a third time the New Zealander saw the enemy aircraft inside the luminous ring of his sight and squeezed the button on the stick. The guns roared out and suddenly ceased while he was still pressing the button. His ammunition was exhausted.

The amazing thing was that even in the heat of battle the young New Zealander remained cool enough not only to assess but to appreciate the flying abilities of the foe he was seeking to destroy.

"This pilot was exceptionally good," he stated, "and I had the greatest difficulty in getting my sights on him. He very nearly got on my tail. Once he did a half roll at about 300 miles an hour and then pulled sharply out of the dive, climbing vertically for about half a minute. Suddenly he pushed his stick hard forward and started a steep dive. I did the same with different results. My engine coughed and spluttered and I was left suspended as it were in mid-air with my speed quickly approaching stalling point. He took good advantage of this, for I lost sight of him, while he pulled sharply out of his dive into a climbing turn and was nearly on my tail when I saw him again. I went into a turn in the opposite direction and having practically no speed was able to turn inside him.

"When he saw I was once again on his tail he tried to repeat the manœuvre. But this time I was wise to it and rolled on my back as he pushed the stick forward, thus avoiding losing sight of him and the inconvenience of the loss of engine power. With a quick aileron turn I was able to maintain my position on his tail. This duel lasted another five minutes or ten minutes in all, the height varying from between ground level and 2,000 feet above Calais town. When I had proved to myself that a Spitfire could stay on the tail of a Messerschmitt 109 throughout any manœuvre, I broke off the engagement and started off home."

Although death was likely to drop out of the skies on him at any second, Pilot Officer Deere took the opportunity of using that German pilot as a tutor in order to master his tactics. His quick reply when the German tried to fool him in the same way a second time proves how well his critical faculties were developed and how coolly they were working at that moment. He also proved to his own satisfaction that the Spitfire had nothing to fear from the Messerschmitt 109 if handled with skill.

As he turned away for home he saw the enemy aircraft flying low with smoke pouring from its engine.

"How did you get on, Johnnie?" he asked over the radio-telephone as he fell in with his fellow pilot while crossing the English coast.

"One destroyed and two probables. How about you?"

"Two destroyed and one probable," was the reply.

Without hesitation they had grappled with a dozen Messerschmitts, at odds of six to one, and had completely routed them, destroying three for certain and probably another three as well.

Pilot Officer Deere, although he had seen only one German aircraft in the air before, fought like a pilot of long experience. He proved his mettle. His chase of the German pilot just to test out the qualities of the Spitfire probably laid the foundations of his future successes, for he could not fail to have faith in his aircraft after that encounter.

As for Pilot Officer John Laurence Allen, he had already proved his mettle two days previously when, going out to intercept an enemy aircraft that was approaching the shores of England, he saw thirty Junkers 88 bombing Calais to pieces. The fact that he was alone, that there was no possibility of support and that the odds against him were thirty to one, in no way deterred him. Climbing swiftly to the attack, he pounced on a Junkers and put in a burst of fire which drove the rest of the enemy into the clouds for cover, where he lost them. Then he flew home.

That afternoon of May 23, 1940, when the two fighter pilots arrived over their aerodrome, both did the victory roll to tell of their success.

Flight Lieutenant Leathart and Squadron Leader White, waiting until the roar of battle ceased, got into the Miles Master and took off. They were quite unarmed, except for the service revolver of the Squadron Leader, and they had no knowledge of what had happened to their escort, so in the circumstances they kept an extra sharp look-out for the enemy as they flew across the Channel for home. Fortunately the skies were clear of enemy aircraft and the Miles Master made a safe landing.

The rescue of Squadron Leader White from Calais Marck aerodrome proved how highly the Royal Air Force prized the life of every single man. Amid the turmoil of battle, one pilot was seen to go down and alight in what was virtually no-man's-land. That officer made his way to the nearest town and, after overcoming various difficulties, calmly rang through to his headquarters to ask them to send out a new radiator. Notwithstanding the cataclysm of work which must have fallen on headquarters at that time, the officer receiving the call quietly checked up to see that a radiator was available and then promised to send one out.

Incidentally Squadron Leader White forgot nothing. Determined if possible to save his new Spitfire, he gave the men on the aerodrome full instructions on how to destroy it if it were necessary. Next day he flew out and found that the Spitfire had been destroyed to prevent it from falling into German hands.

But it was the officer in France, and not the aircraft, that was the concern of the Command. Aircraft could be replaced more easily than trained officers and leaders of men. To save a man—this was the overriding impulse which sent Flight Lieutenant Leathart and his escort out to Calais Marck aerodrome to rescue Squadron Leader F. L. White, D.S.O.

That rescue which Flight Lieutenant Leathart performed during those arduous days of May brought him the D.S.O., while Pilot Officer A. C. Deere and Pilot Officer J. L. Allen were each awarded the D.F.C. for putting the enemy to rout.

Subsequently Pilot Officer J. L. Allen went down before the Germans, but promotion came to all the rest, and Pilot Officer Deere attained the rank of Wing Commander with further decorations.

CHAPTER XIV

THE BROKEN TAIL

PILOT Officer Kenneth William Mackenzie, who achieved fame and won the Distinguished Flying Cross by his unorthodox method of destroying a Messerschmitt 109 by slapping off its tail, was one of the new generation who took to flying as early and easily as previous generations took to cycling and motoring. Though his name may suggest that he was a Scotsman, he was actually an Irishman, having been born in Belfast on June 8, 1916, during the last great war against Germany.

If the loyal Ulstermen who cling so closely to Great Britain lay claim to him as one of their gallant sons, the English may console themselves by the fact that although his father was Irish, his mother was English, so it would be reasonable to infer that he had inherited some of the qualities of both nations. His exploit proved that he possessed the famous fighting spirit of the Irish, but in the very heat of the fight he displayed a coolness which may easily have been derived from the English.

Educated at the Methodist College in Belfast, he was so interested in flying that he was no more than a mere boy of sixteen years old when he passed his tests and qualified for his "A" pilot's licence. During the following years he studied technical engineering at the Queen's University, Belfast; and, like other keen young men, this young Irishman with the dark brown wavy hair, brown eyes and sandy moustache joined the Volunteer Reserve of the Royal Air Force.

Called up at the outbreak of war, he crossed over to England on December 19, 1939, and took a refresher course to equip him for flying the modern fighters, and after getting his hand in on Hawker Harts and Hinds stepped into his first Hurricane. Thenceforward, for day after day he flew and dived and looped and performed aerobatics until he became so used to the aircraft that it seemed almost a part of himself when he was in the sky. He practised evasive tactics and methods of attack and shooting and interceptions until he was as highly trained as he could be. But weeks became months without his desire to go up to fight the enemy being fulfilled. Many other pilots all over England were like him—anxious to win their spurs against the enemy, yet compelled to remain in reserve and wait as patiently as they could for the great day when they could fly on active service.

During the German attack on France in May, 1940, he listened in the mess to the wireless news of the exploits of the Air Advanced Striking Force in France and was anxious to join them; day after day as the wireless gave news of the Dunkirk evacuation, he longed to be there doing his share. The Battle of Dover found him still in reserve; and not until the Battle of London was dying away toward the end of September did he go up for the first time on active service with the County of Gloucester Auxiliary Squardon No. 501.

On October 5th he scored his first victory by shooting down a Messerschmitt 109. On the morning of October 7th just before 11 o'clock he shut the hood of his Hurricane and took off with the squadron to intercept raiders. There was haze up to about 8,000 feet with thin cirrus cloud above, but at 10,000 feet they emerged into the clear sunshine and left the cloud below them. Continuing to climb, they had just reached 19,000 feet when they saw about a dozen Messerschmitt 109s. Attacking at once, the Hurricanes in a second were split up all over the place, fighting their individual battles.

Wing Commander Hogan who led the Hurricanes got in a burst which damaged one of the enemy and sent it diving. In a flash Pilot Officer Mackenzie went after the enemy and, diving below it just astern, pressed the button and saw his bullets streaming into the petrol tank and the radiator for which he was aiming. A three second burst and the German went down, followed by his antagonist who watched him crash into the sea off Dungeness.

By the time Pilot Officer Mackenzie had made a climbing turn and looked around, he found he was alone in the sky. Where previously aircraft were whirling about in all directions, now there was nothing to be seen at all. Their great speed had carried them out of sight, and the dog fight in which he had just been engaged might have been a dream, but for that white patch marking the spot on the sea where the enemy had dived in.

Pulling the stick back, Pilot Officer Mackenzie began to climb. Soon he came out of the mist and cirrus into the clear blue sky and the sunshine. Turning on his oxygen, he continued to climb until his altimeter recorded 26,000 feet, or five miles. Then he started to patrol between Folkestone and Dover. He was quite happy, not at all worried by being alone. Through gaps in the clouds he saw the breakwaters and ships and houses of Dover appearing like the little cardboard models seen at an exhibition.

Suddenly he caught sight of some specks in the sky over the Channel moving towards him. They soon resolved themselves into eight Messerschmitt 109s flying in two sections at about 28,000 feet. In the lead was a "vic" formation of four, followed by another "vic" formation of three, with a single fighter weaving about behind to keep watch over his companions.

That the odds of eight to one were rather excessive did not enter the Irishman's mind. On the contrary he regarded the appearance of the Messerschmitts as a heaven-sent opportunity. Here were the enemies he had been longing to meet for months and without a second thought he pulled back his control column to climb to the attack. Flying up under them as they approached, he pressed the button and sprayed them with a hail of bullets.

The Hurricane pilot saw the last Messerschmitt do a half roll and turn back in the direction of the English coast, going down in a terrific dive. Pilot Officer Mackenzie pushed his control column forward and dived fast after him, going down one, two, three miles, flashing out of the bright sunshine into the light cloud and mist until he overtook the enemy at 8,000 feet and, keeping below and behind him, poured bullets into him for three seconds.

Watching the Messerschmitt intently, the Irish pilot saw glycol spray out of the radiator and white smoke begin to stream from the engine. The air speed of the German dropped to between 250 and 200 miles an hour as, sweeping over Folkestone at a height of 200 feet, he headed out to sea with the hunting Hurricane on his tail about 200 yards away. The sky by now was clearing and the sun was shining through.

After chasing the Messerschmitt for about a mile, and maintaining his position on the enemy's tail, Pilot Officer Mackenzie pressed the button on the control column, fully expecting to shatter the enemy and send him crashing into the sea. Instead his guns remained silent. He had no idea until he pressed the button that he had used up all his ammunition.

Fully determined that the enemy should not escape, he was at a loss to know what to do. Flying up alongside the German, the Irish pilot saw him gripping the control column as though he were hypnotised. The Nazi glanced up out of the corner of his eye at his adversary, then glued his eyes on the instrument board and flew doggedly forward. From first to last he made no attempt to attack or evade the Hurricane, but just flew straight forward.

Pilot Officer Mackenzie, as the German glanced up at him again, waved him down to land in the Channel. The enemy took no notice. They were flying then at about 180 miles an hour and not more than 100 feet above the sea.

Climbing a little, Pilot Officer Mackenzie side slipped right under the German and up on the other side. The enemy flew straight on.

The Irish pilot repeated the manœuvre, but the enemy held doggedly to the control column and his course, giving an occasional glance out of the corner of his eye and ignoring the Irishman's imperative signals to go down.

"It was exactly as though he was hypnotised," Pilot Officer Mackenzie said afterwards. "I didn't know what to do. I climbed to about 1,800 feet and put out my undercarriage, thinking to take his tail off with it, but I found I had not enough air speed to do him any harm, so I pulled up the undercarriage. At that time we were flying within 80 or 100 feet of the sea and I could just see the French coast. Then the idea occurred to me that I might knock his tail off with my wing. I flew on his port side just above him and came up until the end of my wing was just over his tail plane. Then I gave a huge amount of right aileron which brought my starboard wing slap down on his port tail plane. At once I saw the tip of my wing fly off up into the air while his tail plane collapsed and he simply dived straight into the sea and never reappeared.''

The clever Irish pilot later gave some idea of the mental processes which led up to his defeat of the German. It seemed to him in the first place incredible that two sworn enemies could be flying side by side just as though they were flying in formation as members of the same squadron, without being able to do anything to each other. The position appeared to be so hopeless. Then, as the British pilot vainly waved the Nazi down and flew over him and under him in futile attempts to force him down, the idea came into his mind to knock him down. It was quite involuntary. Never in his life had he imagined that such a thing was likely to occur. The dilemma itself made him think out the solution to his apparently insoluble problem—it suggests that although the Irish fighting spirit was fully roused, there was the restraining influence of reason to guide him to experiment with the undercarriage and so lead him on to triumph by slapping the tail off the Messerschmitt with his wing.

As he saw about three feet of his wing-tip go flying into the air and the Nazi dive straight into the sea amid a fountain of spray, he did a steep climbing turn to make for home. It was then between 11.30 a.m. and 12 o'clock. Fortunately for Pilot Officer Mackenzie, the tip of his wing snapped off cleanly without interfering with the aileron. Had the aileron broken off, it is doubtful if he would ever have returned.

Being naturally elated at his triumph, he was metaphorically patting himself on the back when he saw tracer bullets going into each wing. A quick glance in his mirror disclosed two Messerschmitt 109s right on his tail firing for all they were worth. There is not much doubt that while he was chasing the Nazi the latter had called for help on the radio-telephone and brought these two Messerschmitts to his aid. They were too late to save their companion, but it was a very open question whether they were going to avenge him on the spot.

Utterly defenceless, with his wing-tip gone, the pilot of the Hurricane gave his aircraft full boost and flung it about all over the place to evade the attackers. The Messerschmitts sprayed the fleeing Hurricane with machine-gun bullets and cannon shell and despite the brilliant flying of the British pilot, some of them went home.

The positions were reversed with a vengeance, for the hunter was being hunted with the utmost ferocity. The engine of the Hurricane began to fail. Oil and thick black smoke poured into the cockpit. Pilot Officer Mackenzie headed as desperately for the white cliffs of England as the Nazi pilot had been heading for France a minute or two earlier. Half blinded by escaping glycol and oil, he was awfully afraid he might have to come down in the sea, so he heaved off his helmet and Sutton harness just to be ready in case the worst happened. As he said later: "I oozed more sweat than ever before in my life. You could have taken my pants off and wrung them!"

Flying madly towards England and safety, he saw with relief the
two enemy aircraft break off the attack and turn for France when he
was about half a mile from the cliffs of Folkestone. He had just enough
power in his engine to lift him over the cliff, then it petered out completely. As it was impossible to lower the undercarriage, he was forced
to land on the fuselage and make what is generally known in the service
as a "belly landing" in a field 300 yards from the edge of the cliff.
He made a good landing, but the impact threw him forward against the
reflector sight which cut right through his lower lip just above his chin
and knocked out a tooth and his eyes suffered badly from the glycol
and oil.

By the time he had climbed out of his Hurricane, the men from the
nearest anti-aircraft post were on the spot to help him. Putting him in
a car, they rushed him off to get a clean-up, after which he insisted on
returning to see if his Hurricane was all right. Then they took him to
hospital where he remained half an hour while the doctor put four
stitches in his lip, which healed perfectly without further trouble.
Everyone was kindness itself. An admiral insisted on entertaining him
to tea, and the pilot's one regret was that he could not do justice to the
cake owing to the injury to his mouth.

During the week's leave which followed, he returned to Ireland
where he found it necessary to have three more teeth removed, so he
wrote off to his Commanding Officer to inform him that his mouth was
slow in healing and to know whether his leave could be extended for
three days. The most surprised man in the world was Pilot Officer
Mackenzie when he received an affirmative reply and learned that he
had been awarded the D.F.C. for knocking the tail off the Messerschmitt.

His unique triumph was followed by further successes until eight
German aircraft had fallen to his guns. Then one unlucky day he was
shot down into the English Channel from which the Germans rescued
him to hold him prisoner until the end of 1944, when he was repatriated.

CHAPTER XV

THE ORDEAL OF PILOT OFFICER ROMANS, D.F.C.

ABOUT 9 o'clock in the dusk of a September evening in 1940 a Hampden
bomber took off from its English base to bomb Eschwege aerodrome.
The great black shape of the bomber rose as it circled the air field, and
the voice of the pilot came through to his young Canadian navigator,
Pilot Officer David A. A. Romans, to ask for his course. The navigator,
making a few swift calculations, gave the course to the pilot who
adjusted his gyroscopic compass and climbed on his way.

Fair at the start, the weather worsened a bit over the sea, but this bad patch was gradually left behind them and by the time they reached the other side the weather had cleared and there was a good moon to aid them in their task.

Flying at 4,000 feet, the bomber approached its target. In the front cockpit, Pilot Officer Romans, making his preparations to bomb, saw the searchlights feeling about for them. The anti-aircraft fire began to increase. Watching the sudden flashes of the guns below, the navigator saw numerous shells bursting around him.

In a Hampden the crew were more or less isolated from each other. They relied upon the intercommunication system to a greater extent than did the crews of other aircraft where the seating arrangements enabled the men to see each other as well as speak to each other on the "intercom." The pilot sat in his cockpit above the wing, which gave him a good view forward and around. At the back of his seat there was an opening perhaps four feet deep, just big enough for a man to get down, which continued in a sloping tunnel under the pilot's seat leading into the front cockpit. Here the navigator sat right forward in the nose of the aircraft. His bomb sights were placed under the table near his feet, so he stretched flat on the floor to manipulate them and drop the bombs.

Before the pilot could get to his seat he had to lower the back, which was hinged to fall down across the well leading to the front cockpit. He then had to slide over the back of the seat and pull it up behind him to leave the entrance to the front cockpit open. When seated, he could not see the navigator, who had to crawl or slide through the passage or tunnel under the pilot's seat, owing to lack of headroom, to get in and out of the front of the aircraft.

In the centre section, behind the entrance to the front cockpit, was a small well in which the collapsible dinghy and other things were stored; then came a metal door which completely cut off the wireless operator who sat with his wireless panel and two machine-guns facing aft in a turret with a sliding dome. Further aft, his head on a level with the wireless operator's feet, the rear-gunner sat with his legs stretched out on the padded floor of the fuselage in the rear turret.

Space was used to such good advantage in the Hampden that it was not easy for the crew to move about, and it would be impossible for anyone to appreciate the dangers and difficulties which were overcome in the bomber that night without having an idea of the positions of the crew. Each sat alone in his cockpit, unable to see or be seen by the pilot who gave his orders through the "intercom."

As the ack-ack grew in intensity, the bomber began to swing about to evade it. Such action is so common during an attack that bomber crews expect it as a matter of course and pay little attention to it.

Suddenly the navigator felt two severe jolts on the aircraft which at once began to stall and dive. Thinking that the pilot, who was his friend, was merely taking evasive action, Pilot Officer Romans paid no attention for a second or two. All his faculties were alert. "Watch your speed!" he called to the pilot through the "intercom."

There was no answer. He sensed that something was wrong. The aircraft was going down. There was silence instead of the voice he knew so well.

Ripping off his helmet, he moved through the tunnel quicker than ever before as the aircraft continued to go down. Bobbing up behind the pilot's seat, he saw him slumped over the controls.

In an instant he was up on the padded rest of the main spar tugging at the pilot's straps in order to let down the back of the seat. All the time he struggled to release the pilot, the Hampden dropped.

His friend made no movement. There was no sign of blood, nothing to tell what had happened.

The navigator got the back of the seat down at last. Kneeling upon it, he shifted the limp body of the pilot off the control column until he was lying flat on the lowered back of the seat.

The needle of the altimeter gradually moved round. The speed had dropped to no more than eighty miles an hour and they were down to 2,000 feet. He clambered over his recumbent friend and sat on top of him while he grabbed the control column and, easing it back, pulled the bomber out of her dive. Then he managed to get the feet of the pilot out of the rudder controls and insert his own.

"I managed to pull the aircraft up and got her under control again," he said afterwards. "During this time the wireless operator simply thought we were doing evasive action, but I succeeded after a while in letting him know what was wrong. As I took the aircraft up to 6,000 feet, the wireless operator struggled to pull the pilot out from underneath me. It was an awful job in the cramped space, but he got him out, took off his parachute and helmet and saw that he was hit at the side of the head."

The navigator estimated that from the instant he felt the shells bursting until he succeeded in pulling up the aircraft and saving it from crashing, a bare minute, or at most a minute and a half, elapsed. If he had hesitated for a few seconds longer, the B.B.C. would probably have announced that "one of our aircraft did not return." It proves how swift the mental and muscular reactions of the crews in the R.A.F. must be in an emergency if they are to escape disaster.

Who can know the thoughts of the navigator when he found his friend unconscious over the controls? It was as well, perhaps, that the task of flying the aircraft was so onerous that there was no time for personal feelings to obtrude. Fortunately he was a trained pilot, for it devolved upon him not only to fly the Hampden in the face of all the difficulties that had arisen, but to navigate it also.

The shells, which hit the aircraft between the starboard engine and the fuselage, had wrought havoc with the instruments. The gyroscope controlling the automatic compass was put out of action, so he was

Plate 7.—The damaged wing of the Hurricane flown by Pilot Officer K. W. Mackenzie, D.F.C., after he had accomplished his unique feat of deliberately knocking the tail off a Messerschmitt 109 in order to drive it down into the sea, as described on page 106.

Plate 8.—The King decorating WING COMMANDER A. C. DEERE, the famous
New Zealand fighter pilot whose prowess accounted for 17 enemy aircraft and
whose escapes after being shot down seven times border on the miraculous.

robbed of the assistance of one of the most valuable aids to navigation.

A glance at the revolution counter shocked him. It was not registering at all. Through his mind flashed the thought that the engines were stopped.

Swiftly he looked out of the sides of the cockpit.

The propellers were working! He breathed freely once more, knowing the engines were all right and that it was the revolution counter that had been smashed.

Meanwhile the wireless operator, getting the first-aid kit, attended to the stricken pilot, who was quite unconscious. Giving him a dose of morphia, he found a tiny puncture behind the pilot's ear. It was hardly discernible. Very carefully he bandaged up the pilot's head and made him as comfortable as possible.

Unhappily the pilot was mortally wounded. Through that tiny puncture a small fragment of shell had entered and pierced the brain.

"Get my map and instruments from down below," said the navigator to the wireless operator. Pilot Officer Romans was anxious to find out his position to fix his course, and directly the wireless operator returned, the navigator successfully took a sight while piloting the aircraft.

Twice later he was able to check his position. After flying for three hours over the sea against a head wind of twenty-five miles an hour, he made his landfall on the east coast and landed safely at his home station.

The gallantry of Pilot Officer David A. A. Romans that night, his swift reactions which saved the bomber from crashing with her crew will be understood by all; but only those with an intimate knowledge of the cramped space in a Hampden can realize to the full the difficulties which he overcame. The better a Hampden is known, the more impossible the feat seems, yet he accomplished it.

That is why Pilot Officer David A. A. Romans was awarded the D.F.C.

CHAPTER XVI

SHOT DOWN SEVEN TIMES

ALAN CHRISTOPHER DEERE, who was born in New Zealand at Auckland, sailed from that lovely land in September, 1937, to join the Royal Air Force. Keen to fly, he frequently wilted under the blunt words of the English instructor and sometimes despaired of ever flying at all; and it still remains a mystery to him how he managed to land safely after his first solo flight. But those teething troubles were overcome and on January 24, 1938, he received his appointment as Pilot Officer in the Royal Air Force. By the last day in December, 1938, he was certified as a fully trained day and night fighter pilot.

His reactions the first time he sat in a Spitfire in February, 1940, are worth recording: "At first the speed amazed me. I was frightened out of my life and absolutely scared to do other than fly straight and level. This soon wore off, and before long Spitfires were being aerobated to the utmost. A Spitfire is the most beautiful and easy aircraft to fly and has no tricks or peculiarities normally attributable to high speed fighters."

Like many another fighter pilot, he cooled his heels in England while he longed to be in France emulating the exploits of his fellow New Zealand pilot "Cobber" Kain, who attained fame in March, 1940, by winning the D.F.C. for outmanœuvring and destroying an enemy fighter while his own aircraft was so badly damaged that he was nearly asphyxiated and blinded by the smoke and fumes from the fractured pipes. Kain got back from that fight and landed safely, but it was tragic that he should lose his life as the result of a flying accident just when he was about to go on leave. Instead of Flying Officer Edgar James Kain receiving his decoration, it devolved upon his mother, who had travelled from New Zealand, to receive it in September, 1940, from the hands of His Majesty the King, who told her how sorry he was that he had been unable to present it to her son. The skill and courage of Flying Officer Kain in those days inspired many fighter pilots in England whose duties consisted of unexciting patrols while they longed to be in action in France.

Things changed for Pilot Officer Deere on May 15, 1940, when he learned he had been selected to patrol over France with Squadron No. 54. He was so excited at the prospect that he could not sleep. During the ensuing week the peace of England seemed to have spread to the French skies, for the squadron sighted only one enemy aircraft all the time, although red war was raging on the earth below.

On May 23rd his real adventures began by shooting down two Messerschmitts during the rescue from Calais Marck aerodrome as described in Chapter 13. Thenceforward adventure piled on adventure and escape on escape. Within two hours of the Calais Marck rescue he was back over Calais climbing with his squadron to attack fifteen Heinkel 111s and a formation of nine Messerschmitt 110s. For months those Spitfire pilots had hungered for such an opportunity. Just as they were about to sail in to attack, a yell came over the radio-telephone: "Watch out—Messerschmitts!"

Coveys of Messerschmitt 109s dropped out of the skies at immense speed. The mix-up became general. The British pilots did the most amazing things with their Spitfires, and when the tally came at the end they found they had destroyed eleven and damaged two without suffering any loss themselves—not a bad beginning for Squadron No. 54.

During the fight Pilot Officer Deere, turning steeply, found himself on the tail of a Messerschmitt 109 which flicked and rolled away, to dive madly for the cover of a cumulus cloud at 10,000 feet, with the

Spitfire hard after him just beyond range. As the New Zealand pilot dropped into the cloud his instruments gyrated crazily owing to the static electricity. Flashing out of the cloud at 400 miles an hour, he saw the enemy 1,000 feet below him and dropped on his tail, but before he could get within range the Messerschmitt opened all out and fled, climbing at full speed.

Unfortunately for the German the Spitfire was the faster. The queer thing was that the German, when he found he was being pursued, made no attempt to dodge. He simply flew straight ahead and climbed. At 13,000 feet Pilot Officer Deere got him right in his sights and held him there while he squeezed the button on his control column for ten seconds. With flames flickering around the cockpit, the enemy went down, followed by the Spitfire pilot, who saw him hit the ground and explode in a sheet of flame.

With three victories that day to his credit, Deere went out again at dusk to help to cover the evacuation from Boulogne. Fires were raging below. A British cruiser plastered German batteries somewhere inland. But not an enemy appeared in the skies, so at 10 o'clock the flight of Spitfires turned for home and, flying in sections in line astern with navigation lights burning, crossed the English coast, making an impressive sight in the night sky. On that first day of high adventure Deere flew for seven hours and twenty minutes.

No enemy came within his sights the next day, although he saw two with a Spitfire going down in flames. The following day, about 10 o'clock, while flying at 20,000 feet over Dunkirk, the squadron attacked a formation of Junkers 88 bombers and twenty Messerschmitt 110s which were making for two British destroyers. The Spitfires dived to the attack. The New Zealand pilot soon set one alight and followed it down to see it crash on the beach near Dunkirk.

During that dive he experienced for the first time what it was like to be attacked. For an instant he was spellbound by the sight of the tracer bullets streaming past his wings. There was a terrific bang. He was flung upside down, diving straight at the sea 1,000 feet below, and only managed to pull out of his dive just above the surface. As he headed for home, he saw a hole in his port wing nearly big enough to crawl through, but he managed to fly the Spitfire to England and land safely on a flat tyre. It was a cannon shell exploding in the tyre that upset him and all but sent him crashing in the sea. That was the first time he was shot down.

A fellow-countryman of his in the same squadron displayed even greater skill during the next patrol by flying and landing his Spitfire without flaps, air speed indicator, brakes or aileron control, while his control wires were cut by a cannon shell and the duplicate set just held by a single strand of wire. It was a striking testimony to the fine training of the fighter pilots of the Royal Air Force, as well as to the construction of the Spitfire.

Next day the evacuation of the British forces from Dunkirk was in full swing, and Squadron No. 54 went over to protect the troops from the German bombers. Deere dived after a Junkers 88 at 400 miles an hour and sent the enemy down in flames before the end of that patrol.

On the following morning he was given the command of "A" flight and sent to patrol the beaches again. They were crowded with troops. A dense cloud of smoke from the burning oil tanks blotted out the sky over the port. It was a few minutes after 4 o'clock in the morning when he arrived with his Spitfires over the beaches. He at once began to chase and close in to attack a Dornier 17. The tail-gunner of the Dornier, opening fire at extreme range to try to drive the Spitfire off, got in some shots which luckily for him started the glycol pouring out of the pursuing aircraft. The Spitfire pilot began to fire back and continued to fire into the Dornier so long as he could see ahead.

But the German had completely disabled the Spitfire and there was nothing for the pilot to do except make a crash landing on the beach. Knocked unconscious by the impact, he fortunately came to a few minutes later, to see the engine smoking furiously. Not wishing to be burned to death, he ripped off his straps, got clear and sat down on the beach and literally cursed his luck. Disappointment overwhelmed him. He had barely commanded his flight for an hour before being shot down—for the second time in three days.

Cheering up at the sight of some Spitfires overhead playing havoc with a flock of Messerschmitts, he considered what to do. He gazed at his Spitfire with the Kiwi, the lucky bird of New Zealand, painted on the cockpit, and felt sad at the idea of destroying it. But there was nothing else to be done, so he thought out the best way of doing it. Taking out his revolver, he shot a hole in the bottom petrol tank. As the petrol poured out, he cut about nine feet of the silken cord from his parachute which he soaked in petrol to make a fuse. Inserting one end of the cord in the petrol tank, he laid the cord along the sands, lit the end with a match, and bolted for his life as the flame ran along the cord. There was a big explosion, and he turned to see Kiwi I, as he named his aircraft, engulfed in flames.

Then he trekked along the beach in the direction of Dunkirk. A walk of five miles brought him to a town where he found a pretty Belgian girl who dressed the wound on his head. Not knowing how to repay her kindness, he stripped off his yellow Mae West, on which his name was painted in bold red letters, and gave it to her as a souvenir. Her first aid soothed his aching head and made him feel more comfortable.

Now he boarded a Belgian troop bus, which carried him about five miles before it stopped. All along the roads were abandoned motor cars in which he noticed the owners had left the ignition keys. Selecting a likely-looking one, he borrowed it. Ramming his foot down on the self-starter, he roared down the road in the direction of Dunkirk.

Possessing very little petrol in the tank, it came to a standstill a few miles further on, so he was obliged to transfer to another abandoned car in which he carried on for a mile or two further.

He was very hungry and thirsty, but his attempts to obtain a drink of water and something to eat at the wayside places were quite unavailing. He craved for water, would have given anything for it, but no one seemed to have had any for days. There was plenty of wine, but no water.

Time after time he took the wrong turnings and got lost. His efforts to find his way by inquiring of the Belgians would have been funny on a film, but they were not amusing to him then. He did not understand the Belgians, nor did they understand him; when they did understand his inquiry concerning the whereabouts of the German army they either did not know or would not tell.

His position was not enviable. He had no desire to be taken prisoner or to spend the duration of the war in a German prison camp, but with the Germans advancing all around him, he might come upon them at any minute. Consequently if he found himself on a road heading inland, he did his best to get back to the coast as quickly as possible.

At last he came to a Belgian town where an hotel proprietress was glad to provide him with eggs and bacon. But even here there was no water to be had. As she had been to school in England, she was able to talk to him. From her he learned that most of the Belgian soldiers in the restaurant knew nothing of the fighting and had no idea where the British or German armies were. Feeling much better after his meal, he got a ride in another Belgian troop bus for a mile or two, after which he again borrowed an abandoned car.

As he drove, his eye caught sight of a British army truck among the abandoned vehicles at the side of the road, then a light tank. From then on the evidence of the British retreat grew plainer. Bomb craters became more frequent in the road. Some had been partly filled, and he switchbacked down and up them, following the cars in front. After using up the petrol in five different cars, he was obliged to make use of a motor cycle which had a little petrol left and this brought him to the outskirts of Dunkirk about 11 o'clock that morning.

The place was like a scene from Dante's inferno. Over the town hung the thick black pall of smoke, completely obscuring the sky.

Bomb craters were all over the place. The roads were so jammed with traffic and retreating French and British soldiers that he was obliged to push his motor cycle to the side among the ruins and leave it, because walking was quicker than attempting to ride.

Never in his life had he seen anything so terrible as the ruins of Dunkirk. Cables and wires were dangling in all directions; masses of rubble which were once houses were heaped all over the place; great girders were twisted and distorted into the most grotesque shapes; wrecked buildings were still burning and smouldering and filling the air with acrid fumes. Not a single civilian did he see, only the crowds of tired soldiers, many limping painfully along carrying their boots in which they had found it physically impossible to march farther, making their way down to the beaches. The roads were almost impassable, owing to the buildings which had collapsed across them, so the tired streams of soldiers had to twist and turn and make their tortuous way as best they could, climbing over the wreckage where necessary in order to reach the shore.

He got to the beach at last and was so worn out that he crept into an old ice-cream shed and fell sound asleep. When he wakened there were crowds of soldiers on the beach looking heavy-eyed and fatigued from lack of sleep and constant marching to escape the encircling German armies, yet all were in the best of spirits and could still crack a joke and raise a laugh. In retreat, they remained unbeaten.

"I had seen many formations of aircraft, both friendly and enemy, and had heard many a whistling bomb come screeching down, only to land somewhere unseen," said Pilot Officer Deere on his return. "I had been on the beach only a short time when I saw a Dornier 215 making inland with both motors on fire. A few minutes later a Spitfire appeared out of the smoke pall, with glycol streaming behind. The pilot crash-landed on the beach about two miles from the troops and was afterwards brought back with his arm in a sling. Many bombs were landing in the water and round about, but the low cloud—it was now raining and quite cold—prevented me from seeing the aircraft responsible. I saw one bomb drop on the pier and go clean through without exploding.

"I had pushed myself in the queue of soldiers awaiting their turn to board the destroyers continually arriving at the pier. After what seemed an eternity I found myself aboard together with about 1,000 troops and thirty officers. I was just preparing to go below deck when a Heinkel 111 appeared at about 4,000 feet. The destroyer began to shake with the effect of the terrific gunfire from 3-inch and pom-pom and before a bomb had been dropped a 3-inch shell scored a direct hit. Exit Heinkel.

"We soon got under way. Below deck I enjoyed coffee and sandwiches. We didn't have to be told enemy bombers were overhead. Suddenly we all shot on to the floor and cups and sandwiches cannoned in all directions. The destroyer had taken evasive action. For very nearly two hours we were harassed by formations of Heinkels and Junkers, but only once did they come near hitting us. It must have been very close, because we were hurled violently on to our side and all the lights went out. It was simply horrible in the darkness and trapped below deck. It was impossible to get a square inch of room on deck, which was crammed with troops.

"After nearly five hours of dodging bombs we sighted the white cliffs of Dover. Here we berthed and I was soon clambering ashore thankful to be on good old English soil again. I arrived back at my home station next day hardly twenty-four hours after my departure, twenty-four of the most adventurous hours I shall ever hope to spend.''

After twelve days of continuous action around and over Dunkirk, his squadron was taken out for a rest, to return to active service in the middle of June, when the days were filled with the usual patrols and fighting whenever they could get into touch with the enemy. Going out to intercept enemy raiders that were leaving Calais in the early days of July, he took his flight up to 8,000 feet to patrol over the Goodwin Sands about ten miles off Deal. At last a silver seaplane was seen approaching close to the water, with an escort of twelve Messerschmitt 109s flying at about 1,000 feet, and another five Messerschmitts flying well behind at 6,000 feet ready to roar down on any attackers.

While a section of Spitfires dived down to give the seaplane its quietus, Deere led a section to attack the five Messerschmitts which at once began to go round after each other in a defensive circle. Diving on the last one, the New Zealander gave it a burst and shot it straight down in flames into the sea. As he climbed he saw the seaplane crew getting into their rubber boat and was so high-spirited that he called over the radio-telephone to Control: ''Send help, they're invading us!''

A few seconds later, while diving down to the seaplane, he saw a Messerschmitt 109 coming up on his tail. Doing a steep turn to meet the enemy head on, he started to fire at the same time as the Nazi. Deere felt the German bullets thudding home in his wings. ''We were dead head-on and he was right in my sights,'' he related afterwards. ''I don't remember whether I thought about avoiding a collision by breaking away, but things seemed to happen so suddenly. The first awakening was a large nose looming in front of me. There was a terrific and horrible thud and then my aircraft began to vibrate so violently that I thought my engine must surely shake itself off the bearers. Black smoke poured into the cockpit and flames appeared from the engines. I reached to open the hood in order to bale out, only to discover that his propeller had struck the front of my windscreen and the whole fixture was so twisted that I could not move the hood.

''I could not see for smoke, but managed to ascertain that I was headed inland. Nearly blinded and choked, I succeeded in keeping the air-speed at about 100 miles an hour. The engine had now seized and I just waited to hit the ground. Suddenly there was a terrific jerk and I was tossed left, then right and finally pitched hard forward on my straps, which fortunately held fast. I seemed to plough through all sorts of things and then stop. The remains of my ammunition were going off in a series of pops and the flames were getting very near the cockpit. I frantically broke open the hood and undoing my harness ran to a safe distance. My eyebrows were singed. Both my knees were bruised, but otherwise I was uninjured. The Spitfire was blazing furiously in the middle of a cornfield and had left a trail of broken posts and pieces of wing, plus the complete tail unit, extending for two hundred yards.''

If not exactly a happy landing, it was certainly a lucky one, due mainly to his foresight in tightening his straps after the collision in preparation for the impact. Quick thinking probably saved him on that occasion. He was back on patrol next day as if nothing had happened.

Days followed when his squadron scoured the skies in vain for the enemy. Then they intercepted twenty Dorniers with an escort of Messerschmitt 109s heading for the Thames and were surprised by another formation of Messerschmitts which had been stalking them along the coast at a higher level. In the dog fight which followed, with Spitfires and Messerschmitts sweeping in and out of the clouds and the air thick with tracer and incendiary smoke, Deere turned on one wing-tip round and round the peak of a great cloud which stood up as solid as a snow-covered mountain top until he spotted a Messerschmitt making for home, when he sped after it and gave it a burst which brought glycol streaming from it.

In that dog fight the squadron destroyed eight of the enemy. Two crashed in the main streets of Margate and the convoy which the bombers were going to attack in the Thames estuary escaped untouched. Unhappily Deere's friend, Pilot Officer J. Allen, D.F.C., who took part in the Calais Marck rescue, was killed during a forced-landing.

Next day, going up to protect a convoy off Dover, they saw a sea-plane laying a smoke screen, under cover of which five German motor torpedo boats sped in the direction of the ships. In the distance loomed a large formation of Junkers 87 dive bombers with so many Messer-schmitt fighters that they were uncountable.

Control was informed over the radio-telephone. Deere saw two British torpedo boats racing down the Channel to meet the enemy, while the two escorting destroyers laid a smoke screen between the convoy and the approaching attackers.

"We had by this time received instructions to engage the fighters, as a formation of Hurricanes was there to deal with the dive bombers," explained Deere later. "We were forced to lose height because of a heavy rainstorm, and when we came out on the other side of the storm, there seemed to be so many enemy fighters that the sky was black. This descent put us at a complete disadvantage and we were pounced on from all directions. By now there was a terrific battle in progress between the destroyers, our torpedo boats and the enemy boats. How any of us came out of that battle alive is a miracle."

So busy did the Spitfires keep the Messerschmitts that the Hurricanes were able to destroy many Dorniers and rout the survivors.

The odds faced by the pilots of the Spitfires and Hurricanes ought to have overwhelmed them, instead of which the dauntless courage and superior skill of the British pilots shattered the enemy and sent them fleeing for home. On August 10th Deere led his squadron to attack

100 Messerschmitt 109s while a squadron of Hurricanes dealt with fifty Dornier and Messerschmitt 110 bombers. During the dog fight Deere caught a German so intent on a flaming Hurricane that he failed to see the Spitfire pilot, who blew him to bits in the air and was amazed at the sight of the victim's tail sticking out of an immense cloud of black smoke and flame. A minute or two later Deere himself, intent on another victim, was caught in the same way and compelled to land.

Another day Squadron No. 54 fearlessly attacked a formation of 200 bombers before the flocks of escorting fighters could come down. The ensuing dog fight was so fast and furious that it was almost impossible to tell friend from foe in the masses of whirling aircraft. This was the reason why the Germans coloured the noses of their Messerschmitts yellow, so that the Nazi pilots would be able to tell instantly whether the aircraft flashing in and out of their sights was a friend or enemy.

He added another to his score in that fight. During his next fight, after watching three German bombers floating down in flames in line abreast with two or three Germans dangling from parachutes in the sky, he chased two enemy fighters right across the Channel and was quite surprised to find himself over Calais Marck aerodrome. As he turned, five Messerschmitt 109s dived on top of him.

"Bullets seemed to be coming from everywhere and pieces were flying off my aircraft. My instrument panel was shattered, my eye was bleeding from a splinter, my watch had been shot clean off my wrist by an incendiary bullet which left a nice diagonal burn across my wrist and it seemed only a matter of moments before the end," he remarked after the fight. "Never did it take so long to get across thirty miles of sea and never had my aircraft gone so slowly. My good old Merlin carried me safely across, however, and I had just reached Folkestone when my pursuers broke off the engagement. None too soon. Two minutes later my engine—I was now at 800 feet—burst into flames.

"Desperately I tore my straps off, pulled back the hood and prepared to bale out. I was still doing about 300 miles an hour, so I pulled the stick back to get a bit more height. At about 1,500 feet I turned on my back and pushed the stick hard forward. I shot out a few feet and somehow became caught up by the bottom of my parachute. I twisted and turned, but wasn't able to get either in or out. The nose had now dropped below the horizontal and was pointing at the ground which appeared to be rushing up at a terrific speed. Suddenly I was blown along the side of the fuselage, hitting my wrist a nasty smack on the tail. Then I was clear. I made a desperate grab at the rip-cord and with a jolt the parachute opened. None too soon. I hadn't time to breathe a sigh of relief before I landed with a mighty thud in a plantation of thick shrubs."

Those shrubs probably saved his life. As he lay there shaken, but unharmed, his Spitfire went up in flames in the next field. The following day he was on duty with only a strapped-up wrist as evidence of his adventure.

Two days afterwards he had just shot down an enemy in flames when his own Spitfire was disabled and he had to make a forced landing. In a fight which started a few days later at 34,000 feet, when the aircraft were weaving white trails in the air, he was diving after an enemy which he had shot down in flames when he found himself in the middle of another formation of Messerschmitts flying at 28,000 feet. One of the enemy promptly shot away his rudder controls.

As he dived away, his engine began to smoke, which indicated that the aircraft would probably go up in flames if he made a crash landing, so he decided to bale out. Controlling the Spitfire by using the ailerons until he was down to 10,000 feet, he prepared to abandon his aircraft. The vivid memory of how he was caught on the previous occasion led him this time to adopt another method, so he stalled the burning Spitfire and took a header over the side as though he were diving off a spring-board into a swimming pool. Directly he saw the tail of his aircraft overhead he pulled his ripcord and floated gently down, taking the opportunity of practising side-slipping by working the lines of his parachute.

It was as well that he practised, for he was obliged to side-slip to miss a farmhouse. He landed plumb in the middle of a heavily-laden plum tree, the whole crop of which he brought to the ground. It was the only tree which still bore fruit and the farmer had been saving the plums until they were in perfect condition—his indignation when he found all his beautiful plums lying on the ground with a hefty New Zealander sprawling among the branches will not bear thinking of. "I think that had I been a Hun he would have shot me on the spot!" Deere subsequently remarked.

The next day, after making two sorties, the New Zealand fighter pilot was just about to take off for a third sortie when a formation of Heinkels began to bomb the aerodrome. As he opened up, a bomb fell right in front of him. He seemed to be flung miles in the air, then he felt himself careering along the ground upside down with his head scraping over the earth and squeezing him into a ball in the cockpit. He thought it was the finish, but the aircraft stopped at last and he was still alive. All was darkness. The earth shook with the explosion of bombs. Then a voice of a comrade shouted: "Are you all right?" Spitting the dirt out of his mouth, he managed at last to reply.

Every moment he thought the flames would creep in on him, but his friend, Pilot Officer E. Edsall, managed to get the door off and haul him out. "I was balanced on my head, so there was no danger of breaking my neck when I released my Sutton harness," Deere explained humorously. His scalp was bleeding and caked with earth, he was very dazed, but otherwise unharmed.

"When I saw the wreckage of my aircraft afterwards I just didn't believe that I had come out alive. The engine had been blown completely off, the starboard wing was some hundreds of yards away, the tail unit was nowhere to be seen and there was a furrow about a hundred yards in length where I had ploughed along upside down. I think the engine being blown off saved me from fire, as there was a considerable amount of petrol in the tank."

The wing and the tail were blown off his rescuer's Spitfire which drove ahead on the fuselage and came to a stop with the pilot unharmed. There was no trace of the third pilot who was taking off when the bombs dropped, and he was not found until about a couple of hours later, when he was discovered knocked out, but completely unscarred and uninjured, along with his wrecked aircraft two fields away from the aerodrome. All three of the fighter pilots had amazing escapes.

Flight Lieutenant Deere, D.F.C., as he was then, had his head bandaged by the medical officer who ordered him to bed, diagnosing slight concussion which, in the circumstances, was not to be wondered at. That night the fighter pilot dreamed of bursting bombs and wakened continually in a cold sweat. Next day he felt as though he had been on the rack and his head was very sore and swollen. All the same he got up and sat in a chair on the grass to enjoy the sunshine.

After lunch came the warning of an approaching raid. Although he had been grounded by the medical officer, it was more than he could do to keep out of action, and he somehow found himself in a Spitfire stalking a Dornier which he shot down into the Thames. Whereupon the doctor could not disagree with such indisputable evidence that he was fit for flying!

No one could deny that Wing Commander A. C. Deere, in those very hectic days, had some extraordinary escapes. Once he was seeking to pass on some of his priceless knowledge by teaching tactics to a pupil pilot, when the pupil unfortunately misjudged the distances and flew right into his instructor's Spitfire which was cut in two. The instructor was so caught up among the wreckage that he found it impossible to bale out, and while struggling to disentangle himself he dropped several thousand feet.

Eventually he won free, but his parachute harness was half torn off and the rip-cord handle was dangling out of his reach six feet below. He tried to get at it in vain. The earth rushed up at him. Feeling that his end was nigh, he closed his eyes and waited.

A mighty jerk on his shoulders made him open them again in astonishment. The parachute had functioned of its own accord.

His lucky Kiwi must have been watching over him, for when an examination was made it was found that the rip-cord pin had never been pulled.

That was not the least of his astonishing adventures.

In the roll of Squadron No. 54, whose fearless fighter pilots helped to bear the brunt of the Battle of Britain and did so much to break the German morale, the name of Wing Commander A. C. Deere, D.F.C. and Bar bears an honoured place. His valour destroyed seventeen German aircraft and added to the glory of the Royal Air Force and to the pride of New Zealand.

CHAPTER XVII

THE PILOT OFFICER

TOWARD the latter half of June, 1940, appeared the following announcement:

"Awarded a Bar to the Distinguished Flying Cross. Pilot Officer Louis Arbon Strange, D.S.O., M.C., D.F.C."

The decorations after the name of a Pilot Officer were unusual. They connoted brilliant ability and outstanding courage, yet the rank was the lowest commissioned rank in the Royal Air Force. Thoroughly intrigued, I pursued the matter and learned of the experiences of an Englishman who was so anxious to help his country in the war that although he had played his part in creating the Royal Air Force and had retired with the rank of Lieutenant Colonel and Wing Commander he was happy to rejoin as a Pilot Officer. At the age of forty-nine he was as keen to strike a blow for England as he had been at the age of twenty-three. Moreover he proved himself capable of striking as strong a blow in these latter days as in the earlier days, as the award of that Bar to his Distinguished Flying Cross, which was won in 1918, served to show.

He was once asked what his real rank was. "What does it matter?" he replied, a gleam of amusement in his blue eyes. He was tall and slender with greying hair and thoughtful lines on his lean brown face, and his words recall the words of Burns—"The rank is but the guinea stamp, a man's a man for a' that."

Here was an Englishman who loved his country and was doing his best for her; one who loved the soil which his forefathers had cultivated for generations; one who has seen the whole panorama of aviation unfold and has helped to unfold it; one who at the age of fifty loved flying as devotedly as he did when he took his Royal Aero Club certificate No. 575 on August 5, 1913, and applied for a commission in the Royal Flying Corps. In those days he was farming 600 acres, but flying won him over to join the Royal Flying Corps and his brother looked after his farm.

His friends were amused one day to find him referred to in the same official publication as Lt. Col. L. A. Strange, D.S.O., M.C., D.F.C., and as Pilot Officer L. A. Strange, D.S.O., M.C., D.F.C., so someone was apparently rather bewildered. As he once more attained the rank of

Wing Commander, the puzzle of his rank may best be solved by referring to him as Colonel Strange.

Born at Blandford in Dorsetshire in 1891, he was educated at St. Edward's School, Oxford, where Wing Commander D. R. S. Bader was educated in later years, and in May, 1914, nine months after taking his pilot's certificate, he donned the uniform of the Royal Flying Corps. Three months later, on August 16, 1914, he flew over to France in a Henri Farman biplane which was fitted with a Lewis gun on a mounting of his own design, the first aircraft to be fitted with the gun which afterwards became the main fighting weapon of the air.

Unable at his first attempt to climb within 1,500 feet of the enemy, he was ordered to take out his Lewis gun and use a rifle for fighting in the future. To use a rifle the observer was compelled to stand up in the cockpit, and it was difficult to aim straight owing to the movements of the aircraft, so the inventive mind of Colonel Strange overcame this drawback by fitting a safety strap to the leading edge of the top plane. With Lieutenant E. Rabagliati as his gunner, he went up on October 2nd to try out his idea, the success of which led to its adoption in other aircraft.

Within twelve days of landing in France he experimented with the forerunners of fire bombs in the shape of petrol bombs which set fire to two German lorries; on October 6th he dived down on German troops to attack them with a machine-gun in what was probably the first ground strafe; towards the end of November he originated leaflet raids by dropping French news bulletins, printed by a French priest, over occupied parts of France; he designed the standard mounting for the Lewis gun used on the army biplane known as B.E. 2c; and being one of the earliest advocates of arming aircraft who preached the importance of the gun and the gunner, he may truly be regarded as a pioneer of air warfare.

The army of those days had little faith in aeroplanes and the men who flew them. On September 4th when Colonel Strange and other pilots in his squadron saw Von Kluck swerving away from Paris, the Higher Command could not credit it, with the result that the "Old Contemptibles" were compelled to continue their desperate retreat from Mons for a day longer than they need have done. It was all so plain to the pilot in the air, but it took twenty-four hours to convince the Higher Command on the ground.

Colonel Strange happened to be the first to observe the initial German gas attack at Ypres on April 22, 1915. He was flying in the evening when he saw what appeared to be streams of yellowish-green smoke rolling from the German front trenches toward the British lines. A German soldier captured ten days earlier had mentioned a forthcoming gas attack, but as no signs of preparation could be detected from the air the information was discredited. Looking down, Colonel Strange was puzzled by the phenomenon; then he remembered what the German had said and flew full speed back to his base, whence he was rushed straight into the presence of General Plumer to report.

Of his adventures in peace and war there is no end. Once during his training days at the Central Flying School, Upavon, a petrol tap in his Bleriot snapped at 5,000 feet and the fumes rendered him unconscious. The Bleriot started to side-slip out of control, but in side-slipping the spray of petrol was blown away from him and the fresh air brought him round. Seeing the way to salvation, he continued to side-slip down to the aerodrome—an unforgivable crime in the eyes of the commanding officer who, thinking he had been deliberately stunting in defiance of orders, gave forth a flow of admonition which shocked the semi-conscious pilot back to his senses. The pilot, who was expecting praise for saving his life and the aircraft, was surprised to get a wigging. Not until his commandant had exhausted his vocabulary was he able to explain what had happened and prove it by his petrol-soaked clothing.

It recalls an amusing incident in which Colonel Strange administered the reproofs when he was in charge of the Central Flying School at Upavon some three years later. One day he saw a pupil turn upside down at 2,500 feet and glide in this position with propeller stopped down to the golf course, whereupon the tail swung over and the Sopwith Pup turned right way up again. The pupil simply got out of the cockpit, swung the propeller and took off again as though landing upside down were quite the normal thing.

Colonel Strange gasped. Climbing into the nearest aircraft, he sped after the pupil and waved him down. "What on earth do you mean by flying the aircraft straight off again after landing upside down?" he queried.

The pupil looked at his commanding officer in amazement. "The last thing I remember was starting to try a roll," he said. "Then I woke up to find myself sitting on the golf course, and as it is forbidden to land there, I started up and took off again."

Once Colonel Strange was given a sergeant and three men, an Avro, a Bleriot and the remains of two Henri Farmans and told to form a squadron. He did it, too, by making the brilliant pupils teach the slow coaches; but his great accomplishment was obtaining from headquarters orders for three new training Avros. Knowing that someone else would take them from under his nose, orders or no orders, he sent three pilots down to the works to remain there until the aircraft were through their tests and then to fly them straight away. He was taking no chances. His chagrin can be imagined when the day before he was due to take his new Squadron No. 23 to France he had to be rushed to hospital for an immediate operation for appendicitis. To make matters worse, a swab was left inside him after the operation and kept him fourteen weeks in hospital and below par for months after.

That led to some of his finest constructive work for the Royal Flying Corps, for he was given charge of the Machine-Gun School at Hythe which later became No. 1 School of Aerial Gunnery. When he took command the school turned out five pupils a week and on leaving it was turning out five a day. Directly bad weather prevented his pupils from living under canvas, he requisitioned the Imperial Hotel. He knew what he wanted and took it. Removing the aerodrome to Lympe compelled the pupils to go three miles for target practice, and they could not waste time walking six miles. Transport was essential and it was not to be had.

Selecting pupils who could drive, Colonel Strange went down to the bus depot of Messrs. Tilling and Stevens and as each bus came in it was requisitioned and driven off. The company claimed £150,000. But the country got its air gunners who shot the Germans to pieces.

"Every man who goes into the air on a fighting machine is a gun-layer first and last, and so his success and the success of his squadron and the whole R.F.C. depended on his gun-laying ability," he wrote in his book "Recollections of an Airman." "Without the supreme efficiency of the man behind the gun, all other work done by the R.F.C. and other arms of the service, seemed bound to be nullified, because photography, wireless, bomb dropping, etc., could not be carried out without the protection of fighting machines manned by efficient gunners. I therefore threw myself wholeheartedly into the development of the gunnery schools that were to teach and improve shooting from the air and assure the R.F.C. the supremacy over our opponents."

A new generation fighting the same old enemy has learned that the man behind the gun in the aircraft is still the deciding factor, as Colonel Strange preached and practised in the last war. The far-sighted Englishman who joined up as a Pilot Officer in this war laid down the foundations of gunnery for the Royal Air Force.

His escapes in the air have been legion, but the most hair-raising of all took place on May 10, 1915, when he was fighting a German at 8,500 feet over Menin. An empty ammunition drum jammed in his Lewis gun, so he controlled his aircraft by holding the stick between his knees while he started to tug at the drum with both hands. At that instant the stick slipped and the Martynside stalled and flicked over into a spin. He was still gripping the jammed drum with both hands when he was flung clean out of the aircraft, and he hung there with only that jammed drum between him and instant death.

"I knew it might come off at any moment, however, and as its edge was cutting my fingers badly, I had to get a firmer hold of something more reliable. The first thing I thought of was the top of the centre section strut which at that time was behind and below the Lewis gun, but as the machine was now flying upside down, I had sufficient wits left to realize that it was behind and above me, though where it was exactly I could not tell," he wrote in his book.

"Dare I let go the drum with one hand and make a grab for it? Well, there was nothing else for it but to take the risk; I let go and found the strut all right, and then I released my other hand and gripped the strut on the other side. I was then in a more comfortable position, and at least I felt rather more part of my machine than I had done in my original attitude.

"My chin was rammed against the top plane behind the gun, while my legs were waving about in empty air. The Martynside was upside down in a flat spin, and from my precarious position the only thing I could see was the propeller (which seemed unpleasantly close to my face) the town of Menin, and the adjacent countryside. Menin and its environs were revolving at an impossible angle—apparently above me—and getting larger with every turn. I began to wonder what sort of a spot I was going to crash on.

"Then I got angry and cursed myself for a fool for wasting time on such idle speculations, while at the same time it dawned on me that my only chance of righting the machine lay in getting my feet into the cockpit. If I could manage it, I knew that I was bound to fall automatically into the cockpit when the machine came over. I kept on kicking upwards behind me until at last I got first one foot and then the other hooked inside the cockpit. Somehow I got the stick between my legs again, and jammed on full aileron and elevator; I do not know exactly what happened then, but somehow the trick was done. The machine came over the right way up and I fell off the top plane into my seat with a bump."

Even then he was in dire danger, for he crashed right through the seat and jammed all the controls. It became a desperate fight to pull out the bits of seat from the controls before the aircraft crashed. He had, of course, kicked all his instruments to bits in trying to get his feet back into the cockpit. He just escaped death by a few seconds. "I rose and cleared the trees on the Menin road with very little to spare," he added, to round off a double escape as dramatic as any in the history of aviation.

Retiring from the service in 1921, he devoted his energies and remarkable organizing ability and knowledge of flying to the development of civil aviation, in conjunction with Whitney Straight, the wealthy young American, and in a few years they developed a fine business as well as new types of aircraft.

At the outbreak of war Whitney Straight was at once called up for service in the Royal Air Force—his experiences in Norway are worth a chapter to themselves—and official instructions were issued that all the resources and ground organization of the firm were to be devoted to "work of national importance." That work consisted mainly of teaching young men to fly for the Royal Air Force.

Colonel L. A. Strange, who was one of the directors, buckled to the task. His only remaining director was a retired officer of the Royal Air Force who was eventually recalled for duty, leaving Colonel Strange to shoulder the burden alone. No one will ever know what he endured. The firm, which he had worked so hard to build, was not taken over by the Government, but its commercial activities were entirely suspended

Plate 9.—Wing Commander L. A. Strange, D.S.O., D.F.C. and Bar, leaving
Buckingham Palace in September, 1940, with Miss Susan Strange, after being
presented by the King with a Bar to the D.F.C. which he won in the last war.
Squadron Leader Strange, who helped to create the Royal Air Force, retired as a
Wing Commander, but joined up in this war as a Pilot Officer, and after an
adventurous escape from France in a Hurricane took over the secret training of
the British parachute troops.

Plate 10.—Sergeant G. H. Riley just about to be picked up by a destroyer's boat after drifting in the North Sea for three and a half days. The two aircraft which found him are flying around, and the photograph proves the difficulty of detecting so small an object as a rubber dinghy even from close quarters. Relays of aircraft covered thousands of square miles during this great search, in which the Coastal Command co-operated with the Royal Navy, as described in Chapter XVIII.

with the consequent closing down of its usual source of revenue. A large staff had to be paid every week, but to get money out of the Treasury was extremely difficult.

"I must have next week's wages. I must pay the staff their wages," he insisted to the Treasury officials responsible for dealing with the matter. "If you don't give me a cheque for the wages I'll ground the aircraft!" he threatened more than once.

After struggling along in these conditions for six months, the notice arrived that the Government was requisitioning the entire organisation. "This means that the firm has ceased to exist," said Colonel Strange when the order came through. "The interests of the trustees must be protected. We've got no aircraft now, so we've got no business left. We must close down. We shall have to write 600 letters giving everyone a week's notice."

This was done. He actually sat down and wrote a letter to himself giving himself a week's notice to terminate his employment as managing director of the business which he had nurtured. It was the legal thing to do, and he did it. That was worthy of W. S. Gilbert at his best.

"Now," he thought to himself, "I shall be able to fly for the country."

So, having put in his application to rejoin the Royal Air Force which he had served so nobly in the past, he called one day upon the selection board for an interview just like thousands of other unknown men who were burning to serve their country. The officer, to whom the name of Louis Arbon Strange meant less than the name of Adam, glanced at the tall bronzed figure, and wasted no time. He was very busy.

"How old are you?" said the officer.

"Forty-nine," was the reply.

"You can't fly at that age!" said the officer bluntly.

"But I do," insisted Colonel Strange.

"You can't do it," repeated the officer.

"But I do," insisted Colonel Strange.

"We can't take a pilot over thirty. You'll have to do administrative duties," was the rejoinder.

"No, I want flying duties," protested Colonel Strange, who was adamant.

"All right," came the reply at last. "Give him a test on a Tiger Moth."

So the man who had been in charge of the Central Flying School and who had helped to create the modern gunnery schools of the Royal Air Force and had been the Wing Commander of the 23rd Wing went to have his test on a Tiger Moth. The youthful pilot who was ordered to test him grinned when he saw him.

"What are you smiling at?" asked Colonel Strange.

"Well, sir," was the reply, "I've got in my pocket my father's pilot's certificate and it is signed by you. It's rather funny!"

I—8

Which goes to show that the youngsters in the Royal Air Force have a sense of humour.

In the most serious way Colonel Strange was made to pass tests on all types of training aircraft, even the types which his own organization had developed and launched in the air.

That is the simple truth.

In April, 1940, after he had given convincing proof that he could fly, he was granted his commission as a Pilot Officer.

No man in the whole service was happier than Colonel Strange when he donned the uniform of the Royal Air Force again as Pilot Officer Strange. The nightmare of the past six months, of trying to get money out of the Treasury to pay wages, of coping with difficulties day after day, was over. He was back in the service he loved, helping the country. His responsibilities had fallen away from him. The Wing Commander of the last war was glad to be the Pilot Officer of this.

Within weeks of his rejoining the Royal Air Force the Germans vanquished Holland and Belgium and began to roll back the French. Under the German pressure the bases of the British squadrons operating in France were continually being shifted. Pilots flew until they were nearly overcome with fatigue; aircraftmen toiled all the time to make adjustments and service the aircraft in order to keep the fighting pilots in the air. It was impossible to take either pilots or aircraftmen off their operational duties to fly away or repair the aircraft collected in the aerodromes further back. The British army, moving rapidly and fighting night and day, called for rations; the tanks and anti-tank guns kept up an insatiable demand for ammunition.

Such were the conditions pertaining in the latter half of May which led to one more remarkable exploit on the part of Colonel Strange. As supplies were being demanded and several damaged aircraft were grounded at Merville aerodrome, it was decided on May 23rd to send Colonel Strange over to Merville with a fleet of civil aircraft to deliver supplies and a party of mechanics to effect temporary repairs to any aircraft in order to get them home.

It was a fine morning when they took off from an aerodrome somewhere in England, and headed for the Channel across which Colonel Strange had flown so often in the old days of war and peace. His pilot, Bill Ledlie, who was famous in civil aviation, knew his way about the air lanes of the continent as surely as a London bus driver knows his way from Oxford Circus to Marble Arch.

The tragic panorama of war unfolded as Colonel Strange looked down on the roads of France. Refugees on foot and in cars were streaming along, the cars looking ridiculously like sheep owing to the fact that they mostly had mattresses rolled up and fastened to the top of them.

"When we arrived at Merville the great fleet of civil air transport quickly unloaded their food and ammunition and left for England to obtain more," he said afterwards. "There were some losses, but it was worth while. The rest of us quickly got busy servicing the Hurricanes we had come to rescue. The first was soon away, a good many bullet holes in it, the variable pitch airscrew control tied into fine pitch with a bit of copper wire, and a piece of telephone cable back to the cockpit to enable the pilot to change pitch by breaking the copper wire with a good tug and other simple devices to make good broken controls and shot-away instruments.''

The pilot who flew this Hurricane away was reported to his base as having been shot down near Merville and his commanding officer was rather surprised when he landed at his home station in a second Hurricane. Meanwhile Colonel Strange was busy trying to get another Hurricane patched up sufficiently to enable it to fly. Bombs dropped from time to time, sniping took place along the road. Bursts of gunfire broke out and died away, but Colonel Strange and his mechanics toiled away at the Hurricane to make it work.

Just before midday a proper dog fight broke out high in the sky near the aerodrome. The deadly stutter of the machine-guns made Colonel Strange pause in his task and look up, just as a white parachute billowed out near a burning Hurricane which dived away to crash nearby. The fighter pilot landed right on the aerodrome.

''Would you like another aircraft?'' Colonel Strange asked him.

The fighter pilot was delighted. It was true that the Hurricane offered to him was a little the worse for wear. There were various bits missing and odd lengths of telephone cable and copper wire attached to it here and there as well as a plentiful supply of bullet holes. But the engine worked all right and it flew, so that was good enough for him. Thanking the tanned pilot officer with the greying hair, the young fighter pilot got into the cockpit and flew off to England.

Amid all the stress of work in those desperate days his commanding officer recalled that he was the second pilot who had been shot down that morning at Merville and had flown back in another Hurricane.''I'd like to see that officer at Merville. Just send out and drop a message asking him to fly the next Hurricane back here himself,'' he said.

The message was duly sent.

''Later in the afternoon, about the time we got the third Hurricane working properly, I was surprised to see one of our own aircraft leave a busy little dog fight and streak down to drop one of the familiar little red and blue message bags telling me to bring the next serviceable Hurricane back to England before nightfall,'' explained Colonel Strange. ''It was a strange sight in a sky—with a Tiger Moth and an Autogyro, bringing back sharp memories of peacetime flying, now floating around absolutely unconcerned on their message-carrying jobs. You might have thought they were helping the police to handle the traffic on Derby Day.''

The order to fly the Hurricane home delighted him, because it gave him the chance of testing his theory that once a man has been taught to fly by the R.A.F. he can fly anything, no matter what type, providing he remembers "to turn all the taps and push and pull all the knobs of a modern aircraft in their proper sequence and has the good sense to inquire about the aircraft's peculiar habits from someone who knows her ways," as he once remarked.

But there was no one at Merville who could explain to him, and although he had never flown a Hurricane before and had no guns with which to defend himself he calmly climbed into the patched-up aircraft and flew it off as though it were a Tiger Moth or one of his old Henri Farmans of the last war. Far from being worried, he was as happy as an undergraduate going on holiday. The undercarriage came up at his touch and the Merlin engine ran like silk.

Then his troubles began. Tracer began to come up at him from the hillsides as the Germans attacked him. Being anxious to save the Hurricane which he had gone to such pains to repair, he decided to climb. Pulling back the stick, he sailed up to 8,000 feet. Like magic the sky ahead became filled with the bursting of anti-aircraft shells as the Germans put up a fierce barrage. In the eyes of an old campaigner, the position was decidedly unhealthy, so he side-slipped down to avoid disaster.

But the leader of six Messerschmitts looking for stragglers noticed him and dived down to shoot him to bits. Colonel Strange, seeing the tracer and feeling the bullets ripping into one wing, side-slipped the other way to meet with similar treatment from an attacker on that side. If he could have pressed the button on his control column and set his guns blazing he would have been quite happy to take on the Messerschmitts, but he had nothing with which to hit back. His only defence was his skill as a pilot. He was compelled to match his mature experience against armed might and youth.

There followed the maddest chase he has ever taken part in, one which called out all the old evasive tactics to defeat the enemy, while the German guns stuttered and Colonel Strange hedge-hopped over the tops of trees, skimming the roofs of cottages and showing those Germans that his hand had lost none of its cunning even if he was turning grey. He roared between the dwellings in a village street, turned on one wing and shot between the trees down the drive of a chateau. When it seemed that he must surely crash into the front door, he pulled back the stick and leapt over the roof and dived down the other side, giving the enemy such a run as they had never had before.

Superb judgment and brilliant flying kept his pursuers at bay as he hugged the ground down a wooded valley which led him at last skimming over the sand dunes out to sea. The navy was there. Directly the naval gunners saw the hard-pressed Hurricane they sent such a hail of fire at the Messerschmitts that the Germans turned and fled. Breathing freely once more, Colonel Strange pulled back the stick and climbed into the heavens to take a farewell look at the French coast where the smoke

of battle hung over Calais and Boulogne to make a Turneresque picture
in the setting sun. He had safely run the gauntlet and could not help
wondering what was happening to his son who at that moment was
somewhere down there in France fighting his way to Dunkirk.

And that was how the man who was supposed to be too old to fly
saved a modern aircraft he had never flown before and won the Bar to
his D.F.C.

During the bad weather in January, 1941, I was forced by snowbound
roads to take refuge in a wayside inn somewhere in England, where I got
into conversation with a Canadian airman who touched on the unbelievable happenings of those days. ''Yes, and there was a pilot officer
who managed to bring out a Hurricane. When he got home he refused
to give it up. He said he'd saved it, so it was his and he was darn well
going to fly it.''

I smiled. ''That was Strange!'' I said to my companion, an officer in
the Royal Air Force.

Truth is stranger than fiction.

CHAPTER XVIII

SAVED FROM THE SEA

To the Royal Air Force nothing was more precious than the lives of
the airmen who fought to overthrow the Nazis and their foul creed;
and of the unsparing efforts made to save British airmen, few were
so prolonged or all-embracing as the rescue of Sergeant G. H. Riley.

At 10 o'clock on the night of September 23, 1940, a Whitley bomber
with a crew of five took off from an English aerodrome to bomb the big
aeroplane factory at Spandau, on the outskirts of Berlin. There were a
few clouds about, but conditions were not too bad as they sped across
Germany. The Whitley was a big bomber, with a roomy fuselage 85 feet
long, and every available inch of the space in the cabins of the captain
and second pilot and navigator and wireless operator was crowded with
dials and levers and switches. On the wireless operator's switchboard
alone were thirty-three switches; his little desk with the brown key on
which to tap out messages to base was no more than fourteen inches by
eight. Above it was the knob which enabled him to switch over his set
from sending to receiving; there were batteries, a priming pump for the
engines, amplifying valves, oscillating valves and all the other valves
without which the modern bomber was lost.

The aircraft was heated by hot air from the engines, and the pipe con-
ducting the hot air to the various cabins and to the rear turret was
lagged with a non-conducting material to conserve the heat. Oxygen
bottles provided the crew with oxygen at high altitudes; great flares a
yard long stood ready by the big chute down which they were launched

to light up the ground below, and two self-sealing tanks of petrol for use in emergencies each held about seventy gallons, enough to keep the aircraft flying for two hours.

For emergency landings on the sea, the rubber dinghy was stowed beside the escape door, which was on the port side of the fuselage about midway between the wing and tail. This door was hinged at the top and opened outwards to provide a good emergency exit downwards while the aircraft was in the air; but the door hampered the movements of those who sought to escape when the Whitley fell in the sea, and in consequence it was usually chopped off at the hinges if the crew was forced down at sea. Among the equipment, such as first-aid outfits, bottles of water, fire extinguishers and other things, was an axe of a peculiar shape specially designed for several emergency uses.

Sergeant Riley in the rear turret kept a sharp look out in the darkness for enemy fighters. His four guns were ready to blaze away instantly, but no enemy troubled him on the long trip over. He sat there on his little seat with the turret control column in his hands and very little room to move his legs, in front of which the spare ammunition was packed in special containers. Had he wished to relax, he could have opened the turret doors behind him to bring into use the tandem seats on which he could lean back or even lie down.

Directly the bomber reached the outskirts of Spandau the search-lights began to move round. The Whitley could not dodge the beams. The vivid flashes of anti-aircraft guns lit up the ground like sheet lightning as the shells began to come up. Dropping their flares as they roared over Spandau, the Whitley crew had no difficulty in locating the aeroplane works. It was too immense to be missed.

As they turned and made their run over the target, the guns put up a fierce barrage. Now and again they felt bits of bursting shells jar the aircraft, but they held their course and dropped their full load of high explosives and incendiaries dead on the target. Sergeant Riley watched the bombs strike home and the factory burst into flames.

Unfortunately for the crew of the Whitley, a piece of shell holed one of the petrol tanks, and made it problematical whether they would be able to reach their base.

Conserving his fuel as much as possible, the pilot made his way back across Germany. He flew over Holland, fighting to maintain every inch of height which was so precious to him, then crossed the Dutch coast and headed over the North Sea. He watched the pointer of the altimeter sliding back inexorably as he slowly lost height. His eye from time to time glanced at the dwindling fuel reserves from the emergency tanks.

There was too far to go and too little fuel. He faced the fact calmly.

When the Whitley was eighty miles from the Dutch coast, the wireless operator got into touch with the home stations, fixed his position and advised them that they were in difficulties.

They flew on, getting lower, looking eagerly for some ship which might assist them. There was nothing, only the empty seas heaving around them. It was so rough that some of the crew wondered whether they could make a safe landing. But on this point Sergeant Riley was convinced. "I knew we were going to do it," he said afterwards.

The crew got ready to abandon the aircraft. They chopped off the escape door so that they could launch the rubber dinghy and get into it without delay. Meanwhile the wireless operator so long as the power lasted gave their position to enable a ship to be sent to their rescue. The second pilot came up from the forward cockpit and crawled under the main spar into the fuselage where the other three members of the crew clustered round the escape door. All braced themselves for the shock. They were thrown about as the Whitley hit the water, but the pilot made a magnificent landing in the rough seas and soon joined his crew. The dinghy was safely launched. One of the men took the Very pistol for signalling purposes, another a flask of water, and another a packet of biscuits. Quickly the five men got into the rubber dinghy and pushed away from the sinking Whitley. It was exactly 5.50 on the morning of September 24th, for Sergeant Riley's wrist watch was stopped by the jolt of the Whitley hitting the sea. They had been flying for seven hours and fifty minutes and were then 100 miles away from the English coast.

From that moment all the resources of the Royal Air Force and the Royal Navy were concentrated on their rescue. A Hudson was instructed to locate them, but failed to do so; but at 10.50 a.m., five hours after they took to the dinghy, another Hudson, detailed for the search, managed to come on the little boat amid the rough seas, and at once signalled its position. The dinghy was then a hundred miles to the east of Hartlepool. This Hudson flew around until relieved at 12.35 by another which in its turn was relieved just before 2 o'clock.

Meanwhile a high speed launch was dispatched to pick up the Whitley crew. But about midday the weather grew worse and heavy rains hid the dinghy while the wind swung right round from the south-west to the north-west thus changing completely the direction in which the airmen were drifting. The weather grew so bad that the rescue launch was unable to stand up against it, and signalled to the base that they were taking in a lot of water, after which all efforts to contact the launch failed.

Those rough seas which battered and defeated the launch fell still more heavily upon the drifting airmen. The waves broke continually over them. Seated in the flooded dinghy, they were wet through and very cold. They sought to warm themselves by taking their emergency spirit ration, but it made Sergeant Riley rather sick. Waving to the first Hudson about 11 o'clock, they wondered how long they would have to wait before they were rescued. Tired out by their long flight, exhausted by the incessant action of the rough seas, some of them started to doze.

So difficult became conditions that the Hudson lost sight of them; but another went out in the afternoon and accompanied a launch to the position where the dinghy was last seen. Neither the aircraft nor launch could find any trace of the airmen. After searching round for an hour and a half they were driven back to their base by the bad weather.

A second Hudson, however, was luckier in its search. The little bunch of men in the dinghy were not easily seen in the high seas, off which a thirty miles an hour wind was whipping the tops. Approaching as closely as possible, the Hudson dropped a container of food and comforts for the men. It fell only ten yards away, but although Sergeant Riley and his companions paddled hard to reach it, the seas were too much for them and they suffered the disappointment of seeing the parcel vanish.

Their position was carefully marked, as was the direction in which they were drifting at about three knots; but the wind by now had swung round still more to the north and every change in the wind changed their direction and increased the difficulty of finding them again. Just after seven o'clock in the evening the Hudson was forced to return to base by shortage of fuel, and the weather was so bad that operations had to be suspended for the night. Meanwhile the base was without news of the missing launch.

The continual pounding of the seas had its effect on the drifting men. One grew lightheaded and fell overboard, but his companions managed to get him back again. Shortly afterwards he dropped in again, but once more his companions dragged him out. They were growing weak, and the struggle exhausted them, but they still mustered enough strength to haul him into the dinghy when he slipped in for the third time. All grew very quiet. Then they saw him fall in again and the seas closed on him for ever.

During the day they had finished the flask of water. Sergeant Riley and the others had eaten a couple of biscuits. Now they were thirsty and cold as they huddled together in an exhausted state and dozed in the flooded dinghy throughout the night.

Just after 6 o'clock on the morning of September 25th, four Hudsons flew off in formation to try to find the dinghy. A search along the track where the dinghy was last sighted yielded no result. Below them two destroyers cast around to find the hapless airmen. One Hudson was cheered by the sight of the missing launch making for land and reported the news to base.

Their search along the supposed course proving futile, the Hudsons began a square search, and about 11 o'clock one of them detected the dinghy. Circling around, the Hudson dropped another parcel of comforts, but the rough seas again prevented the airmen from picking it up. The navigator of the Hudson fixed the position with the utmost care before the pilot flew off to find the destroyers to bring them to the spot. At that critical hour when the rescue of the airmen seemed almost certain, the shortage of petrol drove the aircraft back to its base before it could find the destroyers. It was as though Fate mocked their efforts.

However, another Hudson went off and found the destroyers, which thereupon made a careful search for the dinghy, but they could not locate it. Meanwhile another Hudson came on the dinghy miles away just after 11 o'clock and circled it until nearly 1 o'clock, when it was relieved by yet another Hudson. On the way back to its base, the first Hudson came up with the destroyers about sixteen miles distant from the dinghy and directed them to the spot.

In the morning the men on board had all waved to the first Hudson. The last Hudson to come on them saw only one man make any movement at all. Circling round, the Hudson came as close as possible and dropped some flame floats and a parcel of emergency rations, but again the waves carried the parcel out of the reach of the airmen. It was not possible to see the dinghy for more than 400 yards, and as the Hudson came round it was lost to sight in a squall and the rough seas. The destroyers were then eight miles away, so the Hudson strove to attract their attention, but they also vanished in a great storm of rain about 2.30 p.m.

The Hudson held doggedly to the search. It sighted two Heinkel 115 seaplanes, but before it could attack them they disappeared into the clouds. Another Hudson and two Ansons were sent out. Hundreds of square miles of sea were covered, yet that little dinghy with the four exhausted men eluded them all. The seas were running high, and the dinghy when the Hudson lost sight of it early in the afternoon was drifting at over four knots. The chances of the airmen were hourly growing less.

"A Hudson found us and dropped flares. It followed us for a long time," stated Sergeant Riley. "We sighted a destroyer later in the afternoon, and the Hudson seemed to direct it to us, but as soon as the Hudson went off we lost sight of the destroyer."

Night closed down on the tragic group of airmen drifting on the waves. Lack of food and the long exposure of the seas were telling on them. That night another man grew lightheaded and imagined he was back walking on the aerodrome. In his delusion he walked overboard and was lost.

For two days the Royal Air Force and the Royal Navy had been seeking them, sparing no resources and no effort. At dawn on the morning of September 26th, five Hudsons took up the task. They were detailed to search an area off Flamborough Head some ninety miles long by fifty-nine miles wide—over 5,000 square miles. All the morning they continued their search, fighting now and again with German aircraft that sought to interfere with them. Once a Hudson came on two Heinkel 115s circling the two destroyers *Ashanti* and *Bedouin* which were prosecuting the search down below, and it promptly attacked the Heinkels and drove them into the clouds. A Blenheim went out to join in the hunt. A motor launch engaged on the same errand of mercy was so battered by the heavy seas that she sprang a leak and was obliged to return.

Time and again during the morning the Hudsons fought short engagements with enemy aircraft which always succeeded in escaping in the clouds. From dawn until the early afternoon they kept up a continuous search, but not a sight of the missing airmen cheered their eyes. A few minutes after 2 o'clock they were all obliged to return to their base because they were at the end of their fuel.

In the afternoon four Ansons went out to resume the quest, but they, too, failed to locate the missing airmen. Hopeless though further search seemed, neither the Royal Air Force nor the Royal Navy would abandon it.

At dawn the next day, September 27th, five Hudsons and four Ansons flew off to quarter the seas and try to find and save the missing airmen. Visibility was poor, the seas were rough, and as they swept down from time to time to look closer at the surface, their windows were coated with brine. At last a Hudson saw the missing dinghy, but it was able to keep it in sight for only five minutes. The position, however, was marked, and at 11.15 a.m. another Hudson flew to the position, and searched the seas around it. It found nothing. An hour later another aircraft went to the same spot, with the same result.

Baffled and disappointed, they returned to base, and three Ansons flew off to continue the search. These found the destroyers and escorted them to the spot where the missing dinghy was last seen—they saw nothing but the empty seas heaving in all directions.

A Hudson took off at 1 o'clock to resume the search. At 1.30 another Hudson followed. Just after 2 o'clock the missing dinghy was seen ahead by one of the Hudsons whose pilot, coming down very low, manœuvred as close as possible and dropped a float and with it a watertight bag of comforts. Luckily they dropped just within the reach of Sergeant Riley who with an effort managed to secure the bag. Although very weak after all he had suffered and endured, Sergeant Riley was still in fair condition, and the first thing he did was to light up a cigarette. His two companions were far gone, and remained in a comatose state.

From the moment that the Hudson sighted the dinghy it started to circle round and would not let it out of sight for a second. An hour later the other Hudson came on the scene and for hour after hour the two aircraft followed each other round and round that pitiful little group on the sea below. Just after four o'clock they saw one of the airmen fall out of the dinghy and vanish. He had already fallen into the sea earlier in the day and been helped back by Sergeant Riley.

"The last day aircraft were above all the time. We had seen so many of them that we took no notice. It was a boat we wanted," he remarked, when he had recovered from his ordeal.

So from 2 o'clock until 5.30 those Hudsons went round and round
that little dinghy which the Royal Air Force and the Royal Navy
had sought for more than three days. The crews of the Hudsons were
determined not to lose it again. At last the destroyers *Ashanti* and
Bedouin steamed up in answer to the signals, and the Hudsons dropped
flares by the dinghy and kept diving over it to lead them to the position.

At 5.35 a boat was launched from one of the destroyers and Sergeant
Riley and his companion were tenderly lifted from the rubber dinghy
and taken on board. The Hudsons waited awhile to learn the condition
of the rescued men. "One fair, one very ill," signalled the destroyer.

Of those five men who so bravely launched the little dinghy when
their Whitley came down in the North Sea, only Sergeant G. H. Riley
survived, and after being picked up the next thing he remembered was
waking in Rosyth hospital on the following day. Drifting for eighty-
four hours, he was carried a distance of about ninety miles.

That intensive search prosecuted by aircraft of the Coastal Command
for three and a half days will go down to history as the act of a true
democracy. Not to rescue an officer of the highest rank were all those
aircraft sent out in relays for day after day to fly in the aggregate
thousands of miles and search thousands of square miles of sea, but
simply to save a young sergeant. Here was irrefutable proof that to the
High Command of the Royal Air Force the lives of the airmen were
beyond price, and that to preserve the life of a single one of these
defenders of civilization it did not hesitate to use all its vast resources.

As if the agony of that ordeal were not enough, Sergeant Riley
had barely recovered and gone on leave to his home when he was
subjected to the terrible raid in Manchester which laid the heart of the
city in ruins. Many died that night, but Sergeant Riley escaped.

"The Germans can't kill me!" the gallant young sergeant remarked
when it was all over.

Nor could they ever conquer those who showed such courage.

CHAPTER XIX

GREAT ODDS AND LIGHTER MOMENTS

ON the evening of May 31, 1940, in a mess somewhere on the east
coast of England, Flying Officer R. N. Selley read with troubled eyes
a note advising him that his brother was missing. He turned to his
friend Flying Officer H. A. Haarhoff. "If we do meet anything we'll
give them what for," he said quietly.

Both the young men were South Africans who flew together in a
Hudson aircraft which was manned by a crew of four, a wireless
operator, a navigator, an air gunner who was Flying Officer Haarhoff,
and the pilot Flying Officer Selley. The Hudson was a useful long

distance reconnaissance aircraft which could carry a good load of bombs for offensive purposes and was armed with twin guns in the pilot's cockpit and a nice sting in the tail where Flying Officer Haarhoff sat in the turret with his two guns. But in those Dunkirk days all aircraft became fighters, as the German dive bombers over the beaches learned to their cost.

On June 1st a battle flight of three Hudsons took off to relieve the dawn patrol over Dunkirk. It met the other battle flight about midday over Dover, inward bound for their base. Flying Officer Selley flew on the port side of the outward bound formation at about 1,000 feet. In the Channel, sea-power was working its miracle. Flying Officer Haarhoff gazed on the greatest and most miscellaneous collection of shipping he had ever seen in his life. There were tugs towing barges and tugs towing yachts, with motor boats of all sizes, some towing lifeboats, with torpedo boats and destroyers coming and going on their errand of mercy and deliverance.

Up and down the coast by Dunkirk the formation of Hudsons patrolled for fifteen minutes each way. Once some Spitfires dropped out of the clouds and mistakenly attacked the leader, who had difficulty in evading them. Another time a Hudson chased an enemy aircraft which fled for its life right into the fog of black smoke with which the burning oil blanketed the town, and the smoke, seeping into the cockpit of the Hudson, nearly choked the gunner.

Not a ripple stirred the sea. It was so calm that Flying Officer Haarhoff could see bottles floating about; once or twice he saw a body amid rafts and overturned boats and drums and barrels; a bombed destroyer was lying on its beam near the beach. There was the remarkable pier of lorries formed by army drivers to help the evacuation and one or two other wrecks nearby, among them an overturned steamer about which we shall hear later.

"It was a miracle: not a breath of wind during the vital days. When I saw all the little craft passing across I was thrilled," said Wing Commander T. H. Carr, D.F.C., who flew another Hudson during those historic hours.

Flying Officer Selley noted the moving figures and boats and all the wrecks and the flotsam and jetsam on the sea, with its huge patches to tell of oil which would never fall into the German hands. A couple of days earlier he had seen a table floating four miles from shore with three men upon it, and closer examination revealed a bicycle. In that emergency one of those men was literally fighting for his life, yet he still refused to relinquish his bicycle and had dragged it after him on to the table before they floated away. The pilot of the Hudson soon brought a steamer to the spot, but the captain was out to save life, not bicycles, and the South African pilot watched the men being picked up while the cycle which one had risked so much to save went floating away on the table top.

About 3 o'clock in the afternoon the Hudson sighted forty Junkers 87s. As these were unseen by the Spitfires patrolling above open cloud at 4,000 feet, the three Hudsons were ordered to break formation and attack.

Flying Officer Selley sped off to attack eight Junkers 87s that were about five miles away. "As we approached," said Flying Officer Haarhoff afterwards, "we could see them circling in about a two mile radius. Each one was doing a steep climb with a stall turn at the top and then came over in a very steep dive straight down. It was a very pretty and impressive sight, and they were doing it with such regularity and uniformity that they might have been at Hendon flying pageant."

"I'll never forget it as long as I live," reported Flying Officer Selley. "We saw about forty altogether and they seemed to split up into two bunches of twenty. I took a bunch of eight Junkers 87s which had twelve more flying at 200 feet above them. When we came in to attack they all joined in one big circle at about 1,200 feet. We just went straight into them. We thought there were a lot, but we didn't mind. It was our job to look after the fellows below and we had to do it."

Regardless of the risk, Flying Officer Selley flew alone in that ring of twenty enemies. It might have been a performing circus with the South African as the ring-master. Round and round he went with them. He tried at first to follow one down and get it while it was diving, but the dive was too steep for the Hudson to follow, so he decided to time his attack to coincide with the moment that an enemy aircraft climbed in front of him before it did its stall turn and dive.

"We attacked as one came up and as he stall turned we just leapt across and shot him down. As we circled with them, Haarhoff picked them off going round, and as they came up I got them with my front guns. I shot down two with my front guns and damaged two more, one badly, but we did not see him go in. Haarhoff shot one down into the sea and damaged another, but we did not see that go in either."

The extraordinary thing is that the Hudson was not hit.

Unable to stand up to the guns of the avenging South Africans, the Germans fled and gave them the skies to themselves.

That was how Flying Officer Ronald Nicholas Selley and Flying Officer Hilton Aubrey Haarhoff eagerly and fearlessly attacked twenty enemy aircraft and each won the D.F.C.

Five minutes after routing the Junkers they saw two lifeboats adrift full of men which they circled while the other Hudsons flew off to find a ship to pick them up. Almost simultaneously three Junkers 88s and three Heinkel 111s with an escort of two Messerschmitt 109s hove in view to bomb the boats. At once the South African made a head-on attack. Those eight German aircraft had not the courage to face that lone Hudson. They turned away over Dunkirk and gave the tugs which came on the scene a chance to take the lifeboats in tow.

Later in the week a Wing Commander of the Coastal Command

beheld not the least amazing sight in those amazing times. "For two or three days after the evacuation ended, Tommies were leaving the coast in rowing boats, on rafts, bits of wreckage, in fact anything that would float, and putting out in the Channel where we were sighting them and sending ships to pick them up," he remarked when it was all over. "Some Tommies swam out to a ship that was lying on her side and took refuge in her. When I came along, the ship seemed to be deserted. Then I saw a man poke his head through a porthole and look up very cautiously. He observed us carefully and when he saw it was a British aircraft he started to wave frantically. In a few seconds men's heads began to pop up through the portholes to right and left and hands began to wave to us for succour. It was a most astounding sight. At one moment the ship was dead, the next it sprang to life. The men had been in hiding there for three days when we saw them and directed a ship to their rescue."

The British pilots who witnessed Dunkirk from the air conjure up an unforgettable picture of the continual pall of smoke under which they flew, of beaches lined with men walking into the water with their rifles held over their heads as they climbed into little boats which rowed them to the bigger boats further out. "It was," as Pilot Officer Lloyd Bennett, D.F.C., remarked afterwards, "one continual traffic, almost a bridge of boats. The Channel was very small for our Hudsons, and I circled so much one day that I mistook a burning town on the other side for Dover and thought the war had moved over to our side. I was quite surprised to find we were all right."

If it is possible to make a mistake like that in daylight, the difficulty of fixing a position at night after taking violent evasive action can be imagined.

Serious as was Dunkirk, it had its lighter side. A Hurricane pilot who baled out on the last day of the evacuation was seen by a Hudson pilot to make a nasty landing. It was some months before the Hudson pilot came across the Hurricane pilot again. "Did you hurt yourself?" asked the Hudson pilot.

"Oh, no," came the cheerful response of the Hurricane pilot. "I fell on my head!"

He was apparently a hard-headed young man.

While anything in the way of practical joking is frowned upon by authority, youth cannot always be suppressed. I once found a station chuckling with delight at the discomfiture of a pretty little W.A.A.F. The station was so large that a motor car was really needed to get about it, and this new recruit was sent off one afternoon to an office half a mile away. "I've been sent for the station black-out switch," she said, saluting smartly.

"I'm sorry it isn't here," said the officer very politely. With a friendly smile he directed her to another office and as soon as she had departed he rang up his friend in great glee to tell him to pass her on.

The pretty little W.A.A.F. was passed on to fourteen offices and had walked five miles before she saw the joke.

Another day a sergeant whose aircraft was in a hot spot with some Messerschmitts inquired over the intercommunication system of his captain: "Were you firing at anything with your front guns, sir?"

"Don't be a fool!" was the reply. "That's not my front guns, that's my teeth chattering."

One station chuckled for many a day over a misunderstanding concerning a balloon. News came into the operations room saying that a balloon was down some miles away. At once a sergeant and twenty men were dispatched in a lorry to capture the runaway and restore it to its rightful station.

What the sergeant said when he arrived and was handed one of the little meteorological balloons that are sent up to register atmospheric conditions in the higher levels history does not relate.

Those May days of 1940 were the heydays of courage and self-sacrifice in the Royal Air Force, for British aircrews and aircraft were so outnumbered that it was only by superior skill and a finer fighting spirit that the British fighters and bombers were able to establish their ascendancy over the formidable masses of the German Luftwaffe. One memorable action won the Distinguished Flying Medal for Sergeant James Reginald Paine, the observer in a bomber told off with eight others to bomb the Germans who were breaking across the Belgian frontier. The British bombers made their spirited attack, only to be attacked in their turn by heavy formations of Messerschmitts.

Four of the Messerschmitts marked down the bomber in which Sergeant Paine was carrying out his duties and began to attack it one after another. Presently the voice of the rear-gunner came through on the intercommunication system to say he was hit.

Now this bomber had such a narrow, tapering fuselage that the entrance to the rear cockpit was through a hatch underneath the fuselage at the tail. Normally, no one would attempt to reach the rear cockpit from the central turret because of the difficulty of wriggling along within the aircraft inside so narrow a fuselage.

Immediately Sergeant Paine heard that the rear-gunner was wounded he determined to go to his help. It was impossible, however, for him to wriggle along in his flying kit. He was much too bulky for the confined space along which he would have to move.

Unstrapping his parachute, and thus depriving himself of any chance of escape if it became necessary to bale out, he stripped off his thick flying suit. By reducing his girth in this manner, he discovered he could just make his way along the narrow fuselage to the tail. Even then it was a tight fit, but he managed to get through. Working in the confined space, he succeeded in easing the rear-gunner out of the cockpit, after which he promptly sat in the gunner's place and took up the fight against the Messerschmitts which he fought so effectively that at last he forced them to sheer off.

As soon as the attack ceased, he attended to his wounded companion. It was bitterly cold at that high level, but Sergeant Paine endured it without a murmur. Having discarded the warm clothing which was his sole defence against the low temperature, he ignored the freezing conditions and remained with the wounded gunner until the bomber was approaching home. Then he made his tortuous way forward again to his own turret and assisted the pilot to navigate the bomber to safety.

In that crisis, all thoughts of self were cast away. He thought only of the wounded gunner and the safety of his companions. If he had not been prompted to take off his flying clothes in order to reach the rear cockpit, there is not much doubt that the Germans would have shot the bomber to pieces.

It is not easy to assess courage, for it cannot be measured or weighed like merchandise, yet there is one form of courage that is so high that one can only bow the head in reverence and awe. It is the courage which so ennobles and uplifts a man that of his own free will he will lay down his life for others. Flying Officer Ralph Hope, the nephew of the late Mr. Neville Chamberlain, was faced with this cruel dilemma, whether he should live and let others die, or he should die and let others live. His aircraft was crashing on some London houses. He could easily have baled out and saved his own life. But he thought of the innocent people who would be killed when his aircraft struck.

Instantly and calmly he made his choice and remained at the controls while he steered his flaming aircraft away from the houses to some open land. Then he baled out—too late.

If there be a cross on his grave, is it not the image of another cross which stood upon a hill nearly two thousand years ago?

CHAPTER XX

A MAGNIFICENT LEADER

OFFICIAL citations are factual, prone to understatement and very sparing in the use of adjectives, so if they go so far as to mention "his magnificent leadership" and "his brilliant leadership," nothing can be more certain than the fact that the officer concerned was an outstanding leader; and if they disclose that he had shot down at least eighteen enemy aircraft, he was assuredly a pilot of exceptional skill and courage—which explains why Group Captain A. G. Malan won the D.S.O. and Bar, the D.F.C. and Bar. This fine South African fighter pilot, who trained for the South African navy and joined the Royal Air Force in 1936, was the first airman to shoot down two German bombers in one night over England, a feat which is dealt with in Chapter ix.

He was a leader to whom the squadron came before everything. It was the squadron which counted, and the success of the squadron that mattered. The team spirit which he infused into the pilots whom he led in the days of May, 1940, served in time to turn Squadron No. 74 into a band of cool and resourceful and fearless pilots whose toll of the German Luftwaffe by the end of 1940 raised them to eminence in the Royal Air Force. He knew how to handle young men with the temperament of fighter pilots, how to inspire them, how to lead them and draw the best out of them. He instilled into them something of the spirit of the Canadian North-West Mounted Police. When they followed him into battle, each went with the intention of getting his man. It was their duty to shoot down Germans without being shot down themselves, and if the enemy escaped one day they could bide their time and knock him down the next.

Not until the latter half of May did the South African see a German in the air. Having patrolled the French coast for some days without sighting the enemy, he was sent out from his base to intercept a formation of German bombers whose movements had been notified. The interception was controlled from the base by orders which reached him through the radio-telephone and he altered his course and height according to the information received. Visual evidence in the way of heavy anti-aircraft fire was of considerable help in enabling him to locate the raiders over the French coast.

He was flying across the top of a great cloud hummock which heaped up in the sky like a snowy peak when he nearly flew into a Heinkel 111. The first German he had ever seen was no more than fifty yards away, while fifty yards further on was a Junkers 88. So fast was he moving that only by prompt handling of the stick could he swerve to avoid the Heinkel.

Terrified that the German might drop down into the cloud a hundred feet below and escape, the South African did a steep turn on to the tail of the enemy and actually started firing on his side with full bank on. His attack was shattering. ''As I straightened up I saw my bullets pouring in and large pieces flew off him. He belched heavy smoke, his undercart fell out and he fell down into the cloud,'' he said afterwards.

Anxious to deal with the German bombers further ahead, he called his section together, and then sank down into the clouds to stalk the enemy for fifteen miles on a compass course. Flying blindly under the surface of the cloud, just as a submarine moves under the surface of the sea, the South African concluded after a few minutes that it was time to bob up above the cloud surface to have a look round.

It gave him a second thrill within five minutes, for he came up slap underneath a Junkers 88. A quick glance revealed about ten German bombers ahead. Ordering the other two Spitfires to attack, he let loose on the Junkers 88, which he completely surprised. Opening fire from a distance of a hundred yards, he squeezed the button for six seconds and was amazed to see the Junkers literally blow up in the air. While he was firing, the camera which was synchronized with his guns took photographs of what was happening as his bullets went home, and this film, now historic, was shown on all the news reels in cinemas all over Great Britain.

Needless to add, the other two pilots of his section seized their opportunity. One shot down a Junkers before the rest escaped in the clouds, and it transpired that the other, Flight Lieutenant J. C. Freeborn, who won the D.F.C. and Bar, managed to shoot down two of the Junkers. Unfortunately he caught a bullet in the radiator which drove him down in France.

The Germans were over-running the country all round him, but Flight Lieutenant Freeborn was determined to elude them. The first thing he did was to push his Spitfire among the undergrowth where he landed, then he covered it up with branches so that it was completely concealed not only from the air, but from any passer-by on the ground. Having hidden his Spitfire from prying eyes, he set off to see whether he could secure some petrol to refill his tanks so that he could make the attempt to cross the Channel.

For three exciting days he dodged the Germans and tried to obtain petrol from the friendly French. Not a drop of petrol could he obtain. Once he found a German supply tank full of petrol that was left unattended by the enemy. Boldly seizing the chance, he slipped into the seat and drove it off full speed towards the spot where he had hidden his Spitfire. He was just congratulating himself on his stratagem and concluding that at last he would be able to get away when he came face to face with a long German column. Promptly turning the petrol tanker into the ditch, he bolted for his life.

His flying start enabled him to get away, and later he was picked up at Calais by a Blenheim bomber which was sent out for him with an escort of Spitfires from his own squadron.

Another time the squadron came on fifteen Messerschmitt 109s flying in broken cloud at 8,000 feet. There was abundant cover for all, and in the mix-up that followed Flight Lieutenant Freeborn shot down a Messerschmitt 109 and darted away into a cloud to climb quickly through it. Directly he poked his nose out of the top he saw three Messerschmitts diving on him.

He did not wait. Spinning round, he took a header into the cloud again and went down and down in a screeching dive, shaking off his pursuers in the cloud which blanketed him like a dense fog. As he dropped out of the bottom of the cloud the first thing he saw was a Messerschmitt 109 chasing a Spitfire and automatically he swept round on the Messerschmitt's tail and shot the enemy down before the German knew what was hitting him.

As the German armoured divisions progressed along the coast, the fierce air combats of Malan and his Spitfire pilots grew more numerous. From Boulogne to Dunkirk they patrolled their beat up and down, while the guns below opened up on them at every opportunity. The pilots had no respite. The weather on the whole was good and on no day was it bad enough to give them a breathing spell. On May 24th, by which time Boulogne was in German hands, they came to grips in real earnest with the full weight of the German Luftwaffe. The flight of Spitfires became split up into three sections, one of which was led by the South African who was under severe fire from the German anti-aircraft guns when he got a call over the radio-telephone from his base to say that the Germans were bombing Dunkirk.

At once he screamed flat out along the coast, dropping down to water level so as to see the enemy against the sky. The sight which met his eyes at Dunkirk was amazing. Never before had he seen anything like it. Formations of twenty to thirty bombers flying at 20,000 feet were grouped together and seemed to stretch in an endless chain as they bombed Dunkirk docks. Above the bombers were countless fighters.

"All I saw was the sky black with bombers. I could not see the beginning or end of them," he reported.

Climbing all out, he led the other three Spitfires up to the attack. The whole of the German Luftwaffe seemed to be arrayed against them, but they did not falter.

Straight into one large layer of bombers they sped with guns blazing, cutting deeper and deeper into the formation. The leader gave a Heinkel 111 a burst of five seconds, and as he saw the enemy aircraft take fire he felt a hit by anti-aircraft fire on his starboard wing. At the same moment bullets took a bit out of his flying boot and cut his electric leads.

Turning steeply to starboard, he saw a Messerschmitt 109 firing at him. A glance in his mirror revealed a Messerschmitt 110 firing cannon shell at him from astern. His ring reflector sight with its magic circle of light was put out of action, so his guns were useless without it.

He was beset with enemies seeking to kill him, threatening to riddle him with their fire. Yet in that crisis he was so cool and calm that he remembered there was a spare ring and bead sight in his locker and he decided to fit it then and there in order to carry on his attack. Climbing steeply into the sun, he pulled the spare sight out of his locker and slipped it into place; but by the time he had accomplished this and turned to take up the attack, the battle had rolled on.

Looking down, he saw what he thought were three puffs from exploding anti-aircraft shells. A second look disclosed that they were three of the crew of the Heinkel he had destroyed baling out. Those were the first parachutes he had ever seen open in the sky.

It was such courage displayed by all the British fighter pilots, as well as the pilots and crews of the bombers, which sapped the morale of the German airmen and set the canker of doubt as to their invincibility

gnawing in their brains. The South African and his fellow pilots
gazed upon the fierce fires which showed how well the British naval
units had destroyed Boulogne before giving it over to the enemy.
Calais succumbed despite the efforts of the Royal Air Force to drop
much-needed supplies of water and food and ammunition into the
beleaguered citadel from the air.

Then the whole might of the Luftwaffe was concentrated on Dunkirk.
Every fifteen minutes large masses of German bombers flew over the
port and dropped their loads of bombs. At first they kept formation.
Then they began to break under the harrying of the Spitfires which
seized on the stragglers and shot them down. Seeing their fellows go
down in flames also helped to sap the German morale.

Nightly the Spitfires returned full of bullet holes. Those that could be
patched by next day were patched; the others were discarded and
Squadron No. 74 simply raked together all the aircraft it could and
plunged at dawn into the struggle once more. They were getting too
little sleep, they were working and fighting hard, but the passing of each
May day brought with it the knowledge of their growing ascendancy
over the Germans. They saw the German aircraft begin to waver, then
they saw them start to break formation, and in their last days of fighting
over Dunkirk Malan and the other fighter pilots saw obvious signs of
the loss of German morale, for the enemy bomber formations broke
up directly they caught sight of the Spitfires and put their noses down
and went screaming all out for their own lines and the protection of
their anti-aircraft guns.

When the squadron of Spitfires was taken out of the line for a rest on
May 27th, it had definitely destroyed over thirty German aircraft,
besides a number that were undoubtedly destroyed, although they were
not seen to crash because the pilots were compelled to evade the attacks
of the enemy. The squadron's losses were three pilots, of whom one was
killed and the other two were taken prisoner.

Among crowded days later on was one exciting day at Dover when
Malan led his pilots on four sorties between dawn and 1 o'clock.
During that morning they knocked down twenty-four German aircraft
and damaged at least eighteen more. Their own losses were four aircraft and two pilots, while two of the pilots baled out safely. By
January, 1941, the fighters of Squadron No. 74 under the leadership
of Malan had destroyed 127 enemy aircraft, which were seen to crash,
while their own losses totalled twelve pilots. The last thirty-three
Germans were destroyed without a single loss to themselves.

That is why the official announcements relaxed their usual restraint
and referred to his magnificent and brilliant leadership. Before the end
of July, 1941, his personal victories totalled at least thirty-five German
aircraft which he had shot down and destroyed. Fearlessly he led his
winged crusaders against the German hordes in the Battle of Britain
and every enemy they sent down in flames was another Torch of
Freedom lit in the skies to dispel the darkness.

At the age of thirty, Group Captain Adolph Gysbert Malan, D.S.O. and Bar, D.F.C. and Bar, achieved high honour in the Royal Air Force and added another leaf to the laurels of South Africa.

CHAPTER XXI

NORWEGIAN ADVENTURES

THE sheer necessity of locating aerodromes in Norway sent the great Sunderland flying-boat commanded by Squadron Leader R. E. Craven roaring across the waters of a Scottish station and heading over the North Sea at 12.30 p.m. on the morning of April 27th, 1940. On board were a squadron leader and a warrant officer charged with the difficult task of finding emergency landing grounds, and it was Squadron Leader Craven's duty to place his passengers on board the British destroyer H.M.S. *Witherington* in Molde Fiord.

The weather was execrable. Everything was blotted out by heavy rain and mist. Visibility was about fifty yards and the cloud was down to 100 feet, nearly at sea level. "It was absolutely shocking—almost the worst I've ever flown in," reported Squadron Leader Craven, which, from such an experienced captain of Sunderlands, meant that it was indeed bad.

Directly the Sunderland was settled on her course, there came a welcome call to the ward-room for lunch, which the rigger had prepared on the primus stoves in the galley. Going through to his meal, the captain handed over the controls to the second pilot, Pilot Officer Lawrence Latham Jones, a young Canadian, who was born at Saskatoon on June 21st, 1917. The skipper generally called him Jonah, while other flying-boat officers often referred to him as Slim Jones— a tribute to his spare figure—or Daisy. But during his Norwegian adventure he acquired another nickname, owing to the first-aid which he administered to a wounded man.

"What did you do, Slim?" asked his friends when he got back to the mess. "Did you give him a shot of morphia?"

The Canadian looked surprised. "Gee!" he exclaimed. "I forgot all about it. I gave him a couple of aspirins!"

So for many weeks afterwards they called him Aspirin Jones.

After the captain resumed his seat at the controls, Pilot Officer Jones went through to enjoy his meal in the ward-room. For a couple of hours or more the Sunderland thrashed through the murk. Then the clouds began to break, and by the time they were 300 miles away from their station they emerged into brilliant sunshine with a clear sky ahead.

Squadron Leader Craven, who had taught more than one captain of a Sunderland how to handle these giant aircraft, sat calmly at the controls, glancing automatically at the revolution counter and the oil temperature.

The engines ran sweetly. The pointer of the altimeter remained steady as the Sunderland cruised along.

Like all prudent pilots who have flown through 300 miles of bad weather to come out under clear skies, he had a word with his navigator to check their position, just to make sure that he was not off his course.

The snowcaps of Norway loomed ahead. Making his landfall at Aalesund, the captain flew along Sula Fiord, only to find there was no exit. As German aircraft were busy bombing a wireless station he did a sharp turn and ran out again. That run enabled him to fix his position.

Setting his course to the north-east, he flew to Mia Island where he began the day's adventures by flying under a high tension cable, just as some German bombers appeared. They did not attempt to attack with their machine-guns, but flew overhead and tried to bomb him.

The captain promptly took the Sunderland down to within five feet of the water, using the rudder skilfully and darting from side to side to evade the dropping bombs. The enemy had the speed of him, but they found him much too elusive to hit. As he flew toward Otterö Island the bombers drew off, probably to return for more bombs. Flying round Otterö, he skirted the north of the island and turned into Molde Fiord where he came upon the destroyer *Witherington* with two or three merchant ships nearby.

Just as he touched down on the water he sighted twelve Junkers 88 over the town of Molde flying in sections of three. Sweeping over the houses, they bombed them heavily, starting many fires, and then flew toward the destroyer and flying-boat. Three of the Junkers made straight for the Sunderland whose captain at once opened the throttles and dodged about over the water in the most erratic manner as bomb after bomb came hurtling down. They burst in the sea all around him, but he was too clever for the German bombers.

Coming close to the destroyer as the bombers turned away, he signalled for a boat to be sent off for his passengers. The whaler was quickly alongside. "I had better go over, too," said Squadron Leader Craven to Pilot Officer Jones. "It is up to you to do as you choose. If you think it necessary to go home and leave me, you must do so."

So Pilot Officer Jones took command of the Sunderland while his captain jumped into the whaler with his passengers and was rowed over to the destroyer. A bomb dropped near them on the way. Just as they got on board another fell and the boat in which they had been sitting simply vanished in the explosion, while two of the ratings on the deck of the destroyer were wounded. It was a most astonishing escape.

Then the Junkers took up the attack again, some concentrating on the destroyer and others on the flying-boat. Pilot Officer Jones in the Sunderland began taxi-ing and zigzagging in all directions, as his crew reported the movements of the enemy.

Squadron Leader Craven, who had been invited up to the bridge of the destroyer to help to defeat the attack, watched the Junkers closely and advised the commander how to avoid them. "Port!" he called; "Now starboard!" As the warship slowed and a bomber made to attack he called: "Full speed ahead!" and the destroyer sped swiftly out of the way.

For half an hour the twelve Junkers attacked the destroyer and the flying-boat, but through the skilful manœuvring, both escaped damage. By that time Pilot Officer Jones saw that the engines of the Sunderland were beginning to overheat through taxi-ing about over the water, so he decided to take off in order to cool them.

He was barely in the air when a Messerschmitt 110 appeared to continue the attack. Diving down on the tail of the Sunderland, the German fighter opened fire with all its guns. But the rear-gunner and the midships gunner of the Sunderland were quick on the mark. They met the Messerschmitt with such a heavy fire that in a few seconds it turned away smoking toward the land.

After this fight with the Messerschmitt, which cooled off the engines, Pilot Officer Jones touched down once more. Meanwhile his captain was taken in the destroyer to Aandalsnes which was already a mass of ruins. The wooden houses were burned to the ground, the inhabitants had vanished by coach somewhere over the mountains, all was desolation.

Up on the snowclad hills overlooking the harbour the marines who were the first to land had set up a battery. But the German bombers mostly kept out of range. Those marines were sorely puzzled because one day they saw English fighters flying between formations of German bombers and making no attempt to attack. The men on the ground could not understand it. They did not know that those English fighters had no ammunition left, that for the short space of twenty-four hours the pilots had put up an astounding fight against enormous odds and impossible conditions.

So desperate was the British need for landing grounds that a squadron of Gladiators strove to function from the frozen lake of Lesjeskogen, some forty miles from Aandalsnes. In all that area there was not a flat space of ground. Among the advance party sent to prepare a runway was the famous young racing motorist Whitney Straight, who was naturalized some years ago and had been flying in a fighter squadron of the Royal Air Force since the outbreak of war. His efforts in preparing the lake and his courage during the ensuing attacks won for him the Military Cross.

In a blinding snowstorm, eighteen Gladiators took off from the deck of the aircraft carrier and alighted on the lake. Without delay they were refuelled and hidden round the verge; but their arrival was soon discovered by the Germans, who sent over two aircraft disguised by Norwegian markings, which were promptly intercepted and driven away by the Gladiators.

At three o'clock next morning the pilots and few available staff fought to get the first Gladiators in the air, a task which the intense cold made practically impossible, yet the impossible was accomplished. In an hour came the first clashes with the Germans when the Gladiators shot down a Heinkel and drove off two others. There was a brief breathing space, then the German bombers started to come over at 7.30 in the morning to smash up the surface of the lake and did not cease their attacks until 8 o'clock at night.

There was no cover for the pilots, no protection for the aircraft. Except where the snow had been cleared, the drifts were so deep that no one could move. The pilots were forced to crawl through the snow on their hands and knees. Their clothes froze solid as boards as they struggled in the snow to refuel and restart the engines in order to go up to fight the enemy. They shot down the enemy in the air, but it was the blast of the enemy's bombs which destroyed the Gladiators on the ground and wounded the pilots. Not one Gladiator did the enemy shoot down from the air.

The spirit of that little band of men on the frozen lake was unconquerable. They fought Nature and the enemy at the same time. As they struggled in the snow to refuel, the enemy dived and machine-gunned them. They had no respite. As one aircraft after another was destroyed, and one man after another was wounded, they set up a machine-gun and attacked the bombers from the ground.

Eighty German bombers had the task of wiping them out and nothing could exceed the ferocity of the German attack. Forty times the British pilots succeeded in carrying out sorties against the enemy. At the end when they had used up their ammunition and had little petrol, some of the pilots showed their ascendancy over the Germans by driving them off with feint attacks. One out-manœuvred three of the enemy by trying to crash into them. When they saw him coming at them, they could not face him and turned away, so he managed to land safely.

Four or five days afterwards a marine straight from Aandalsnes told me how discomfited they were by the strange actions of the British aircraft which completely baffled them. I could not explain it then, but the reason is now plain.

One pilot whose aircraft went up in flames as he landed tried to start another, but a bomb destroyed it before he could do so. Another pilot had sixteen fights with the enemy. ''I then attacked another three Heinkels during the course of my patrol. How much damage I inflicted I cannot say as there was always another Heinkel to attack. I broke away as I was running short of petrol and was not certain of my position. I landed on the lake and saw three Junkers approaching, so I took off again and attacked them, eventually 'forced landing' through lack of petrol. In all I had sixteen combats.''

Six Junkers were shot down by the Gladiators. Eight more fled from the British pilots with smoke pouring from them as they disappeared among the mountains. But at the end of the day the squadron of

Gladiators was reduced to five. The surface of the lake was shattered and no longer usable, for there were 132 bomb craters on it.

Despite the losses, the leader was unbeaten. During the night he found a sloping piece of ground on which it was possible by the exercise of superb skill to take off and land, but the slightest vacillation or lack of judgment meant disaster. While the Germans were sleeping, he removed the surviving aircraft to this spot and fought the hordes of Junkers for a few more hours until the Gladiators dwindled to one solitary aircraft. Those magnificent men, who had nothing to fly, remained undefeated. Had they possessed properly defended bases and their usual ground staff they would have dealt with those Junkers as the Spitfires and Hurricanes dealt with the German Luftwaffe in the Battle of Britain.

It was with the survivors of this invincible band that Squadron Leader Craven took his evening meal amid the ruins of Veblungsnes, and they shared with him all they had to offer—corned beef and Canadian whisky! Afterwards he embarked in a launch and made his way back to the Sunderland to see how Pilot Officer Jones had fared and to make things snug in her for the night.

Early next day he heard from Whitney Straight that the Messerschmitt attacked by the Sunderland had definitely crashed. Unfortunately Whitney Straight himself was wounded while locating it and was unable to fly for some time. It may be recalled that Wing Commander Whitney Straight was shot down over the Channel on August 1, 1941, and was driven to make a forced landing in France, after ordering his squadron to return to base. His award of the D.F.C. came later. Not for long were the Germans able to hold him prisoner, for about a year later he managed to reach London, after one of the most thrilling escapes of the war, and early in 1943 he was acting as Air Commodore in the Middle East.

Seating himself at the controls, Squadron Leader Craven started up the Sunderland and in a few hours was back again in Scotland. Although bombed in turn by more than a dozen Junkers and attacked by the cannon shell and machine-gun bullets of the Messerschmitt, no one on board was touched, while the flying-boat itself had only two bullet holes in it. The brilliant way the pilots handled the Sunderland during those sustained bombing attacks brought both of them the award of the D.F.C.

CHAPTER XXII

SURPRISES FOR GERMANY

THE first attack on the Dortmund-Ems Canal was a revelation of the British character as well as the unbelievable lapses of the Nazis. In June, 1940, when the Nazis had crushed the liberties of Norway and Denmark and Holland and Belgium and France with swift, sweeping strokes that have no parallel in history, in those black hours when the people of Great Britain could comprehend neither the defeat nor the miracle of Dunkirk, the men of the Bomber Command of the Royal Air Force calmly considered a counterstroke to shock and surprise the Germans, the raid on that canal which is such an important artery of the Ruhr. The planning of that raid is indicative of the steadfastness of the British character. While everything was collapsing on the Continent and Great Britain had lost all the equipment and guns of its fine army, these few officers and men quietly planned to strike back.

There was nothing haphazard about the operation. It was most carefully conceived. During the last war some of the British attacks were so cleverly organized that exact replicas of the German trenches were dug far behind the British lines and dummy attacks were made on them so that the troops would know their way about and what they had to encounter.

It was obviously not possible nor desirable to construct a full-scale replica of the Dortmund-Ems Canal in England. But the officer commanding this Bomber Group did the next best thing, he looked round and found a stretch of canal that would serve his purpose quite well. The bomber crews were assembled and sent up to make attacks on the canal. They dropped dummy bombs on the target and the spot where each bomb fell was marked by observers on the ground. These practice attacks, three of which were made in daylight and one at night, proved of the utmost value to the pilots and bomb-aimers. Meanwhile the crews studied their maps and the magnificent photographs which had been taken of the area, as well as a model made in plasticine of the two viaducts which carry the canal over the river. Nothing therefore could exceed the care with which the crews were trained for their task.

On the evening of June 19, 1940, nineteen bombers were ready for the raid. Ten of them were detailed to attack the eastern viaduct, which was the older viaduct built of stone, and the other nine were told off to attack the western viaduct which was constructed of concrete. At 9.30 the great bombers began to follow each other into the sky at short intervals and set course for their target. It was rather misty to start with, and there was considerable cloud over Holland, but as they flew inland the clouds dispersed and it developed into a beautiful moonlight night.

The captains of the aircraft, who had been instructed to arrive independently over the target, had no difficulty in locating their position. The moon was almost full and from 1,000 feet visibility on the ground was quite good. The leader of the raiders, who became Wing Commander Walter Charles Sheen, D.S.O., recognized the canal about ten miles from the target and flew straight along it, the reflections of the moon upon the water making an excellent guide. Now and again he saw the dark shapes of barges, while here and there the canal widened out to enable barges to be moored without interfering with the normal traffic.

Dropping down to a height of fifty feet he raced along the canal and made his run over the viaduct. But it did not please him. Flying too fast, he was a little off his target, so he circled to the east and away to the north again. This time he made no mistake, but made a very steady and slow approach at 120 miles an hour. He dropped down to fifty feet and even lower, until the wings of the bomber were almost level with the parapets of the viaduct.

"Bomb gone!" called out Sergeant Bartlett, the bomb-aimer.

"I've seen it splash into the water in the middle of the viaduct!" shouted the rear-gunner, as they climbed and set course for home.

Flight Lieutenant Bernard George Meyer, D.F.C., had a similar experience. Picking up the canal a few miles north of the viaducts, he came down to a height of 250 feet and sped over the great barges. About a mile from the target he took the bomber down to fifty feet. "It was a grand sight to see the moonlight on the canal," he recorded. "As we singled out certain landmarks, we turned up on the western viaduct and dropped our bomb, and the rear-gunner saw it splash into the water as it fell."

One of the attackers, Sergeant Joseph Unsworth, D.F.M., flew around for twenty minutes in order to see what damage he had done. "It was a fine moonlight night and the water shone like silver," he said later. "We got a direct hit on the side of the aqueduct with a heavy bomb and twenty minutes afterwards we saw the water seeping out, so we came back highly delighted."

The inconceivable thing is that the viaducts on the Dortmund-Ems Canal were then quite defenceless. There was not a gun nor a searchlight to defend that target which was so vital to the Germans. The British bombers had the viaducts at their mercy and they made a smashing attack on the safety gates and embankments and the beds of the aqueducts.

From this attack which was a complete and very unpleasant surprise for the Germans, every British bomber returned safely to its base. Photographs taken later by British reconnaissance aircraft showed that the viaducts were badly damaged and that the canal had been rendered unusable, for the water had drained away from it and left barges sitting on the mud. Men were seen doing their best to unload some of them in a field alongside the canal.

The Germans not only worked hard to repair the damage, but they also defended the canal so well with searchlights and guns that they probably considered it impossible for any aircraft ever again to make a successful attack on the position. Nevertheless the British bombers went back from time to time to do their worst. On one occasion, Flight Lieutenant R. A. B. Learoyd acted as a decoy to draw the fire of the defences while other bombers slid down to the attack; another time he made a high level attack.

He was thus not unfamiliar with the Dortmund-Ems Canal when he started out to make his third attack upon it on August 12, 1940. A small force of bombers took off at two minute intervals and settled down on their course. Each had been given a specific time at which to attack, and it was necessary to keep strictly to these times so as not to interfere with the attacks of the preceding and succeeding bombers. It was very cloudy at 2,000 feet when the bombers started out, but Flight Lieutenant Learoyd, who flew across at about 4,500 feet, found the target area free of cloud, so there was nothing to mask his approach.

Locating the canal by the light of the young moon, he looked at the clock and found that he was ten minutes too early, so he began to kill time by circling the target. Waiting for his turn to attack must have been a nerve-racking ordeal. He saw a terrific barrage let loose as his companions made their runs; he watched the Hampdens as they were caught and held in the beams of the searchlights, he beheld one suddenly blaze up in the air and crash in flames.

Certainly the ten minutes which Flight Lieutenant Learoyd spent in watching the German defences vent their fury on his fellow pilots would have shaken most men, but he held resolutely to his task. Warning his crew, he made his approach and dived down on his target. He was compelled to run the gauntlet of the guns which were sited on each side of the canal so that they could blow any attacking aircraft out of the sky. The deadliness of the German fire may be judged by the fact that already two out of four British bombers had been shot down.

Flight Lieutenant Learoyd was undeterred by the fate of those who had gone before. As he dived down, six or eight searchlights flashed into the cockpit and completely blinded him. He was so dazzled by the intense light that he was obliged to bow his head and look only at the instrument panel. It was a physical impossibility for him to see where he was going.

The voice of the navigator came to him over the inter-communication system, directing him into the very heart of that inferno. The thud and shock of shells and bullets hitting the Hampden told of the fury and accuracy of the German fire. But Flight Lieutenant Learoyd did not swerve from his course. Down he dived to 150 feet, right along the centre of the target he flew, with guns blazing at him from both banks at point-blank range. It seemed impossible that the Hampden could survive such intense fire, for it was essential to fly on a steady course over the canal in order to make the attack effective.

"Bomb away!" said the bomb-aimer.

Then the Hampden was away too, swerving all over the sky to get out beyond the range of those terrible guns. Climbing full out, the pilot headed for home. The Hampden was in a sorry state. Large pieces of the main planes were shot away, the landing flaps were out of action and the indicators which told him whether the undercarriage was up or down were quite useless, for the hydraulic system had been cut.

Nevertheless Flight Lieutenant Learoyd flew the Hampden safely home. But it was far too dangerous for him to land in the dark, so he circled round until dawn, when he managed to get the undercarriage to operate by the emergency system and thus make a safe landing.

That was how Squadron Leader R. A. B. Learoyd won the Victoria Cross.

The damage wrought by the British attacks on the Dortmund-Ems Canal caused such interference with the traffic of raw materials to the Ruhr that the Germans were obliged to cover the canal completely and carry it through a camouflaged tunnel.

The Magdeburg ship lifts were another vulnerable point in the canal system of Germany and in the early months many wondered whether the Royal Air Force would ever attack them. On August 21, 1940, all doubts were resolved, for on that night the British bombers struck for the first time at the ship lifts, and struck hard.

For some days previously the men detailed for the task studied a model of the lifts as well as very fine enlargements of photographs that were taken from all angles by the clever pilots of the R.A.F. who had specialized in this work. The two lifts were really huge troughs, each being roughly about 275 feet long by 50 or 60 feet wide, and capable of carrying ships or barges up to about 1,000 tons. The big barges on the German canals equalled in carrying capacity two train loads of fifty trucks each, so if vital canals could be put out of action for a few days the matter was a grave one for the enemy. Each ship lift had lock gates to seal the ends and enable the ships to pass in and out and rise with the lift to the high-level canal or drop down to the canal at the low level. The construction of the Magdeburg ship lifts was a fine engineering feat of which the Germans were very proud.

The weather on the night of the operation was not conducive to success, and of the pilots who started out, only two found the target. These were Squadron Leader C. J. F. Kydd, D.F.C., who that night won the D.S.O., and Pilot Officer Alexander Webster, D.F.C., who won a Bar to his decoration.

Squadron Leader Kydd and his crew made out the ship lifts quite clearly just as the defences opened up on them. The Germans, who knew better than anyone how important the ship lifts were to their war effort, had brought up so many anti-aircraft guns and searchlights that they regarded the area as a death trap for raiders. As soon as Squadron Leader Kydd straightened out to make his run over the lifts, the full blast of the guns met him, the searchlights blinded him with their glare, and the gunfire was so fierce that he was driven off his target.

But the fair-haired, blue-eyed pilot had come a long way to reach his goal, and having achieved the feat of finding it in the face of all the difficulties which Nature could impose, he was fully resolved to carry through his task. Circling into the clouds, he dived down to make another run; but the hell of fire turned him away before the bomb-aimer could get his sights properly on the target.

A lesser man would have been content with those two attempts and would have flown off to drop his bombs on some other target. That thought never entered the head of the pilot. He had one supreme task to perform and, if it were humanly possible, he was determined to do it. For the third time he straightened out on his target, only to be deflected off it once more by the weight of the fire.

No near misses or probables were good enough for him. Only a certainty would satisfy him. His persistence and courage were extraordinary. For the fourth time he dived into the inferno and the German gunners again succeeded in putting him off his target.

If ever a man stuck to the precept of "try, try again," Squadron Leader Kydd did so that night. He would not give up. For the fifth time he dived down and straightened out to make his run over the target. The deadly guns and blinding searchlights blazed at him, but this time he kept his course through it all. Straight and true he held the Hampden along the canal and right over the centre of the lifts.

"Bombs away," said the bomb-aimer over the inter-communication system, and Squadron Leader Kydd swept into the clouds and flew home.

"There was low cloud from the Dutch coast all across Germany and visibility was only one mile," he reported. "The clouds became a little more broken over the target and we flew low to identify the place. The first time we made our run the searchlights were so blinding and the anti-aircraft fire was so heavy that we were put off. I made another run and again the defences deflected us off our target; so I tried again, with the same result. The fourth time it was the same, but the fifth time the bomb aimer got right on the target from 500 feet and let go our bombs. Strangely enough, we were not hit. We could hear everything exploding all round us and bumping us about, but we escaped damage."

Only five days earlier on August 16th Squadron Leader Kydd led the British bombers to attack the immense oil plant at Leuna. It was a glorious night with a bright moon when he dropped his load of bombs full on his target, which was the hydrogenation plant. He and his crew expected to see the whole plant go up in flames, but to their bitter disappointment nothing happened. For twenty minutes they cruised around, watching the buildings on which their bombs had fallen. Then all of a sudden they saw it burst into flames which grew so intense that they could still see it when they were fifty miles away on their homeward journey. They enjoyed their sandwiches and hot drink from the thermos after that raid.

On the way out they were only attacked at Hanover and Brunswick by the anti-aircraft defences. ''But on the way back the Germans went completely mad and seemed to be letting fly all over the place at nobody in particular—they were swishing it all over the sky,'' he remarked afterwards.

They noticed in several raids that a man used to wait for them at one particular spot and blaze away with a rifle, no matter how high they were flying. This sportsman always delighted them. Another laugh came when the rear-gunner requested his captain's permission to shoot a star out of the sky, under the impression that it was the light of an enemy aircraft. He was not the only gunner to be misled by a star, for some have tried to shoot out the light of Jupiter, under the impression that the planet was stalking them. But one of the most uncanny experiences befell the captain and crew of a bomber who were haunted near their target by a weird light which followed them around in the dark. The pilot tried all sorts of tactics to shake off the pursuer, but he could not get away. Wherever he went, whatever he did that menacing light maintained its position astern. The guns on the ground fired on them madly, and every second they were expecting their pursuer to open fire.

Then they discovered that one of their own flares had somehow become entangled by the parachute in the tail of the bomber!

Pilot Officer Alexander Webster who also got through to the Magdeburg ship lifts on that foul night of August 21st faced the concerted fire of twelve anti-aircraft guns with the same unshakable determination as that displayed by Squadron Leader Kydd. He dived down until he was flying at only fifty feet and dropped a delayed-action bomb in the great troughs.

He also distinguished himself at the Leuna raid on August 16th; but one of his most desperate and gallant exploits, which won for him the D.F.C., was his attack on the 26,000 ton battle cruiser *Scharnhorst* against which vessel the Royal Navy and the Royal Air Force carried out a vendetta which is unique in warfare. It began during the Norwegian campaign in April, 1940, when H.M.S. *Renown* got within range and scored several hits on her, but she fled to some secret lair where her wounds were patched.

For some weeks she vanished completely, and the eyes of the keenest British observers failed to detect her. Then on June 13th—an unlucky day for her—she was sighted by a British reconnaissance aircraft in Trondhjem Fiord and was quickly attacked by aircraft of the Fleet Air Arm, which scored at least one hit with a heavy bomb.

To leave her at Trondhjem was to invite her total destruction, so a few days later the enemy sought to take her under escort to Germany, but the British submarine H.M.S. *Clyde* was on guard at the entrance to Trondhjem Fiord and at once hit her with a torpedo. Needless to add, the British authorities were advised that the *Scharnhorst* was at sea with a strong escort of destroyers and Messerschmitt fighters, and a naval force was sent at full speed to try to intercept her. Meanwhile the Coastal Command dispatched a Sunderland flying-boat and relays of Hudson aircraft to shadow the *Scharnhorst* for nine hours, fighting off the Messerschmitts from time to time, until conditions grew suitable about dusk for an attack.

Then a force of torpedo bomber aircraft of the Fleet Air Arm arrived and launched their torpedoes. The barrage put up by the escorts was so heavy that two of the aircraft were shot down. The *Scharnhorst* came unscathed through the attack, but one of the destroyers was torpedoed.

An hour later the attack was resumed by a force of Hudsons and Beauforts which bombed the *Scharnhorst* and scored three direct hits on her. A heavy bomb exploded alongside number one gun turret, another by number two turret, while the third hit her full on the stern and the attackers saw a shower of debris rise into the air as the bomb exploded.

Three of these aircraft were shot down either by the intense gunfire of the ships or by the Messerschmitts. But the Messerschmitts also had to pay the price, for at least two were shot down, one by the Sunderland.

Once more the *Scharnhorst* escaped, and she was next located in the floating dock at Kiel where Pilot Officer Alexander Webster, who gained the D.F.C., went with others to attack her.

Of the eight bombers told off for this operation, four were to make a high level attack and circle around while the other four stole in to make a low level attack. The weather that night was shocking. Flying at 9,000 feet over Sylt, Pilot Officer Webster found thick snow getting inside the cockpit and billowing round him. His instruments began to ice up, the engine cowlings glowed red with heat and the engines and propellers were encompassed in a blue light which ran along the leading edge of the aircraft; the wireless crackled viciously and now and again blue sparks leapt out. It was not pleasant to be caught in such an electrical disturbance.

Circling over Kiel, the pilot saw the flashes of the heavy guns and watched the searchlights groping up for them. A cone of red, green and white searchlights seemed to be following the aircraft around. Clearing the throttles to stop most of the noise of the engines, he said to his crew: "Let's go in for that ship. Let's have a crack at it."

Approaching from over the town, he glided down from 9,000 to 500 feet. Not a gun fired at them. There was absolute silence.

"When it is quiet like that you feel that they are waiting for you, watching for you, laughing at you," Pilot Officer Webster remarked. "By that time we were all keyed up and tense, wondering what was going on and why they were not doing something about it. The climax came when the searchlights got us and the guns started. For about sixty seconds we roared over Kiel at nought feet. I was blinded by the searchlights, so I steered by my instruments while Bisset directed me

Plate 11.—A Spitfire among the clouds. This was the aircraft of his dreams conjured up by the genius of R. J. Mitchell, the designer of the Schneider Trophy seaplanes, in his last days while stricken with an incurable disease. Before dying he gave Great Britain an aircraft which helped to save civilization.

Plate 12.—WING COMMANDER H. M. STEPHEN, D.S.O., D.F.C. and Bar, who shot down five German aircraft in one day, and in November, 1940, was awarded the D.S.O. in the field for shooting down three enemy bombers in one sortie. He is standing talking to his friend, SQUADRON LEADER J. C. MUNGO-PARK, another outstanding fighter pilot, who shot down many of the enemy and was posted as missing in July 1941, after a fighter sweep over France.

on to the target. I'm sure the German shells and machine-gun bullets must have killed off their own people—they seemed to throw everything they'd got at us, except the gun mountings.

"Bisset saw the ship ahead and kept yelling directions to keep me on my course. I flew straight toward the side of the dock. 'Hold it!' he shouted, and let it go. 'Bomb away!' he called, and the rear-gunner saw it head for the right spot and splash in.

"By then we were depending on speed. Keeping very low, we screamed over the harbour and out to sea, where it was now quiet, so we circled and climbed, feeling as happy as sandboys."

CHAPTER XXIII

FLIGHT LIEUTENANT H. M. STEPHEN,
D.S.O., D.F.C. AND BAR

FUTURE generations will want to know what manner of men were these young fighter pilots who saved the freedom of the world, and what were their reactions in those stupendous days when all human progress depended upon their prowess. Such questions will not be easy to answer. Official accounts, cold and impersonal, lack the human touch. Yet although the fighter pilots in the air were as young gods riding their thunderbolts to scourge the Nazis from the skies, on earth they became human once more.

One of the names to assume prominence in the autumn of 1940 was that of Flight Lieutenant Harbourne Mackay Stephen. On August 31, 1940, he was awarded the D.F.C. for shooting down five enemy aircraft in four successive fights with large enemy formations on August 11th over the Thames estuary, making his total up to twelve. On November 14th he won a Bar to his D.F.C. by attacking single-handed four Messerschmitt 109s at 27,000 feet and shooting the tail off one before destroying another. And on December 14th he achieved the distinction of being the first fighter pilot to win the D.S.O. on the field in England.

Obviously, a fighter pilot who succeeded in winning the D.F.C. twice as well as the D.S.O. within the space of five months must possess unusual qualities. H. M. Stephen was a Scot who was born in Elgin on April 18, 1914. Before his school days dawned he disclosed a stubborn will coupled with a fighting spirit, so no doubt he was able to take care of himself at school in Elgin and Edinburgh and Shrewsbury; but what his masters thought of him and what he thought of them remains unknown.

The roads from Scotland to London are well worn, and he followed in the wake of many another Scot who has sought fame and fortune in the capital of the British Empire. The English are rather tolerant and helpful to the Scots, the Irish and the Welsh, but whether these nations appreciate this fine quality in the English as much as the

English appreciate and reward them for their valued services is an open question.

Young H. M. Stephen was lucky, inasmuch as work waited for him in London. His father happened to be a friend of Mr. William Will, of Allied Newspapers, who offered the boy a place in the office in Grays Inn Road, London. The pay was fifteen shillings a week, and the job called neither for skill nor intelligence. He was just the "copy" boy, a very humble cog in the machinery of a modern newspaper office. All he had to do was to take the "copy" from the reporters and sub-editors up to the composing room, where the linotype operators waited to set it up for the next edition of the paper. He learned a lot about newspaper offices and the writers who form public opinion, and if he missed much of the glamour and romance with which the films have so generously endowed the profession, he could not fail to notice the perpetual work and rush inseparable from an endless race with the clock to put the paper to "bed" in time for the newspaper trains.

A spell of some years on the staff of Allied Newspapers brought the opportunity to transfer to the advertising staff of the *Evening Standard*. Flying had long interested him, and in 1937 he made up his mind to join the Volunteer Reserve of the Royal Air Force, which he did in April of that year, when he started his training at Maidenhead.

It was not always easy to get away from the office to carry out his course of instruction. But the difficulties were soon overcome by Mr. J. G. Beaseley, one of the directors of the *Evening Standard*, of whom Flight Lieutenant Stephen often spoke in the warmest terms. "I owe a lot to Mr. Beaseley. He encouraged me to keep on flying, and used to smooth out difficulties about getting time off," he remarked.

One of the good qualities of this brilliant fighter pilot was his appreciation of those who helped him and his recognition of outstanding merit, particularly that of Group Captain Malan, under whom he fought so magnificently in the famous Squadron No. 74.

Stephen and his fellow-enthusiasts who were anxious to fly on Tiger Moths at Maidenhead, used to give up their Saturdays and Sundays to the task. Instead of idling away the week-ends, they devoted them to learning all they could about aviation.

His first thrill came when his instructor took him up and started to throw the Tiger Moth all over the sky. This experience, during which the earth appeared to rotate round the aircraft, gave some pupils a sickening feeling, but he weathered it without turning a hair. After flying under dual control for nine hours with the instructor, he went up for his first solo flight.

"Were you nervous?" he was asked afterwards.

"Not at all. Either you can fly or you can't!" he said decisively.

From Tiger Moths he graduated to Hawker Harts, and before the outbreak of war he was called up to join the Volunteer Reserve of the

Royal Air Force as a sergeant pilot in order to take a course on Hurricanes. So his spare-time hobby was to prove of invaluable service to the nation.

His first reaction to Hurricanes after Hawker Harts was that they were tremendously powerful.

"Were you scared of them?" someone inquired.

"No," came the calm reply.

It was simply a plain statement of fact. He had no fear. This young Scot with the dark, well-brushed hair, who was five feet nine inches tall, was cool, calculating. There was an appraising look in his dark eyes, and flickering at the back of them was a glint of amusement, as though he were enjoying a little joke all to himself; when he smiled, a dimple appeared on his chubby, clean-shaven face.

"You wouldn't think he had shot down all those Germans—he doesn't look a bit like that!" a young lady once remarked.

She was right. He was quiet, modest, with nothing swaggering about him despite the sudden fame and decorations. But still waters run deep, and his opinions were clean-cut, swift and very decided.

When the war started, the routine of training swung automatically into top gear. Instead of working a few hours a day, those volunteer pilots began to work all day for seven days a week. They practised the most amazing evolutions in the air against the day when they would meet the enemy; they tackled the difficulties of interception, giving a section ten minutes start before setting forth to try to locate them. It was like playing hide-and-seek. When the clouds were about, the task was more difficult, so sometimes they succeeded and at others they failed, but success and failures alike enlarged their knowledge and experience.

In April, 1940, he won his commission as a Pilot Officer, and went to cut his flying teeth in Scotland, where he helped to shoot down a Heinkel which they rounded up in those quarters.

His transfer to Squadron No. 74 in the home counties eventually mellowed his experience and gave him the opportunity to shine. When the Germans began their thrust on May 10, 1940, this squadron of Spitfires became one of the British spearheads over the French coast. The British fighters were operating far from their base, and their four patrols a day between dawn and dusk were arduous and exhausting. Theoretically the pilots knew all about air fighting, but their actual experience was extremely limited. Flight Lieutenant Stephen had the advantage of most, inasmuch as he had seen German aircraft in the air and had even played his part in helping to shoot one down. But many of the pilots had not seen an enemy aircraft in flight, and none of them knew much about air fighting or how the theories would work out in practice. We know now that the theory and training were sound, that the pilots were superb, and that everything worked out all right. In those days, however, it was unproved, and the fighters of the Royal

Air Force, although they had gained their wings, had yet to win their spurs.

Up and down between Ostend and Boulogne the Spitfires flew at heights which largely depended on the clouds. If the clouds were at 10,000 feet they flew below them, if the sky were clear they flew at 20,000 feet. For days not a Messerschmitt nor any other enemy aircraft came in sight, then the squadron came on fifteen German aircraft and got their first crack at them. In the dog-fight the British fighters shot down six or seven of the Germans, of which Flight Lieutenant Stephen destroyed one. In the ensuing May days, when they joined issue with the Germans, they inflicted severe losses on them; their own losses in pilots were light, but their losses in aircraft were considerable. Continuous patrols from morning till evening, coupled with the hard fighting, told its tale on the pilots of Squadron No. 74, who grew exhausted and badly in need of a rest and refit, so on May 27th they were withdrawn for ten days, consequently they took no part in the evacuation of the British Army from Dunkirk.

"It was only by June or July that we began to learn the technique of air fighting, and Wing Commander Malan was the greatest of leaders," Flight Lieutenant Stephen once remarked.

His own big day of August 11, 1940, when he shot down five of the enemy, was perfect in every way. Just after 6.30 in the morning he took off with the squadron to patrol over the Channel, and climbed to 17,000 feet. About 6.45 a.m. they sighted between twenty and thirty Messerschmitt 109s, and in a minute or two they were all involved in a dog-fight. "I had a quick bang at one of the enemy, then at another," said Flight Lieutenant Stephen. "Then I happened to turn up sun and joined two aircraft that were climbing, when I discovered that I was following two Messerschmitt 109 fighters at only a few yards distance; in fact, I was formating on them. By the time I'd realised my mistake they had turned away from the sun, and I opened fire on the leader. I came up behind him and gave him a burst, and he dropped down into the Channel. When I gave the second one a burst he just exploded in mid-air."

After the fight the squadron returned to the aerodrome and ordered coffee and toast to be sent to the hut at the dispersal point, where the aircraft were being refuelled; but before they could take their coffee they were ordered up again. This time Flight Lieutenant Stephen was out of luck, but the squadron landed with three more added to its total and one to the score of Wing Commander Malan. They were in the mood to enjoy some fresh coffee and a cigarette.

"Stand by," came the order to them at 10.30 a.m.

All climbed into their Spitfires, strapped themselves in and donned their oxygen masks ready to start up the engines and get away. Soon after taking off to guard a convoy in the Thames estuary, they were cheered by the sight of about forty bombers flying in groups of three,

spread out over a front about a mile wide. One of the flight commanders, thinking the bombers had already attacked the convoy and were
retreating, was surprised to find himself in the middle of them before
he knew it. The Germans were still more surprised, for they at once
broke up their formation before the blazing guns of the leader and his
section, and moments later aircraft were whirling all over the sky.

"The German aircraft were going round in steep turns. Imagine
them, forty light bombers—very manœuvrable and fast, the famous
Messerschmitt Jaguar 110 fighter-bombers. We were chasing them,
and they were chasing us in and out of the clouds. In a few minutes
they started to form one of their well-known defensive circles. By
this time several Germans were lying smashed up in the water, with
the crews swimming round. The Spitfires were now diving in and out
of the circle and never letting them complete it. I got my sights on one
bomber and gave him a long burst, and one of my tracer bullets must
have hit his petrol tank, as in a few seconds he went down flaming into
the sea. I climbed into clouds just as another bomber darted at me,
and we passed each other so closely that I do not know how we avoided
a smash. Turning on his tail, I silenced his rear-gunner with a burst,
and as I closed the range the Messerschmitt rolled over and fell upside
down in the sea."

That was his fourth enemy aircraft in three sorties, and by shooting
down four in one morning, Flight Lieutenant Stephen accomplished a
remarkable feat. Nor was his run of luck yet over, for when the
squadron flew off after lunch they saw twenty Junker dive-bombers
escorted by Messerschmitt fighters. The Germans turned tail at the
sight of the Spitfires, but one was slow in getting away.

Flight Lieutenant Stephen sped after him and got in a burst of
machine-gun fire. "He dived and I followed him down, giving him
another burst just before the pilot jumped out. He was so low that his
parachute did not open, and his aircraft crashed and burst into flames
on the beach," said Flight Lieutenant Stephen in summing up his
record day.

Over twenty of the enemy fell to his guns by December, 1940, so he
did his share in helping to win the Battle of Britain. Once he flew so
high that he reached the very limit of the aircraft's climb and flopped
about in the air like a pigeon with a broken wing. Another time, when
flying at 35,000 feet, he saw two Messerschmitts flying 2,000 feet above
him. "I was jolly glad they didn't attack. I don't think they noticed
me," he commented.

His abiding impressions of those heroic days will probably be of
simple things—the blazing sunshine, which made it so hot in the
cockpits that the pilots flew in their shirt-sleeves and helmets; the
striking resemblance to a jigsaw puzzle of the clusters of islands in the
north of Scotland when viewed from 20,000 feet; the ant-hill that was
London seen from a height of about six miles, when the Thames was

a tiny silver streak that could barely be seen and the high-flying balloons seemed no bigger than peapods.

One day while up with the squadron during the Battle of London he saw a black mass of about 200 bombers protected by fighters flying up the Thames estuary. Despite their overwhelming numbers, the Germans, at the sight of the two squadrons of Spitfires, turned tail—jettisoning their bombs around Tilbury as they were actually making their turn—and fled for their lives. No better proof of indiscriminate bombing by the Germans can be adduced than that, for it is impossible to aim at a target and hit it on a turn.

About that gigantic fire in September on Thameside, which lit up the place like daylight, Flight Lieutenant Stephen was afterwards quite impersonal. "We had to prepare our aircraft for next day and patch the bullet holes. We had our own job to do."

And if they had failed to do that job, the Dark Ages would have shut down once more on Great Britain and the whole civilised world. Shooting down Germans took courage and resource, and a keen eye and a clear head. The pilot who could make decisions coolly and instantaneously stood the better chance of vanquishing his opponent. The young Scot gave indisputable proof of his ability and in due course was posted as a Wing Commander.

The British technique of dealing with the German masses which sometimes seemed to fill the sky was cleverly conceived and brilliantly executed. The Spitfires, which could climb higher than the Hurricanes, guarded the higher levels and dealt with the enemy fighters, while the Hurricanes at the lower levels concentrated on the bombers. The enemy aircraft which managed to evade the first line of defenders were attacked by the squadrons posted further back. In those incredible air battles many a damaged Heinkel or Junkers turned and limped for home. It was the practice of the Spitfire pilots to conserve their ammunition as much as possible by firing short bursts at the German fighters, then directly the Messerschmitts were driven back the Spitfires could turn and use their remaining ammunition to help the Hurricanes finish off the damaged bombers.

At nightfall the Spitfires flew off from the station where they had been operating all day to a safer station around which the aircraft were dispersed to minimize losses in the event of a night attack. Here the pilots could generally get a good night's sleep to fit them for the morrow's fight. Before dawn the pilots rose and flew the Spitfires back to the station from which they were to operate during the day.

These were some of the methods by which the smaller numbers of the Royal Air Force dealt such a crushing defeat in the autumn of 1940 to the vast German Luftwaffe, which was considered by Hitler and Goering to be invincible.

CHAPTER XXIV

TALES OF THE BOMBERS

THERE was no end to the amusing and amazing stories that were related quite casually in the messes of the bomber stations. There was the night, for instance, when Squadron Leader R. L. Oxley, D.F.C., who was known among his service friends as "Beetle," showed as much effrontery as his namesake in Kipling's *Stalky and Co.*, with results that surprised him—as well as the enemy. It started with his bomber acting as a decoy over Magdeburg, making as much noise as possible in order to draw the fire and let his companions go in and do their work before he went off to do his. Low cloud baffled the searchlights, and Squadron Leader Oxley was not worried by the guns, which were firing blindly.

Having roared about over Magdeburg to scare the Germans, he climbed to 6,000 feet to bomb his target, which had shown up for a moment through a gap in the clouds. Swiftly, unexpectedly, the sinister shape of a German balloon threatened death only fifty yards away. It gave him a shock.

"I thought of the chances I'd been running, flying in and out of those cables for half an hour," he said later. "As I turned and climbed I saw five or six dirty, grey shapes, just like the British balloons." Incidentally, he once saw a German balloon as high as 13,000 feet.

Dodging the balloons, he dropped a bomb or two on his target and turned to find another target where he could drop the rest. Flying south-west of Bremen at 10,000 feet, he saw an enemy aircraft landing on the illuminated flare path of an aerodrome. The red lamp was left on, and the captain of the bomber was not slow to seize his opportunity. Gliding down to 4,000 feet, he fired off a signal cartridge to see whether the enemy would put the lights on. The Germans fired up a signal consisting of three yellow and three white lights in reply.

"The nearest thing I had that night was a red-yellow, so I fired that," recorded Squadron Leader Oxley. "I was quite enjoying myself to see if we could fix them. They fired another signal, so I switched the navigation lights on, but these had no effect. Then I started morsing on the recognition lights, and for want of anything better to send I sent 'Heil Hitler.' That had the pleasing and astonishing effect of getting them to put all the lights on. They gave me a green to come in and land, which was just what I wanted. I went round the circuit as though to land—and opened up and let our bombs go into the hangars. Then I went off and returned about twenty minutes later. They must have been convinced that no enemy would hang about so long, for when I again signalled with my recognition lights they gave us another green to land. But we had nothing more to drop. I wonder what they told the C.O. next day!"

Which incident goes far toward explaining his nickname. Yet there was nothing of the dare-devil about his appearance. He looked far too good-natured to go bull-baiting Germans in their own arenas. He spoke quietly, and moved with an easy step. About five feet five inches in height, he was inclined to be tubby, with a clean-shaven face and fair hair that was going thin on the top, though he was still in his twenties. It was when his vivid blue eyes lit up with a mischievous twinkle that he betrayed a hint of that sense of humour which found such free expression over Germany, although the Germans could never see his jokes.

Like other pilots, he struck a good blow for England when Hitler was preparing to invade Great Britain during the crisis of 1940, and Squadron Leader Oxley twice ran the gauntlet of the heavy enemy defences in order to bomb the barges being collected for the transport of German troops. The Germans had mounted large numbers of machine-guns controlled electrically from a distance, and during his first attack Squadron Leader Oxley was so blinded by the searchlights that he had to keep his eyes on the instrument panel and steer as instructed by the navigator.

A few nights later he arrived at the same spot at 10.2 p.m. and dropped a flare.

"Oh, my God, sir! You can't miss. This is wonderful!" exclaimed Sergeant Horner, the navigator.

There were about a hundred barges arranged in arrowhead formation along the shore. The flare set all the guns firing in the neighbourhood as Squadron Leader Oxley circled to make a dive-bombing attack. At 5,000 feet the searchlights picked up the bomber and made it impossible for the pilot to see, so he flew once more under the instructions of the navigator. "Push her down a bit, sir!" the latter exclaimed when they were down to about 3,000 feet. A moment later he added: "Bombs gone!"

"What do we do now?" asked the captain.

"Keep on going down," came the reply, as the captain closed the bomb doors. "Now turn left," said the navigator when they were down to 300 feet.

Escaping the dazzling lights, the captain dropped still lower, leaping a sand dune like a horse going over a hurdle at Aintree, and climbing out to sea for home. His bombs shattered the barges, covered with black tarpaulins, but none of the bomber crew saw any German troops on board, which was not surprising considering that it was at night. The bomber's attack lasted exactly four minutes.

An ingenuity rivalling that of Heath Robinson was developed by Pilot Officer W. F. Tudhope, D.F.C., the navigator of the bomber piloted by Flight Lieutenant B. J. Meyer, D.F.C. Among other things which used to be served out to the crews who took part in long bombing raids were cold meat pies. These were palatable when hot, but not quite so appetising when cold. Now the bomber crews, being young and healthy, used to get hungry after spending six or eight hours in the air, but even so Flight Lieutenant Meyer and Pilot Officer Tudhope found that the cold meat pies still left much to be desired.

It was then that the navigator had his brilliant idea. Tying up the meat pies in a paper bag, he tied the closed mouth of the paper bag against the side of the hot-air pipe which was used for heating the cabin, then he inserted the mouth of the hot-air pipe, with its bag of meat pies attached, into a bigger paper bag, the mouth of which was tied securely round the hot-air pipe to prevent the hot air from escaping. By the time they had reached Berlin their cold pies were deliciously hot, and after bombing their targets they used to settle down and enjoy a good hot meal.

They were a happy crew, who used to sing all sorts of popular songs while they were flying over Germany. Sometimes they transmitted on their wireless to tell the Germans what they thought of them, and if their language was a little strong they were perhaps to be excused.

Of course the weather often played the most extraordinary tricks. Once over Hanover Flight Lieutenant Meyer found that the port engine had frozen at 8,000 feet and so much snow came into the aircraft that he was able to scoop it off his sleeve to make a snowball for the navigator. Another time he ran into thick cumulus cloud at 15,000 feet and soon heard the buzzing on the intercommunication system which presaged an electrical storm.

"I noticed a little blue ball of fire on my front gun," he reported. "It got larger until it was as big as a grape fruit, and my navigator looked ghastly in the blue light. The propellers from boss to tip were one mass of blue flame, and the whole of the leading edge of each wing was lit up; while a vivid blue flame three feet long streamed out *in front* of each wing-tip. My wireless operator did not dare touch anything. He got shocks right and left, and saw a trail of blue sparks flowing out of the aerial."

Pilot Officer A. A. Halley, who started out on the night of January 14, 1941, to bomb aerodromes in Norway, had similar disturbing experiences. Getting into a gigantic cumulus cloud which towered up for about 16,000 feet, he saw a purplish glow develop on the right wing-tip, and then it seemed that the wing-tip was on fire, but instead of the fire streaming back, as one would expect, it vibrated in front of the wing-tip. He dodged out of that cloud as quickly as possible and thereafter went round the massive cloud peaks or navigated between them so far as was possible. Nevertheless, he got caught in another disturbance which lit up the leading edges of the wings and the wing-tips in blue light, while the propellers became arcs of blue flame.

Suddenly from the starboard wing-tip a great jagged spark of a bright purple colour shot out like forked lightning—it was huge, about thirty feet long. There was an explosion followed by a bright flash inside the cockpit, and all the luminous dials and instruments stood out brighter than ever before. At the same time the wireless apparatus blew up and a bit just missed the face of the wireless operator, who was temporarily blinded by the flash. The bomber crew were lucky, inasmuch as they had only just received a wireless bearing from their base which enabled them to navigate safely back to Scotland.

Flight Lieutenant A. de Villiers Leach was caught in similar electrical storms on that night of January 14th. Flying at the two-mile level to escape the lower cloud, he saw the cumulo-nimbus clouds reaching up and up to 20,000 feet, two miles above him. "They were lit up by the moon, and looked like giant peaks," he said when he landed. "They got higher and higher and surrounded me, and it was getting so cold that I thought it better not to go over them, and came down through a gap to 4,000 feet, where we flew in cloud. A bluish flame two or three inches wide appeared at the tip of the propeller arc and gradually increased to about a foot in depth. When I looked out to port I saw the whole wing fringed with the flame, which looked like a bluish-white aura. Suddenly there was a terrific flash—I was absolutely blinded for a moment—and when I looked again the aura had vanished."

Another pilot that night saw the whole of the metal surfaces of his wings covered with a bluish light and dancing tongues of fire, yet these young men who rode the storms and set the lightning flashing treated their terrifying experiences just as coolly as they staged their lighter interludes in the air.

For instance, Pilot Officer John de Lacy Wooldridge, D.F.M., hit very hard for Britain—and none the less hard because he struck so cheerfully. He and his crew did not take their bombing operations sadly, despite the risks they ran. Time and again the wireless operator, Sergeant Buck, played practical jokes on the Germans by tuning in to their wave length. "Hallo, hallo, this is Jairmany calling. This is station XYZ, and here is the news in English." Then all the members of that happy crew would take their turn in giving a fake news item in English.

The red-headed rear-gunner, who was a bit of a wag, improved the programme on one occasion by announcing: "We will now give you a selection from Gilbert and Sullivan." And all the crew solemnly sang "Tit-Willow."

It would be interesting to know what the Germans thought. It must have been something quite beyond their comprehension, another manifestation of the "mad English" who defied death with laughter and cheerfully sang their way across Germany to Berlin and back. On September 6, 1940, when they made the long trip to Politz and Stettin to show how the strong air arm of Britain could reach out, they were flying quite low when a whole concentration of searchlights suddenly blazed up and trapped them. Instantly the wireless operator switched over to the German wave length. "Put out those lights. This is Goering up here!" he called in a mock German accent.

The disobliging Germans refused to put out the lights, so Pilot Officer Wooldridge simply evaded them. He and the crew had some exciting experiences when they went to bomb the oil refineries at Hanover. It was a perfect night, clear and starry with a full moon, and they bombed the refineries good and well, but found to their chagrin that two of the bombs would not come off the racks.

Pilot Officer Wooldridge set course for home and cruised along, looking for anything he could find. To his joy he saw an enemy aerodrome with the flare path lit and three aircraft flying round with navigation lights on. The first thing the captain of the English bomber did was to run over the flare path and try to drop those two bombs. They were stubborn and refused to budge. Owing to the noise made by the three Heinkel 111s, the English bomber remained unnoticed, so Pilot Officer Wooldridge calmly dived down to 1,000 feet, switched on his lights and joined the Heinkels that were circling the aerodrome.

He did not lack nerve.

Flying round, he waited for a chance to shoot down one of the Heinkels. It came as the first Heinkel turned in to land. Cutting across the aerodrome, Pilot Officer Wooldridge attacked the Heinkel head on, giving him a good burst with his own gun.

"As I turned, both rear-gunners shot him up," he stated. "All the flare path lights were switched off at the critical moment just when the Heinkel was about to land, and we saw him crash and go up in flames. We sailed around once more, letting fly at the others as they appeared. The other two switched off their lights as soon as the flare path lights went out, and the anti-aircraft fire, with nothing to shoot at, was very erratic. Then one of the Heinkels switched his lights on to show he was a friend, and promptly got shot at by his own defences."

The happy bombing crew that went singing into battle chuckled at the sight of the Heinkel being pasted by its own defences. Having made one of the Heinkels pay the penalty for raiding England, Pilot Officer Wooldridge flew off to the aerodrome at Nordenay, which was only seven minutes away.

"We still had our two bombs to dispose of," he added.

Seeing that the hangar lights were on, he audaciously turned on his navigation lights, at which the Germans signalled with white flashes. Without delay he replied with a haphazard series of white flashes, just to see what would happen. The enemy, completely misled, gave him the green signal to land. They had no idea it was a British bomber they were signalling in.

Pilot Officer Wooldridge, doing a close approach right over the hangars with bomb doors open, started to shake the bomber up and down and did it so vigorously that he succeeded in shaking off the two recalcitrant bombs. One hit the edge of the hangar and the other hit the tarmac. The explosion shot the bomber up a hundred feet and nearly turned it upside down.

"Then I dived straight to sea level and pushed off home—calling it a day," he remarked.

Most people would have called it a day *and* a night. The same crew were coming back from the Ruhr one night when the captain saw a light in the sky. Ten minutes later he saw the light still in the same position on their tail. Convinced that it was an enemy fighter, he told his crew to train all the guns they could upon the light. "I'm going to throttle back to let the Jerry overtake us, and we'll get a sitter," he told them.

"Now!" he added, and jerked the throttles back and held up the nose, waiting expectantly for the pursuing aircraft to speed past in flames. Unable to understand why nothing happened, he glanced back again. The light was still in the same position.

It was Sirius.

How they laughed when they realized the way in which they had been caught!

The last time I saw Wing Commander Wooldridge, D.F.C. and Bar, D.F.M., was when he walked in to take over command of some very secret squadrons of Mosquito bombers. He was as cheery as ever.

An assignment to bomb the railway junction at Rheims in the summer of 1940 gave Flying Officer Alexander Webster, D.F.C. and Bar, a very uneasy moment, although it had its amusing side—afterwards. Rheims was duly located, and the captain of the aircraft had what he called a "beautiful horizon" as he went down to 2,000 feet. Then the search-lights caught them and the tracer started to come up.

The pilot, thinking he would be clever, did a stall turn, but it did not work out as he intended. He closed the throttles as he put the nose up until the bomber slowed and stalled, then he kicked the rudder hard over while it turned to go down steeply.

Unexpected things happened. He not only lost the searchlights, but also his beautiful horizon; all the instruments on the panel went completely mad. Sergeant Bisset, who a moment before had been shooting from the rear cockpit at the searchlights on the ground, found himself on his back, with drums of ammunition falling around him, shooting at the clouds.

The captain, struggling with the control column while the altimeter touched zero, was staggered. He simply could not understand what had happened. A crash seemed certain, when he regained control.

At once the insistent voice of the navigator came to his ears. "There's something wrong. It's oil—I can smell it, feel it and taste it. . . . You'd better get ready in case something happens." There was a short pause as the navigator investigated in the dark. "I think there's a bomb in front. I'm leaning against it!" he added.

A minute or two later when they were safely over the sea and getting their breath, they switched on the lights to see what had happened.

A yell came from the navigaor. "It's not a bomb—it's the lava-tory!" he cried in amazement.

It was, and its normal position was in the back of the aircraft.

No magician ever performed a more difficult or dramatic conjuring trick on the stage than Flying Officer Webster performed that night in the air without any rehearsal. Before the remarkable feat could be accomplished, the Hampden had first to turn on its back, then dive for a while until the portable lavatory slid exactly opposite the well leading to the front cockpit. Only the most perfect timing could turn the Hampden right side up at that exact moment to enable the lavatory to drop into the well. A fraction of a second's delay would have sent it too far and made it fall on the head of the pilot. After turning right way up at that psychological moment, the Hampden had to dive again and do a bit of a climb.

Then, hey, presto! the "bomb," which happened to be neither unclean nor deadly, was transferred in a twinkling from the back of the aircraft to the back of the navigator in the front cockpit.

The only explosion which took place was one of uproarious laughter from all concerned.

CHAPTER XXV

WINGED CRUSADERS

EACH fighter pilot who took part in the Battle of London cherished his own individual impressions, and Pilot Officer G. H. Bennions, D.F.C., was no exception. "We really began to earn our pay then," he once remarked modestly—and posterity will not disagree with him.

Hearing the call of the Royal Air Force as long ago as 1929, when he was a boy still under 16 years old, he learned so much about aero-engines in the following years that he could diagnose an unusual sound in an engine as easily and accurately as a heart specialist diagnoses a murmur in the heart. But it was when he trained as a fighter pilot that his early dreams began to come true, and the experience he gained over the Arabian coast, where the landing grounds were so small that the pilot who failed to drop in at 60 miles an hour with his nose well up was bound to find trouble by over-shooting the boundaries—that experience confirmed his choice of a pilot's life. Step by step he gained promotion until he won his commission.

By the time his squadron was ordered, on September 3, 1940, to take part in the defence of London he had already shot down two or three of the enemy. The first day they hurled themselves into the conflict against the Heinkels and Junkers and Messerschmitts was marked by the loss of their two leaders. They were very preoccupied in the mess that night.

Next morning they were out at 6.30 on their first patrol, and they set forth on their last patrol an hour before dusk. For day after day their normal routine was to get up at dawn, make three or four patrols of 90 minutes, attacking the enemy with more avidity than a well-trained terrier seizes a rat, and grounding their Spitfires at night to repair them and prepare for the morrow, before dropping into bed, dead tired, to be kept awake half the night by the battery of big guns just outside their windows.

As for food, they took it when they could. Often as not when they sat down to a meal in the mess they would be called away to go up to fight the massed German formations. All the time they were in the mess, transport waited outside to rush them to their Spitfires at the dispersal point. The instant they were ordered up, the ground staff would start the engines to have the aircraft waiting ready for the pilots to take off directly they arrived from the mess. To save time, the pilots generally kept on their flying boots, and left their other kit on the seat or wings of the aircraft, where they could grab it and don it quickly.

It says much for the fitness of the pilots that they endured those gruelling days for so long. Towards the end of September they began to show signs of getting a little stale. They displayed a lack of interest in anything on the ground. Men would fall asleep at odd moments during the day between patrols. One or two said they felt tired. They began to look up for a cloudy day that might give them a bit of a rest. Yet this lassitude vanished like magic and they became as keen as ever directly they went roaring up into the skies to meet the Germans.

They were hard days for the fighter pilots and grim days for Great Britain and humanity. Toward the end of September the German losses had so shaken the German command that the character of the air war changed, and instead of immense formations of bombers, the enemy began to send over high-flying fighters. This made the work of the fighter pilots much more difficult. It took longer for the Spitfires to climb and intercept. Sometimes they were dived upon by the Messerschmitts before they could reach the patrol line. In spite of the big advance made in aircraft and engines, it was a wearisome business to climb five miles, and as the enemy began to send fighters over at 25,000 and 30,000 feet it was impossible to make contact with them at under five miles.

On one occasion Pilot Officer Bennions climbed over seven miles to 37,500 feet—a long and arduous climb—after two enemy fighters with the intention of engaging them. He could get no higher, although he kept the nose of his aircraft hard up in the air. Any little movement disturbed the balance and sent him flopping down 300 or 400 feet. The two enemy aircraft, which flew 1,000 feet above him, must have been fitted with two-stage superchargers to compress the rarefied air sufficiently to give the engines enough oxygen at the right pressure.

"They were leaving white trails in the air," reported Pilot Officer Bennions after he landed. "I thought I would just get up behind them to shoot them out of the sky, but I couldn't. They kept diving at me, just putting their noses down and sweeping up to their old level again like a switchback; but they did not fire or come within 400 yards of me. Once I got into their slipstream, and my perspex iced up instantly and I could not see anything at all. My screen became quite opaque and I had to open the hood to see where the two Huns had got to. I felt like a kite balloon being dived upon as my aircraft stood up at a ridiculous angle. In opening the hood I lost 1,000 feet, so I had to break off and come down without firing a shot. They were still patrolling when I went home.''

This explains some of the extraordinary difficulties of fighting on the verge of the stratosphere, so high in the sky that the aircraft are invisible to the naked eye.

On October 1, 1940, after fighting for a month in the greatest air battle the world had so far known, Pilot Officer Bennions was due to go on leave for six days. His pass and railway warrant were made out all ready for him. During that nightmare month he had raised his victories to eleven and had probably destroyed five others.

''I thought I'd like to shoot down one more Hun before going for a rest,'' he stated.

Accordingly he took off with his squadron and patrolled with them at 30,000 feet for 90 minutes, when the oxygen began to dwindle and they turned for home. On the way Pilot Officer Bennions sighted some Hurricanes, with about 40 Messerschmitt 109s above them. Calling up the leader, who acknowledged the message, he flew ahead to indicate the position of the enemy, and the squadron split up into two formations.

Turning right to take up a favourable position for attack, Pilot Officer Bennions arrived at the Messerschmitts—to find he was alone in the sky.

His companions had seen the Hurricanes, but had not sighted the Messerschmitts, so they had just carried on and flown to base.

It never entered his head to follow them. Undeterred by the odds, the lone English pilot turned to attack the rear of the pack. Singling out a Messerschmitt, he pressed the button twice and saw it fall away in smoke and flames, to bring his score to twelve. As it went a cannon shell exploded by the left side of his face. There was a short sharp pain in his eyes, he was momentarily blinded, and the next thing he remembered was pulling his Spitfire out of a steep dive. Pains in his right arm and right leg suggested that they had been wounded.

''I cleared my other eye with my glove and found I was able to see vaguely,'' he said when it was over. ''I could see that the hood and cockpit were shattered, so I decided to bale out. I undid the oxygen tube, disconnected the wireless plug, slid back the hood, opened the door, undid my strap and fell over the side. I don't know what attitude the aircraft was in—I couldn't see. When I felt myself clear and falling through space, I put my left thumb through the ring of my ripcord and gave a slight pull. I felt a terrific jerk as my parachute opened, then I lost consciousness. The next thing I remember is lying on the ground telling my name and squadron to someone attending me.''

It seems impossible that a man who was so terribly wounded as Pilot Officer Bennions could remain conscious and perform all those actions which enabled him to escape. His will-power was almost superhuman. His left eye was destroyed and there was a hole through which his brain was exposed. Within two hours Mr. A. H. McIndoe, the brilliant plastic surgeon, and an eye specialist were operating and doing their best to save him and repair the damage. For five weeks the wounded pilot was in hospital and Mr. McIndoe exercised the art of the plastic surgeon so skilfully that he prevented any disfigurement. Few people ever noticed that the pilot had an artificial eye.

The miracles of healing which Sir Harold Gillies performed in the last war were excelled in this.

More than once Pilot Officer Bennions—who became a Squadron Leader—was heard to express his gratitude for the care and attention of the brilliant surgeon who saved him from disfigurement after a miraculous escape.

Another young officer who was grateful to the doctors was Flight Lieutenant Douglas Hamilton Grice, D.F.C., whose adventure started near Dover on August 14, 1940, when he with nine of his companions in arms sighted a big formation of German bombers north of Dover flying wing-tip to wing-tip. They numbered between thirty and forty, while above were as many Messerschmitts acting as escort. The British fighters although badly outnumbered, hurled themselves at the bombers and just managed to get in an attack as the Messerschmitts came diving down. In the fight which followed, Flight Lieutenant Grice's aircraft was badly hit and the cockpit soon became a mass of flames. He was then flying at 16,000 feet.

"I had either to get out or be frizzled to death," he recorded. "I was very nearly unconscious with the petrol fumes and heat, but I got the hood open and the straps undone. I think the aircraft fell over and I fell out, for the next moment I knew I was in the fresh air. I held on as long as I could without pulling the ripcord, until I started to turn head over heels, then I got so dizzy after I had dropped about 4,000 feet that I just had to pull it. I came down about five miles off Felixstowe between two trawlers steaming about 100 yards apart. I waved to them and although they saw me and one of the fishermen waved back to me, they just steamed on. Five minutes later, however, a launch appeared to pick me up.''

He had some bad moments when the rigging lines of his parachute got entangled round his legs and threatened to drown him, but luckily he was able to get free.

So badly burned were his face and wrists that he was in hospital a month; but he was not permitted to shave for two months, at the

Plate 13.—Squadron Leader G. H. Bennions, D.F.C., leaving Buckingham Palace with his wife and child after receiving his decoration from the hand of the King. Anxious to achieve his twelfth victory before going on leave, he attacked a large formation of Messerschmitts single-handed, and after shooting one down he received a terrible wound that would have proved mortal but for his astonishing will-power.

Plate 14.—This was the amazing sight witnessed by pilots of the Royal Air Force while they thrashed the German Luftwaffe over Dunkirk. Men of the British Expeditionary Force lined up patiently on the beach waiting to be evacuated. Their spirit triumphed over defeat and enabled the big and little ships manned by the men of the navy, the merchant navy, fishermen and amateur yachtsmen, to perform the greatest miracle in maritime history (see page 118):

end of which time he possessed a most luxuriant black beard—as well as a new skin on his face which, thanks to the improved method of treating burns, was left unmarked.

Flight Lieutenant Grice, who had destroyed eight enemy aircraft, was shot down once before over France on June 8, 1940. The weather that afternoon was perfect, with brilliant sunshine and not a cloud to be seen as he turned about 4 o'clock to attack three Heinkel 111s, whose cross-fire punctured his radiator and oil system. Immediately the glycol from the radiator poured into his cockpit and nearly blinded him as he broke off the attack and turned south to land if possible behind the French lines. He glided fifteen miles before he came to earth in a little village ten miles from Rouen, to be met by a French peasant who insisted on shaking him by the hand.

Failing to find anyone in the village who could help him, he returned to his aircraft, to discover that some British gunners, who had just arrived, were willing to give him a lift to Rouen. Here he met another officer who helped himself to an abandoned car, and together they drove from aerodrome to aerodrome until in two or three days they had made an adventurous passage of 400 miles across France.

At Dreux Flight Lieutenant Grice secured an aircraft in which he attempted to cross the English Channel, but the way was barred by an impenetrable fog of black smoke which had drifted from the burning oil tanks at Rouen. He was consequently compelled to change course and make a landing in Jersey, from which little island he flew to England next day to rejoin his squadron.

CHAPTER XXVI

SQUADRON LEADER M. N. CROSSLEY, D.S.O., D.F.C.

To Squadron Leader Michael Nicholson Crossley, D.S.O., D.F.C., the day of June 8, 1940, also brought its thrill, for at that time he was a Flight Lieutenant just starting to shine over France, beginning to pile up the long list of triumphs which led him to become one of the honoured band of fighter pilots who had officially destroyed 22 enemy aircraft—not to mention at least seven others which he had damaged.

He was about 6 feet 3 inches tall, with the slim body of an athlete and the poise of an Etonian. Many a time he had gazed from the playing fields of Eton across the Thames to the venerable grey stones of Windsor Castle piling up in beauty on the opposite bank, but if the playing fields of Eton claimed a deal of credit for his victories, the College of Aeronautical Engineering which he attended at Chelsea certainly claimed more. With lightish hair, a fair clipped moustache and alert blue eyes, he had a clean-cut nose and nostrils which gave him an air of great keenness. Born in Warwickshire in 1912, he concealed a fearless fighting spirit under a delightful sense of humour that drove him to poke fun at himself, as some of his notes testify.

"Whoa! What a shock! Whole outfit up at 3.15 a.m. Going to France. Everyone amazed. Set off to France, land at Abbeville, refuel, hear dreadful stories, get very frightened, do a patrol, see nothing, feel better; do another, see nothing, feel much better; return home, feel grand."

That was the amusing way in which this fighter pilot, who had helped to put the fear of the Royal Air Force into the German Luftwaffe, jested about himself. He was one of those men whose actions speak louder than words, as many misguided Nazis discovered.

Flying with his flight of Hurricanes to patrol between Ostend and Zeebrugge on May 10, 1940, when the Germans began their thrust into Holland and Belgium, he did not observe any of the invaders or their aircraft. And the general impression that anyone flying over the beaches of Dunkirk during the evacuation must have seen everything was not borne out by his own experiences, for he was twice sent with the squadron to Dunkirk and did not know that the beaches were crowded with men until afterwards. "We were the top squadron and at 26,000 feet we saw nothing," he reported when it was over. "Of course, we saw a lot of battles going on, but our job was to keep guard above, and although we saw the beaches were black, we did not know what it was until after Monday, June 3rd."

To his chagrin, the first time he got a Heinkel 111 right in his sights, he discovered that his guns would not operate. But he made up for his disappointment next day on May 19th by shooting down two Messerschmitt 109s during a dog fight in which the squadron as a whole shot down seven of the enemy. On that occasion he had the strange experience, which has aroused the comment of so many fighters, of being in the midst of a mass of whirling aircraft at one minute and climbing up, after seeing his adversary crash in flames, to find the sky empty as though the previous air battle were an hallucination.

It was not easy when moving at speed among the clouds to identify the enemy in the brief glimpses that were sometimes afforded. He was once patrolling with a companion who was on guard higher up when he saw what he termed a "big ship" going past, and thought it was British. "It's a Blenheim!" he shouted on the radio-telephone to his companion.

"Hell! It's a Junkers 88!" was the reply, as the other Hurricane dived on it, just too late to prevent it escaping into a cloud.

"Just after that another came across in the opposite direction," commented Squadron Leader Crossley. "I fixed him up all right. I gave him all I had. He tried to dive into the smoke coming up from Dunkirk, but it wasn't thick enough to hide him. Going in after him, I got him and saw him crash sideways into the sea in flames about a mile out east of Dunkirk."

The great clash of his squadron came on June 8th when he was about to lead them home after their patrol. Flying at 18,000 feet, he detected what appeared to be a black mass moving toward them at a lower level. The squadron followed him down to make the attack from the stern on the back ranks of the enemy, who were stepped up in layers. He put a burst into a Heinkel 111 which flared and crashed in flames, and as he broke away to climb again he found himself half way up a huge line of bombers. "I just spotted one with a section of two and nipped in behind and gave it a clout. Its undercarriage came down and it broke out of line and went down to make a crash landing in a field. I didn't stop to see whether the crew got out. The enemy fighters were so far behind that we got the chance of attacking the bombers before they came up," he explained.

In that battle the Hurricanes destroyed three Messerschmitt 109s and six Heinkel 111s. The two German bombers which fell before the guns of Squadron Leader Crossley brought his score to seven and led to the award of the D.F.C.

His experience when the Germans began to fire their first shells from the French coast over the Channel was not without its funny side. He was patrolling with "A" flight to protect a convoy near Dover when all of a sudden he saw an enormous splash about a mile away. It was followed by three more immense white fountains which shot up out of the sea.

"Good heavens!" he thought. "They're bombing the convoy, and we're supposed to be looking after it."

At once he bobbed up through the clouds, which were at 6,000 feet, to look for the bombers who were engaged in the dirty work. To his surprise he could see nothing at all. Very perplexed, he dived down below again to have another look for the enemy and get to grips with him. Still he could find nothing. Completely baffled, he called up Control.

"They're bombing the convoy," he reported.

"Well, do something about it!" was the laconic reply.

The Hurricanes hunted around like terriers that have lost a rat, but the rats had apparently bolted back to their holes. Squadron Leader Crossley was feeling completely mystified by the affair when Control got into touch with him. "You can't do anything about it. They're shelling from Cape Grisnez!" came the voice over the radio-telephone.

So the Hurricanes were obliged to sit aloft watching the gun flashes at Cape Grisnez, and marking the spots where the shells exploded just 61 seconds later. The German shells fell among the convoy, but they failed to damage a single ship.

Another day he was leading the squadron in to land at the base, and actually had his landing wheels down, when he happened to look back in the direction of Dover and saw some ack ack bursting right over the port. At once he whipped up his wheels and, shouting to the other pilots to re-form, tore back to Dover.

The ships which they had so recently left were being subjected to an intense bombing attack by Junkers 87s and Messerschmitts 110s, otherwise Jaguars, which appeared to be diving down in all directions. The Hurricanes did the only thing possible, each selected an enemy and went for him. Squadron Leader Crossley singled out a Jaguar that was just starting its dive and, waiting until it was half way down, dived after it. A large black bomb dropped from the enemy and fell a hundred yards away from a ship, then the Jaguar pulled out of its dive about twenty feet from the surface and made off toward the French coast.

The squadron leader was about three-quarters of a mile behind, but with all the impetus of an 8,000 foot dive to help him he found himself steadily overtaking the Jaguar. They were travelling so fast that he dared not lose sight of the enemy for a moment to glance in the mirror to see if anyone happened to be chasing him. The slipstream of the Messerschmitt kept hitting the Hurricane and throwing it about, and Squadron Leader Crossley, flying no more than ten feet from the surface, had such difficulty in keeping an even keel that he was afraid his wing might touch—which was not the sort of ending to the chase that he intended.

Gradually the Jaguar grew larger until it filled his sights. Then the eight guns of the Hurricane stuttered for three seconds, and the rear-gunner of the enemy, who had opened fire from a distance of 800 yards, never fired again.

As the Hurricane overhauled the enemy, the German pilot began to try to evade the pursuer by steering from side to side. As a matter of fact, instead of the German making it more difficult for the English fighter, he made it easier, for each time the Jaguar swerved it exposed a greater area, and the British fighter simply sat still and pressed the button every time the Jaguar crossed his sights.

Smoke began to pour out of the starboard engine of the Jaguar and suddenly it did a sharp climbing turn up to about 50 feet. As Squadron Leader Crossley was about to give him the final burst he heard another pilot yelling to him on the radio-telephone: "Look out behind!"

Instinctively Squadron Leader Crossley nipped to the left for a few hundred yards and saw another Jaguar coming up after him. As he flashed across the nose of the Jaguar in turning, he heard an ominous bang. Then the Jaguar roared past with the other Hurricane hard on its tail. For a moment Squadron Leader Crossley wondered what had happened to his own Jaguar, then he saw a large white circle of foaming water which slowly changed to an oily patch to mark the grave of the enemy. On landing he found that a bullet had punctured one of his tyres and missed his ankle by inches.

They were a happy set in his squadron, each of whom was known to the others by a "trade" name, among them being The Mandarin, Jackdaw, Grubby, Hector, Pete B, Polly, Humph, Jimmy, David, while they dubbed Squadron Leader Crossley the Red Knight. They were a deadly team which exacted heavy penalties from the German Luftwaffe every time they could get to grips, and the notes of the leader were expressive. "Later we intercepted a large number of assorted Huns. The following tipped stuff into the Channel—Hector, Pete B, Humph, Red Knight. The Mandarin converted three non-smoking Ju 87s into smoking 87s."

Of Monday, August 12th, he wrote: "Coo! What a blitz! Patrol base. All of a sudden we sight a cloud of Huns, and move unwillingly towards them, but sight another cloud complete with mosquitoes a bit nearer; we move even more unwillingly towards them and attack. Everyone takes a swing at the 50 Dornier 215s and the Messerschmitt 109s. Hell of a lot of zigging. Very hectic. Day's bag nine 109s, three 215s."

His subtle sense of humour was emphasized when he wrote that the fighter pilots who were spoiling all the time for a fight moved "unwillingly" toward the enemy, although top speed was much too slow to please them. A squadron that slapped down twelve of the enemy when it was "unwilling" would give Goering a headache when it was "willing"!

They were one of the squadrons which helped to make the Germans pay so dearly for their surprise attack on Croydon on Thursday, August 15, 1940. If ever Squadron Leader Crossley and his fighter pilots touched the peak of excitement, it must have been that afternoon, which he afterwards referred to as "a remarkable blitz afternoon." Few will disagree with him. They started by chasing some Germans up to Harwich, where they had a mix-up with Messerschmitt 109s. Returning to their base to refuel, they were ordered down to Portsmouth to help beat off a very heavy attack by German bombers, after which they flew to base to refuel again. They were then sent away to patrol off Dover, and had climbed to 10,000 feet in the neighbourhood of Maidstone when the Control called them up and told them an attack on Croydon was pending. They needed no second invitation. Up till then they had destroyed six German aircraft that day and were keen to add to their score.

"We turned round and beat it for Croydon as hard as we could. Sure enough when we approached I saw a large party in progress," recorded Squadron Leader Crossley. "Masses of Me 110s were dive bombing the place. As they did not appear to notice our approach, I steered straight past them, with the object of getting between them and the sun. This was successful and we charged at them. I put a long burst into the first one I saw and he promptly caught fire and went down in flames. Then I saw another detach itself and make off, so I made after it and gave it a long burst, at which the starboard engine caught fire. I broke away and the Mandarin gave it a long burst and it altered course inland as if looking for somewhere to land. I nipped

in and gave it another bang, and as I broke off I saw the starboard
airscrew revolving slowly and then stop. Another burst from the
Mandarin and one of the crew baled out and the aircraft crashed in
flames in a wood near Sevenoaks.''

In that running fight lasting no more than two minutes the antagonists
covered about twelve miles.

That day the fighters led by Squadron Leader Crossley, who won
high promotion, knocked down thirteen enemy aircraft out of the
sky—an unlucky number—for the Germans.

CHAPTER XXVII

HAPPY LANDINGS

ALTHOUGH so many things were foreseen and guarded against in the
Royal Air Force, the unexpected was always happening. It was, for
instance, something quite inexplicable which saved the lives of Flight
Lieutenant David Drakes and his crew in the dark hours of the early
morning of May 13, 1940—which was Whit Monday.

Taking off about 11 o'clock on the Sunday night, the pilot flew to
Cologne where he dropped his bombs with judgment and effect on
troop trains and railway sheds and tracks to hinder enemy troop
movements. He was flying back over Brussels, evading the searchlights and guns, when the fragment of a bursting shell put his starboard
engine out of action. He did all he knew to maintain height on one
engine, but the altimeter moved steadily against him. Arriving at the
coast, he pushed bravely out to sea, but within five minutes saw that
it was impossible for him to reach England, so he turned to follow
the Belgian coast with the intention of making a last-minute dash
across the Channel at Dover, where it was narrow, or else of landing
in France.

He had the greatest difficulty in keeping the bomber straight, and
the strain on his left leg was so great that he was obliged to call on the
navigator to help him by standing up in the tunnel and pushing with
all his strength on the rudder-bar. As they crept down the coast in
the darkness, the pointer of the altimeter slowly moved round to 300
feet. They had been flying about forty-five minutes since the engine
was hit and had dropped from 5,000 feet.

Seeing that they were unlikely to remain in the air more than two
or three minutes, the pilot told the crew to prepare to alight on the
sea. ''Come up and hang on behind me,'' he ordered, which they did.

In the last few seconds as he was about to touch down, he made out
a bit of a beach in the darkness and managed to land the bomber
safely on its belly. As the aircraft made contact with the shingle, the
port engine was flung out by the impetus. For forty yards the bomber
ploughed forward in a straight line up the beach, then it suddenly

did a right-angle turn to the left and came to a stop in a field. It was so dark that the rear-gunner, thinking they had alighted on the sea, pitched out the dinghy and was going to get into it when he found they were on land.

In seconds the crew scrambled out of the aircraft and withdrew to a safe distance. An ominous sizzling came from the bomber. When it failed to go up in flames, the crew, who had no idea of their whereabouts, went back and made a bonfire of their secret codes and maps, after which they destroyed certain important apparatus which it was desirable to keep out of the hands of the enemy. Then they climbed a dune and hailed one or two sailing ships that were passing near the shore. Receiving no answer, they explored a little and found a group of houses at the doors of which they knocked. Nobody took any notice, so they concluded it was better to sit down on a sandhill, enjoy the solace of a cigarette and wait for dawn.

They were sitting there chatting and smoking when a party of about twenty men loomed up out of the darkness and Flight Lieutenant Drakes suddenly found a bayonet prodding him in the stomach while a gruff voice said "Allemand!" It was not so much an inquiry as an accusation.

The Englishmen prudently put up their hands, while Flight Lieutenant Drakes informed the newcomers in his best French that he was English. The Frenchmen, who turned out to be coastguards, were more convinced than ever that they were Germans, and the captain of the bomber got another prod from the bayonet. "Anglais, Anglais," repeated Flight Lieutenant Drakes, without much effect. Then he took a chance. Putting down one hand, he opened his flying coat and pointed to the badge on his tunic and said very slowly "Air . . . Ah . . . Eff."

Flashing a torch at the badge, the coastguards went to the bomber, and were satisfied when they saw its markings. Then they all shook hands before the coastguards led the bomber crew off to their lighthouse and hut about a mile and a half away to prepare a good breakfast for them. The friendly and hospitable Frenchmen insisted on taking them to the village for lunch, after which they gave them a fine send-off at the aerodrome. They were good allies and comrades-in-arms.

Lucky as the bomber crew considered themselves when they landed safely without injury, they did not realise exactly how lucky they were until it got light. Then they discovered that if the bomber had carried on in a straight line instead of turning at right angles, it would have crashed into some houses directly in its course and they would probably all have been killed. Why the bomber changed its course in that abrupt manner in time to save their lives, remains a mystery, for it is obvious that from the moment it touched the shingle it was beyond human control.

The bomber crew of Sergeant Joseph Unsworth, D.F.M., also met with an unexpected, but happy, ending to an adventure which began with the bombing of Kiel Docks on August 4, 1940, when the night was quite clear and starry. On arriving back in England after being up for over nine hours, they found such a thick ground fog with low cloud and rain over their base that Control would not permit them to run the risk of landing. They were accordingly diverted to another aerodrome, where conditions were if anything slightly worse, so they were sent off elsewhere. They wandered round from one aerodrome to another, only to find that visibility on the ground was nil and it was impossible to get down.

"It was a strange sight to see a church spire sticking out through the top of the fog," Sergeant Unsworth reported.

About 6.30 in the morning they made their final attempt at an aerodrome on the East Coast, but conditions were worse than ever. The pilot turned away into the driving rain that was associated with the fog. It was daylight, but he could see nothing. Visibility simply did not exist, and the pilot, who was soon wet through, was obliged to fly with the hatch open in order to maintain control.

For twenty minutes he flew in these conditions, then the port engine cut out. It did not even cough—there could not have been a drop of petrol left.

The rear-gunner, however, did not worry about their desperate plight. He slept as calmly in "the tin" as though he had been in bed. It says much for the nerves of the boys in the Royal Air Force.

"Stand by," ordered Sergeant Unsworth. The wireless operator gave the rear-gunner a kick with his foot to awaken him before tapping out: "Going down in sea. Taking emergency action."

Fifty feet from the surface of the sea the other engine cut out. The captain called the navigator up out of the front cockpit. The rear-gunner got the dinghy ready while the wireless operator still tapped away. Then the captain called to them to stand behind him. "When I looked round it amazed me to see them all so unconcerned, although we all knew that not many had escaped after a crash landing at sea," the pilot said later.

Occasionally a boat loomed up and vanished in the fog. The pilot tried to turn and skate back near a trawler, whose crew thought they were Germans going to machine-gun them. As they skimmed along nearly touching the surface the pilot cut off the petrol and put the switches down. They blew up their Mae Wests. The astrodome was opened for a speedy exit amidships. Then they hit at between ninety and a hundred miles an hour.

"I've never heard a noise like it in my life—like thunder," remarked the pilot when it was all over.

As the cowling touched, both engines shot out, the perspex nose was smashed in and a great wave of water gushed up through the tunnel, drenching the crew as it rushed out of the astrodome. If the hatch had not been open to provide a vent, they might have been seriously injured by that great rush of water. For a moment the bomber dived under the surface and then came up again to stop about thirty yards ahead.

So cleverly did the pilot and other members of the crew brace themselves when the shock came that none was injured. In three seconds the wireless operator, the rear-gunner and the navigator were in the dinghy, while the captain was swimming alongside. It was as much as the other three men could do to haul him in, owing to the weight of his soddened clothing.

In ten minutes they saw the trawler appear out of the fog and rain, and five minutes later they were on board. The skipper was unshakable as an oak. The airmen he had saved might have been paying him a formal call. "It's turned out nice again," he remarked casually to Sergeant Unsworth, whose opinion of the weather can be guessed! The airmen quickly stripped and donned some spare clothes collected by the crew, while their own wet clothing was put to dry in the engine-room, and the skipper served them all with a generous tot of rum, which soon warmed them up.

On their way back they steamed right into a magnetic minefield laid by the enemy. A naval patrol hailed them through the megaphone. "Do you know you're right on top of a minefield?" he called.

"Of course I do, but it doesn't bother us," called the skipper through his megaphone, and they proceeded to port, where the bomber got a fine reception, and in due course Sergeant Unsworth learned that he had won the D.F.M.

In the last resort the lives of the crew were in the hands of the pilot; they depended on his skill and courage, as Wing Commander Arthur Noble Luxmoore proved on May 12, 1940. Starting off from a base in the Midlands to attack an industrial target at Gladbach-Rheydt in the Ruhr, he suffered a savage attack from the pom-poms of a mechanized column of German troops, and suddenly felt the bomber get out of control as it shuddered from a direct hit, which destroyed part of the rudder controls.

With a supreme physical effort, the pilot regained control and, freely accepting the risk, held on his course to his target, where Pilot Officer R. E. Allitt, the second pilot and bomb-aimer, carried out his task and bombed the works. Turning to struggle home, the bomber was subjected to an intense barrage. She shuddered again as a shell blew away a large part of the main plane. Fighting to keep her in the air, Wing Commander Luxmoore carried on. Another hit put the starboard engine out of action. The crew felt the aircraft shudder again and yet again as two more shells struck home.

The bomber started to fly in circles owing to the loss of the rudder control. Wing Commander Luxmoore was obliged to call upon Sergeant H. Wathey, the observer, to enter the tunnel right under the pilot's seat and apply all his strength to the rudder bar to help to regain control and keep the bomber on the right course. Then she started to dive, and only after a fierce fight could they get her on an even keel again. All the time the aircraft kept trying to spin or fly in circles, and it took the utmost physical strength of Sergeant Wathey and the captain to counteract these movements. Once or twice when the unrelenting searchlights held them, Sergeant Wathey rushed to his guns and attacked them to such good purpose that he succeeded in shooting two of them out. Corporal Ronald Jolly, the wireless operator, turned his gun from time to time on the searchlights and had the satisfaction of shooting one out.

By sheer physical strength the pilot and Sergeant Wathey fought to maintain the heavy bomber in the air, while Corporal Jolly worked calmly at the wireless, obtaining fixes to enable the navigator to give the pilot his course.

To all intents the aircraft was unmanageable, and most captains would have given the order to abandon her. But there is no doubt that Wing Commander Luxmoore was determined not to let his crew fall into enemy hands and had made up his mind to bring them back to France.

Fighting all the time to counteract the erratic movements of the bomber, Wing Commander Luxmoore flew safely across the Ardennes and arrived over France, after a nightmare passage of a hundred miles. They were down now to under 1,000 feet, and he gave the crew the order to bale out. Pilot Officer Allitt and Sergeant Herbert Wathey at once got clear. At that moment Corporal Jolly was getting a fix from Le Bourget, and did not receive the order, as he was not on the intercommunication system. When he got through to the captain again he heard his voice saying: "Have you jumped?"

Quickly destroying the aircraft papers and leaving the transmitter key switched on, Corporal Jolly baled out at a low altitude, and while he was floating down to safety he saw the bomber fall out of control and burst into flames.

Wing Commander Luxmoore, disregarding all risk to himself, knowing that he alone would not be able to maintain control, held on long enough to enable his crew to get out safely. But by that time it was too late for him to save himself. So died a brave man who in dying gave living proof of Democracy's belief in the greatest good for the greatest number.

A further series of adventures befell the other members of the crew. As Pilot Officer Allitt got up again after landing in a clearing in a wood he thought: "If only I had my torch and maps I'd escape." A second later he realized that he actually had his torch and maps in his hand— he had grabbed them and retained a grip on them all the way down. Making his way to the nearest village, he was at once challenged by a French soldier, who held him up with his bayonet under the impression that he was a German parachutist, and put him under arrest in the guard room. Allitt explained that he was an English flying officer, but they were taking no chances until a French officer arrived and escorted him to his General.

Sergeant Wathey landed in a big tree down which he climbed with difficulty in the dark. Making his way laboriously, with many a stumble, through the undergrowth of the wood, he suddenly felt himself slipping and rolling downwards. When at last he came to a stop he found he was on the edge of water, so he wisely remained where he was until daylight.

In the dawn he saw he was on the bank of a river, so he set off again to the west, falling in with two Belgian peasants, whom he accompanied along the road. From time to time German aircraft flew over the road and machine-gunned them, but each time they managed to escape. After tramping for eight miles Sergeant Wathey was challenged by some French soldiers, who promptly arrested him, having no doubt that he also was a German parachutist. Marching him to headquarters, they handed over their prisoner.

Corporal Jolly had the strangest experience of all. He landed on a steep slope, which happened to be the roof of a house, down which he slid. The lines of his parachute were entangled somewhere above, and as he tried to make his way forward he felt something give and break at every step he took. Floundering along in the dark, he could not understand where he was or what was happening, and at length he came to the conclusion that he was walking on ice. Not until he fell a few feet did he realise that he had walked the whole length of the roof of a greenhouse!

He banged on the door of the house. There was no answer. Then he walked into the village, where some people, as soon as they saw him, shouted "Boche!" and bolted for their lives. At last he induced the village constable to take him in charge, and eventually all three of the crew met as prisoners at headquarters about fifteen miles away. Here they were properly identified and released, to be entertained most lavishly with wine, when it was food they needed. They will not soon forget the French General kissing them on both cheeks as he bade them adieu before they drove off in a British staff car to the nearest Royal Air Force aerodrome, where they were looked after until an aircraft arrived from their base to pick them up next day.

When His Majesty the King was decorating the three men for their coolness and courage at their base somewhere in England, he listened keenly to their descriptions of what had happened, and Corporal Jolly's account of how he stumbled along the roof of the greenhouse in the dark, thinking it was ice breaking under his feet, was so funny that the King could not help laughing. "Too bad to laugh at them after what they have been through," he said, and continued to chuckle as he moved on.

Feats of flying such as that of the late Wing Commander Luxmoore or the remarkable flight of Flight Lieutenant Henry Bernard Collins, D.F.C., can be appreciated to the full only by trained pilots. It was a fortnight after Wing Commander Luxmoore's nightmare flight, when France was crumbling and the British forces were crying out for anti-tank ammunition to deal with the German tanks, that Flight Lieutenant Collins was asked if he would carry a load of ammunition to France in one of the Imperial Airways Ensigns. The Ensign was a big aircraft of about 20 tons, and it normally needed a long run to take off and land safely. It was a civil aircraft, quite unarmed, and there was no escort available for it.

Flight Lieutenant Collins was keen to go. Discussing the matter with his second pilot, Flying Officer Earl Bateman Fielden, who was well known in civil flying, they calmly took down some of the camou-flage nets at Croydon aerodrome and stowed them away in the aircraft, which was loaded up with nearly four tons of ammunition. Late on the night of May 25th the great Ensign roared along the runway and climbed into the air. She was large enough to provide a first-class target for the anti-aircraft gunners, and slow enough to fall a prey to the first Messerschmitt that came along. One direct hit would have brought about one of the biggest explosions ever seen in the sky. But the men on board did not worry about that. All they were concerned about was helping the men fighting in France, and the duty of Flight Lieutenant Collins was to deliver the ammunition as though he were Carter Paterson to the door of the men who wanted it, at Seclin aero-drome, which was a few miles from Lille.

Flying south, and using the blazing oil tanks at Dunkirk as a beacon, they crossed the French coast, while every gun within range opened up on them and the searchlights swept the skies. For twenty minutes they flew through a pyrotechnic display, which increased over Lille until it was like a Brock's Benefit night at the old Crystal Palace, and Flying Officer Fielden was momentarily expecting the whole lot to blow up.

When they arrived near Seclin their reception was so hot that it was obvious the Germans had already taken possession of the aerodrome. To attempt to land would have been folly. Accordingly they turned away and came low near Armentieres to find a landing ground. Dimly they made out a field. It was only seventy yards wide and about 500 yards long. Any pilot would have sworn it was impossible to land the giant Ensign in so small a space. But Flight Lieutenant Collins did it— he actually landed that great aircraft in a field which was growing a crop of potatoes. By all the rules the aircraft should have sunk in the soft surface and overturned, but by uncanny skill and judgment the pilot brought the aircraft safely to rest.

Without delay they got out their camouflage nets and covered up the Ensign. It was as well they did so, for the first streak of dawn brought a German aircraft over the field at no more than 1,000 feet, but the net camouflaged the Ensign so perfectly that it was not seen.

They worked at top speed unloading the boxes of ammunition and hiding them among the potatoes. The anti-tank brigade at Armentieres were clamouring for it. Before 4 o'clock they were taking breakfast with the anti-tank brigade, and as there was no bacon available, they sat down to fried pork, which was delicious.

Their take-off was even more remarkable than the landing, for with only the light of two hurricane lamps as guides, one planted 300 yards down the field and the other to mark the boundary 200 yards further on, Flight Lieutenant Collins lifted the giant aircraft into the air from that field of potatoes with three tons of letters as well as sundry generals on board and landed them all safely back at Croydon—which was why he was awarded the D.F.C.

He knew all the hazards, realized that a slight error of judgment would bring disaster, but his superb skill and experience enabled him to triumph.

CHAPTER XXVIII

MINES, TORPEDOES AND BOMBS

LEAVING the historians to settle whether June or September, 1940, was the most critical month in the history of Britain and Mankind, my own opinion is that the anxiety in the fighting services was far greater in June than in September because of the general expectation that after Hitler had destroyed the opposition in France he would at once seek to hurl his invading armies across the Channel to crush the British before they could re-equip their magnificent men who had escaped from Dunkirk. Nobody knew then how far the Hitler divisions had been exhausted by their continental onrush, with the result, as usual, that Great Britain at the peak of her peril was improvising her defences and gathering a citizen army to defend their hearths and homes.

In this tense situation the reconnaissance aircraft of the Coastal Command used to go out to see what the enemy was doing and watch for the first sign of the invader. On the night of June 28-29 a patrol returned to an East Coast station with news suggesting that the invasion was about to be launched. A vast convoy of ships had been sighted, and no one doubted that the Germans were on their way. Accordingly the various headquarters were informed, and there were last-minute conferences among the staff of this particular station. Other stations were warned immediately, and pilots and crews were ordered to stand by. All the aircraft were fully armed to attack the ships of the invaders, and everyone was keyed up for the struggle, wondering how soon the clash would come.

As we know, it did not come at all. The reason was simple. The convoy of about eighty ships was a British convoy. They still chuckle on that station when they think about it now—but the comforting thing is that they were prepared to meet whatever was emerging from the darkness over the seas.

If Hitler in those days gave the Royal Air Force something to think about, it is pleasant to know that the Royal Air Force more than reciprocated. For a whole month the German High Command were as anxious and puzzled as they have ever been in their lives. The announcement by the Admiralty on April 12, 1940, that the waters of the Baltic and the Cattegat and Skagerrack were mined, coupled with the unexpected loss of transports full of troops on the way to Norway to prove that it was true, gave the enemy a shock. They could not understand how such extensive areas had been sown so quickly without the mine-layers being observed and attacked.

Those German officers whose duty it was to keep watch on the waters must have suffered many bitter reprimands of the High Command for their laxity. A ship blowing up here and another sinking there provided proof that the claims of the British Admiralty to have sown mines in these waters were not bluff, but reality. And the Germans were convinced that mine-laying surface ships and submarines were solely responsible.

It seems almost unbelievable—but it happens to be true—that although the Germans initiated mine-laying by aircraft when they dropped the first magnetic mines by parachute in the Thames estuary in November, 1939, they failed to realize for a whole month that what they had done, and what the British knew they had done, could be repeated by the British.

It was on the night of April 11, 1940, that Hampden bombers first set out to help to mine those waters. Night after night they went out in secret to drop their mines by parachute and build up more minefields to encompass the enemy. It had all the hazards of long-range work over the sea.

One mine-layer at least got a laugh out of it, for the pilot of a Beaufort of the Coastal Command was approaching the German coast when the captain of a German ship, probably quite assured that only a German aircraft could be flying in that neighbourhood, flashed a warning: "You are running into danger," which was very kind and thoughtful of the enemy.

The Beauforts of the Coastal Command, as already mentioned, along with the Swordfish of the Fleet Air Arm also took part in this hazardous work that yielded none of the spectacular results which whipped up bomber crews to enthusiasm as they saw their bombs burst on the targets. The mine-laying aircraft flew out in secret, deposited their mines in the dark and flew away again without knowing whether their work would prove fruitful or futile. Such work called for a strength of spirit and purpose to sustain men for any length of time. There were no public acclamations to hearten them. They performed their duties out of the sight of human eye and they had for the time being to be upheld by the knowledge that they had sown their mines on the requisite spot.

Not until the mine-laying aircraft started their operations were the full fruits garnered from the many reconnaissances the pilots carried out along the enemy coasts. In their reconnaissances they learned the layout of the confusing indentations of the coasts so well that they were able to go back in the dark and spring a surprise upon the Germans. In the beginning they were able to fly over in formation and split up into sections to drop their mines with precision, and the accuracy insisted upon was within a hundred yards of the spot indicated in orders. If they could not accomplish this, they had to bring the mines back—but few indeed were the cases of mine-layers returning with their mines on board.

The result was that the British authorities had knowledge of where each mine was laid. And as it was duly anchored, Great Britain complied with the international laws on mine-laying and did not break them, whereas the Germans scorned the laws by laying magnetic mines in the international sea lanes to sink neutral as well as belligerent shipping.

At length when the Germans discovered that the minefields which seemed to spring up by magic were in reality laid by British aircraft, the mine-layers were forced to give up mine-laying in formation and dodge in and drop their mines individually as opportunity served. Sometimes indeed a British aircraft would meet with such opposition from the flak ships that it was compelled to fly around for nearly an hour—until, in fact, the enemy felt assured that it had flown off, when it would slip in and out again before the Germans realized what had happened.

The British mine-layers laid dozens of minefields to hem in the enemy on all the coasts which he dominated from the northern coast of Norway right down the French coast to Bayonne on the border of Spain. Nor did the pilots lay their mines in coastal waters only. They stole in and dropped their mines in the German rivers and ports and even in the Kiel Canal itself, where it eventually became known that seven ships were sunk. The Germans alone knew what shipping losses they suffered from the mines which the British aircraft scattered in their ports and waterways, and they dared not reveal the figures to the German nation.

The British pilots who dropped the mines did much to whittle away the German strength. Some of them flew in Swordfish with open cockpits which could not normally have made the long sea passage to their objective and back without being fitted with an extra tank just above the head of the pilot. To enable the aircraft to fly with this additional weight of fuel, one of the crew remained behind and the trip was carried out by a pilot and navigator. The aircraft were slow and vulnerable, and the pilot's position under the petrol tank if a bullet struck it made him particularly liable to be burned to death, but pilots smiled at the risks and did superb work.

As soon as the enemy wakened to the fact that aircraft were responsible, they instituted at their ports a service of fast motor-craft whose crews watched for the mines dropping. Directly they detected a parachute coming down they rushed out to mark the spot with a buoy to enable it to be swept up as soon as possible. But while they were still under the impression that ships were responsible they were sorely puzzled because after sweeping up the mines or clearing a channel through a minefield, they would make losses to prove that the mines had been mysteriously replaced. The British reconnaissance aircraft naturally reported the German sweepers at work, and of course the aircraft would go out that night to lay a surprise for the enemy next day.

A task of such magnitude could not be carried out without some losses, but the silence necessarily surrounding the work tended to obscure the risks. For instance, Flight Lieutenant B. G. Meyer, D.F.C., who had carried out over thirty bombing operations and knew full well what it was to have his aircraft shot about, decided that he would do a spot of mine-laying for a change at Brest. "We thought it would be easy," he recorded, "so we volunteered. But when we got quite close to the port we were met by a terrific barrage. As we went in to Brest, they drove me down to within twenty feet of the water. They were firing so hard that we could see the tracer splashing into the water in front of us. We have never had so much stuff so close before. It was just like turning hoses on us. We skated in about twenty feet off the water, then climbed up to drop our mine in the inner harbour, after which we dropped down and skated out again; but we didn't sing on that trip."

As will be remembered, he and his crew sang their way across Germany and back many a time.

Without doubt the most difficult work of all fell to the torpedo-bombers, who had to come down so low and keep such a straight course before they could launch the torpedo that sometimes they almost collided with the target before they could pull up and away. If the target happened to be a German warship, such as the *Bismarck*, the risk and courage entailed in making a torpedo attack will rightly be judged as exceptional. It called for special training and outstanding skill and judgment in assessing the speed and direction of a moving ship and in launching the torpedo.

Unless a torpedo be launched at the correct angle, it will porpoise, otherwise dive below the surface and then come up again and do another dive, behaving just like a porpoise, instead of speeding straight to its target at the correct depth below the surface. In the earlier aircraft the torpedo was loaded in a line parallel with the fuselage of the aircraft, and the pilot had to approach the surface of the sea at the exact angle at which the torpedo should enter. Then someone had a brain wave and mounted the torpedo under the aircraft at an angle which enabled it to be correctly launched when the aircraft was flying parallel with the surface, or on an even keel!

Squadron No. 22 of the Coastal Command was not only the first to be equipped with Beauforts, but among the first to take part in mine-laying operations. Under the command of Wing Commander M. J. St. G. Braithwaite, it also carried out many torpedo attacks on the shipping in the invasion ports. Its losses in the early days were sometimes due to enemy action, sometimes to circumstances over which the pilots had no control. For a period the squadron suffered heavily, which robbed the Royal Air Force of some of its most highly-trained specialist pilots; among them was Flight Lieutenant A. R. H. Beauman, who carried out thirty operations in all sorts of weather, with many torpedo attacks on ships by day and by night. He was last seen off Wilhelmshaven going in to torpedo a big ship in the face of terrific anti-aircraft fire, but whether he hit the ship before he was hit himself remains unknown. Dicky Beauman, who received the D.F.C., was one of the most popular members of the mess and no finer pilot or braver man ever sat in the cockpit of an aircraft.

While the torpedo aircraft may reap rich rewards, as in the attack of Taranto when their hits on the Italian battleships and cruisers redressed the balance of power in the Mediterranean, this specialized type of job was nevertheless subject to all sorts of unforeseen chances. The pilot flying swiftly through the air as he keeps a moving ship under observation has not only to judge the speed and course of that ship, but must anticipate any change of direction it may make if he is to score a hit. A mere flick of the helm will cause a torpedo to miss—and a miss is as good as a mile. In one respect the pilots who launched torpedoes were realists—they never referred to near misses! With them it was either a hit or a miss.

Splendid work was done by six Beauforts of No. 22 Squadron in Cherbourg Harbour at 11 o'clock on the night of September 17, 1940. The moon was at the full, and bombers were bombing the docks when the first flights of Beauforts were led into Cherbourg at no more than ten feet above the surface. They flew so low that the gun in the fort at the entrance could not be depressed sufficiently and its tracers were seen bouncing off the other breakwater. Squadron Leader Rex Mack, D.F.C., got his torpedo away at a steamer of over 5,000 tons just as five searchlights picked him up. The fire from the breakwater and harbour and ships was so intense that the tracer bullets cannoned off ships and walls in all directions. Flight Lieutenant Francis hit a destroyer and Sergeant N. Hearn-Phillips, D.F.M., torpedoed a vessel of over 5,000 tons—which was not a bad night's work. Against these three successes, one of the Beauforts was lost, but it was a wonder that any escaped at all in such a heavy barrage of fire.

Some weeks later, on November 10, 1940, Wing Commander Braithwaite was about to make a torpedo attack on a steamer which was steaming at five knots. Circling round, he swept in and got his torpedo away. It ran perfectly straight for the steamer which was palpably doomed—or so it seemed. Then, quite unexpectedly, before the torpedo reached the target, there was a gigantic explosion and a great column of water shot up in the air as the torpedo hit the top of a sandbank which lay in its path. At high tide the torpedo would have sped over the top of the sandbank and the steamer would have gone to the bottom.

One more heroic deed out of the endless saga of the Royal Air Force must end this chapter. It was the misfortune of war which led to Pilot Officer John T. Davison, a young New Zealander, receiving a direct hit from a flak ship while he was seeking to bomb German E-boats off the Danish coast. Badly wounded in the thigh and leg, he hung on despite his injuries and flew his aircraft for 300 miles over the sea to his base.

The aircraft itself was considerably damaged, and when it arrived over the aerodrome the undercarriage was seen to be out of order. The bombs were still on board, and the watchers down on the ground fully anticipated that unless the pilot could get the undercarriage to work the aircraft and crew would be blown to pieces when he attempted to land. For half an hour the pilot flew around the aerodrome struggling to make the undercarriage function properly, but the task was beyond him.

"Can you go out over the Wash and jettison your bombs?" asked Control.

"Yes," he replied, and flew off over the sea to drop his bombs; but owing to the damage to the aircraft there was one at the back of the rack which stuck.

Unaware of this menace, he flew straight in to make a crash landing and, as he touched, the bomb exploded and blew the tail to smithereens. The observer and the pilot tumbled out as the engine flamed up and began to run for their lives. Suddenly they thought of the rear-gunner, who was nowhere to be seen.

Those who were hastening to their aid saw them turn back and rush into the flames and smoke. A few moments afterwards they emerged again, dragging Sergeant Aslett, the rear-gunner, as though he were a sack of potatoes. He was peppered with bits of nuts and bolts and scraps of metal, and although he was knocked out by the explosion and would certainly have lost his life if Pilot Officer Davison and the observer Sergeant G. W. Brazier had not gone to his rescue, he recovered along with his companions, to bring their tale of high courage to a happy ending.

CHAPTER XXIX

SQUADRON LEADER A. McKELLAR,
D.S.O., D.F.C. AND BAR

As a boy, Archie McKellar had two ambitions—to become a plasterer and to fly. Born at Paisley in 1912, he was the only child of John McKellar, who had himself served his apprenticeship as a plasterer before launching into business as a contractor, and Archie McKellar was determined to learn his father's trade and follow in his footsteps. No family could have been more united, but when Archie McKellar left Shawlands Academy his father was anxious for him to go on to the university to continue his education and adopt a professional career.

"I want to be a plasterer, Dad," Archie said.

"But a good education will make life so much easier for you," his father urged him. As a compromise the lad went into a stockbroker's office after leaving school, but he did not like it.

"I want to be a plasterer, Dad," he repeated to his father.

"But it's very hard manual labour, and if you join the trade you will have to serve your apprenticeship and get the same pay as any other boy," his father insisted. "If you go to the university, a good education will make life much easier for you."

"Education is only knowing the world and its ways, Dad. I want to be a plasterer," Archie pleaded, so at last his father gave way. Making out his indentures, Mr. McKellar bound his son to serve as an apprentice for five years, during which time Archie McKellar worked on the same terms as the other boys and neither received nor asked one special privilege from his father. He was perfectly happy. It was never necessary to call him in the morning, and not once was he late for work. Every day before dressing he spent half an hour doing physical exercises, with the result that although short in stature he developed great physical strength and endurance.

Wing Commander W. M. Churchill, D.S.O., D.F.C., who became his commanding officer when Archie McKellar transferred from Squadron No. 602 to Squadron No. 605, used to refer to him as the "pocket Hercules," while other companions in the Royal Air Force called him the "pocket battleship," so compact and strong was he.

Keen on all forms of sport, he played rugby for his school, enjoyed a swim, liked a gallop on a horse, drove a good ball in a game of golf and displayed a keen eye and quick muscular reactions at tennis and squash. Many a time when he gazed out of the office window at the works during the lunch hour and saw the schoolboys playing cricket with three stumps chalked upon the wall to serve as the wicket, he would go out and show them how to bowl. The boys doted on him. He was so vital, so happy, so friendly that everyone liked him.

More than once his father noticed that he was immersed in books on flying, that he was very interested in the life stories of the great pilots of the last war, Ball and McCudden, Bishop, Mannock and the rest. After work was finished, Archie would often go out on the moors near Glasgow to watch with delight the gulls and peewits and other birds flying around. He studied their actions closely and used to tell his father how they zoomed and dived and banked, but it was all incomprehensible to his father.

Then one day Archie came in, his blue eyes sparkling with joy, his voice full of excitement. "I can get into 602 Squadron!" he exclaimed. It was the City of Glasgow Auxiliary Squadron of the Royal Air Force.

His father was horrified. "It's a dangerous game, flying. I can't let you do it," he replied.

"I want to learn to fly, Dad," pleaded the son.

"It's too dangerous. I can't allow it."

In vain Archie McKellar pleaded. "All right, when I can afford to pay for lessons, I will learn to fly," he said, and for weeks refused to speak to his father, although they were so deeply attached.

During the last year of his apprenticeship he acted as working foreman for his father and had fifty men working under him, so he gained experience of handling men before he joined the Royal Air Force. Directly his apprenticeship was terminated, he remained in his father's business as working foreman and eventually became general foreman.

He kept his word. As soon as he could afford to pay for lessons, he secretly joined the Scottish Flying Club and in due course gained his pilot's certificate. They knew nothing about it at home, and he was flying for some time before his father discovered it. But the bonds between them were so close that the fact did not disturb the happiness of their family life.

Every week-end when Archie McKellar went flying he flew over the house and waggled the wings of his aircraft in greeting to his mother. He dived so low that more than once it seemed that he would strike the chimneys. "I'll have those chimney pots off yet, mother," he used to say jokingly when he got home.

So far as I can gather, his entry into the City of Glasgow Squadron No. 602 was due to the presence of the Duke of Hamilton at a meeting held by the Scottish Flying Club. Apparently the Duke of Hamilton, who was the Commanding Officer of 602 Squadron, was impressed with the skill and verve of Archie McKellar, who was granted a commission as Pilot Officer in 1936. He won promotion to Flying Officer in 1938 and was at once called up for active service when war broke out.

He proved himself after his course of training to be a superb pilot who could fly the Hurricane and Spitfire with equal confidence and zest. "A Spitfire's just like a soft-mouthed, high-spirited thoroughbred, Dad!" he once told his father.

His hour of glorious life lasted from September 3, 1939, until

November 1, 1940, and he enjoyed every moment of it. His father wrote of him: "He had a happy and cheery word for everybody, rich or poor, young or old, he loved them all and they all loved him." My experience confirms it, for I have never heard anyone spoken of with such deep affection as Archie McKellar by his friends and fellow officers in the Royal Air Force. He was a little man, about 5 feet 3 inches tall, but he possessed a great heart and unflinching courage.

The Scots have a reputation for being dour and taciturn and impassive. But Archie McKellar was the reverse of this. He was demonstrative and voluble. "He would keep up a running commentary over the radio-telephone for miles from the time we first sighted the enemy until we made contact," Wing Commander Churchill once remarked. As for his kindness, Squadron Leader Robert Findlay Boyd, D.F.C. and Bar, who was with him in 602 Squadron, said: "He would share his last ten-shilling note with you."

He radiated cheerfulness, swept away depression. To be with him was as stimulating as a glass of champagne. His popularity was proved by the fact that everyone called him Archie. He had the happy knack of making friends. When the other apprentices in his early days took advantage of his small size, he promptly learned to box so that he could take care of himself.

Always he was immaculate. He looked after his body as carefully as an athlete and kept himself in the pink of condition. No matter what happened, he shaved and groomed himself every morning, even during the Battle of Britain when many a fighter pilot in other squadrons went unshaved for two or three days. He insisted on his squadron following his example. "If I have to die, I want to die clean," he remarked to his colleague, Squadron Leader C. F. Currant, D.F.C.

He was a connoisseur of good food and good wine who smoked a pipe and enjoyed a good cigar. "You can tell Uncle Archie that I shall be looking for that box of cigars," he wrote to his mother in a letter describing how he shot down three of the enemy in a raid on Newcastle. "Dearest Little Mother, I am very well and very pleased with myself. On Thursday at 12 o'clock I was sent off with my flight to patrol Newcastle at 20,000 feet. We all arrived safely and remained there until 1.30, when I saw seventy to eighty Nasties in one big formation followed by a second formation of twenty to thirty. They were approaching Newcastle from the south. I whipped into them with my flight. I got three down, with one possible, and the rest of the boys got five down with seven possible—possible being when the Hun breaks away from the formation with engines out or flames coming, but is not seen to crash. By this time there was a lot more fighters, so everyone gave the Nasties the fright of their lives. I was very proud. The Air Vice-Marshal came along and congratulated the Flight on their good show. It really was, as the majority were all new and inexperienced. Two of the boys were shot down, but without damage to one, and only scalp and head wounds to the other, so I reckon it was pretty good going. Unfortunately I caught my little gold bracelet on one of the clips of my aircraft during the show and broke it and it is lost, so if Dad is feeling pleased about this news I would like another one, please! ! ! All my love, Sonnie.''

He scored his initial success when he helped to destroy the first enemy to be brought down off the British coast, during a raid on Rosyth of which he wrote: ''Spitfires full out, 300 m.p.h., 350, 380, 400 and there was the enemy. I picked mine and attacked. I saw him lurch, a flame from his engine which went out, and then I saw his tracer bullets coming back at me and I broke away like mad. By this time George who had lost his in clouds joined me and we started to beat him up together. The Hun trying to dodge into the clouds all the time, but one of us always headed him off. At last the poor devil crashed into the water. As there was a destroyer near, I circled round them for a little. The pilot was saved, but all the other three had been shot dead.''

His sense of humour peeps out at the end of the letter. ''P.S. There is a lovely line in to-day's *Scottish Express* about a sheep farmer and a plasterer shooting down a Hun.''

Many a time he went up to practise dog fighting with Wing Commander Douglas Farquhar, who exercised a good deal of tact in persuading Archie not to transfer to another squadron where the prospects of fighting seemed rosier. Those early months of enforced idleness when he was so anxious to get at the enemy were as irksome to Archie McKellar as to other fighter pilots. Fortunately he took the advice of Wing Commander Farquhar, who wrote: ''I am glad I was successful and that as a result of staying in 602 he was the first fighter pilot to fire at an enemy machine, took part in the destruction of the first enemy raiding bomber and led the attack on the first enemy bomber to be brought down on land—a magnificent record. He did an enormous amount of flying and his successes were due to careful preparation and thought.''

The way he transferred to Squadron No. 605 discloses his agile brain and how swiftly he saw and seized a chance. When Wing Commander W. M. Churchill, D.S.O., D.F.C., went to Drem to re-form No. 605 Squadron, he was rather gloomy at leaving his old squadron. Preoccupied by the task in hand, he strolled for the first time into the mess where he was promptly approached by a sprightly little man with a twinkle in his eye and every brown hair of his head most immaculately brushed into place. ''I'm sorry to hear that my services will not be required as your squadron leader,'' the smiling Scot remarked in the friendliest manner. ''I understand you are waiting for another member of your old squadron. It was just the job I wanted.''

A telephone call to the Air Officer Commanding, and Archie McKellar had got the job and started his friendship with Wing Commander Churchill as well as with another keen pilot, Gerry Edge. "From that day on began the most charming triangular friendship I have ever known," the Wing Commander wrote. "I used to think that I was a good Flight Commander, but those two boys were marvellous. They used to conspire together to think up new ideas for the squadron and to make things easy for me."

Notwithstanding that Archie McKellar was highly-strung, he had wonderful self-control. Always he was thinking of the squadron, how to improve them and weld them into a finer team. In the end he achieved such a high degree of understanding that he had only to give a flick of his wings and the boys knew at once what he wanted and would automatically take up position.

One extraordinary thing which he did at Drem was considered by the technical experts to be impossible. "He put a permanent wave into the wings of a Spitfire," is the way Wing Commander Churchill described it.

Diving upside down out of a cloud at terrific speed and finding he could not get out of the dive in the normal manner, he managed to roll over out of the dive, placing such a strain on the aircraft that he actually bent the wings. The case was so remarkable that they had the test pilot up specially to examine it and see what the pilot had done.

For a small man, the fighter pilot had a loud voice, and when he grew very excited his Glasgow accent became so broad that many of his English friends found it difficult to understand him. He was very loyal, very truthful, and had intense likes and dislikes—there was no middle course for him. He was intuitive to a degree and had a pretty sense of humour. He sensed if anyone was a bit depressed and would do his best to cheer them. "Let's go to Edinburgh for a dinner," he would remark.

After one such party which he arranged for two of his superior officers, they found the police had let the air out of their motor tyres. The senior officer, who prided himself on his fitness, got out the pump. Archie, who had no intention of doing the work, at once volunteered as the officer started pumping. "Oh, sir, do let me help," he kept saying politely, while his senior went on pumping to show how fit he was. The sight of the senior exerting himself to blow up the tyres while the fighter pilot looked on has raised many a chuckle since.

There was one bombing raid which sent Squadron Leader Currant and three of his colleagues dropping to the floor to gain what protection they could from flying glass by pulling tub chairs over their backs. There they crouched, like dogs in kennels, while bombs exploded and shook the place. During a temporary lull the door suddenly opened and they looked up to observe the ashen face of a sergeant with a mop of red hair staring at them as though he could hardly believe his eyes. They looked at him, then at each other as they crouched on their hands and knees with the chairs over their backs and even the exploding bombs failed to stop their roars of laughter. Never had they seen anything so ridiculous as the figures they cut at that moment.

Once Archie McKellar received a bottle of very special whisky from Edinburgh, which led him to expatiate upon it and promise his friend Bunny Currant the finest drop of whisky he had ever tasted in his life. That evening the whisky was brought out and his friends beamed in anticipation as they took their tumblers and raised them to their lips.

"It's grand stuff!" said Archie, helping himself.

"Jolly good," said Squadron Leader Currant, looking curiously at a companion.

"Very!" agreed that gentleman with the utmost courtesy.

Then Archie took his drink and exploded.

Someone had purloined three-quarters of the whisky and filled the bottle with water.

He had a kind word for all ranks and would stick up for anything which he thought right. "You've no business to tick off my flight sergeant like that," he once said to Wing Commander Churchill after the latter had given the flight sergeant an admonishment which Archie considered was undeserved.

Strangely enough, although he was fond of shooting and had a lovely sporting gun, he generally missed his birds. Yet when it came to shooting down Huns he was deadly. In this respect he was rather like Squadron Leader Currant who won the D.F.C. and Bar for shooting down so many Huns, yet when he went up for a practice shoot at the drogue towed by another aircraft he seldom hit it. More than once he was made to feel an awful fool by a pupil who had riddled the drogue with bullets while he himself was shooting into the blue, yet he had no difficulty in hitting the Germans when he was after them.

Keen as were the other pilots in the squadron, Archie McKellar was sometimes a little too keen for them, especially when they had been patrolling at 28,000 feet and were frozen stiff and anxious to get down. He always wanted to stay up a little longer in the hope of catching the enemy.

"Come on, pancake!" the Controller would remark over the radio-telephone.

"Can't we stay up another ten minutes?" Archie would inquire, and generally got his way.

The sight of the blazing docks on the Thames, when the enemy managed to set an oil tank alight by day to serve as a beacon for them at night, filled him with fury. "We must do something about it," he insisted. Every night he would volunteer to go up. Once he went up without any lights at all and landed safely. But in the end he got his enemy at night. He had been flying around for an hour when he heard the voice of the Controller calling to him to land.

"I've got to get a Hun to-night. I'll give you a bottle of champagne if you put me on to one," he replied.

"All right," came the voice of the Controller. "I'll give you a vector."

The Controller duly gave the Scot a vector, otherwise the course which he hoped would bring him into touch with an enemy. "There's a Hun caught by the searchlights over there," he remarked.

"Fine! I'll go over," replied Archie.

He went and got his Hun.

The Controller got his bottle of champagne.

This phenomenal little fighter pilot shot down for certain twenty enemy aircraft, besides several others that were probably destroyed. During the great air battles over London in September, 1940, he shot down a German a day for eight days in succession. His most extraordinary feat, however, was the destruction of three Heinkel 111s— "great, fat, lazy bombers," as he used to call them—in one long burst.

It was on September 9, 1940, that Wing Commander Churchill led his squadron of fighters into the air from Croydon at 9.30 in the morning to come to grips with the enemy once more. It was a beautiful day, with some cloud at 4,000 feet and a clear sky above. Heading south, the Hurricanes climbed steadily to intercept at 20,000 feet.

They had reached 15,000 feet when the voice of Archie McKellar came to his leader over the radio-telephone. "Enemy ahead, sir," shouted the Scotsman as he caught sight of a cloud of thirty Heinkel 111s with an escort of fifty Messerschmitt 109s about 4,000 feet above them and twenty Messerschmitt 110s to guard the flank.

At that distance Wing Commander Churchill could see no more than six Messerschmitt 109s and at once went in to draw them off with his section in order to give the other fighters a chance to get at the bombers which Archie McKellar told him were present. Directly he had drawn off the first batch of Messerschmitts and seen them go flashing past, he saw six more and as he was forcing them away a bullet grazed his leg and sent him spinning down out of the formation.

By the time he recovered, he had lost the bombers and his squadron, but he headed after them all out on the course they were following. To his amazement, he soon observed the Heinkels still flying in the same direction as though unaware of the British fighters who were stalking them.

As he flew to overtake them, he saw Archie McKellar's section of three turn up sun and swing round to the attack. At that very moment the Heinkels turned into the sun straight toward the Hurricanes which were concealed by the glare. The Germans were, in the parlance of the fighters, "a piece of cake." No deflection was necessary at all. Archie McKellar, seeing the leading Heinkel in front of him, just pressed the button on his control column and squirted at it, and Wing Commander Churchill watched it blow up in the air and knock the wing off the port Heinkel, which immediately went down just as the starboard Heinkel turned straight into Archie McKellar's stream of bullets and got what was known in the service as a "gutser." Black smoke began to pour from the engines, the nose of the bomber reared up for a moment, then the third Heinkel went down on its back.

"It was a most marvellous show," said the commander, who saw it as though he had been sitting in the front seat of the stalls. When he got back to base, he found his pilots at the dispersal point chattering like a lot of magpies, with Archie McKellar, who had knocked down a Messerschmitt 109 on the way home, telling them all about it. To destroy four enemy aircraft in one sortie was indeed a triumph for the fighter pilot, a feat which cost him 1,200 rounds of ammunition. His leader was able to confirm the destruction of the three Heinkels in one burst of fire. But unhappily the triumph was marred by the loss of a friend during the fight, and Archie McKellar never referred to it again.

"I'm sorry I made such a mess of it," said Wing Commander Churchill apologetically.

"Your sight is no good. You are too old—you're an old man!" exclaimed Archie McKellar—which must have been rather a shock for a young man of thirty-two.

"I'm going on flying," the commander replied.

"You'll simply be shot down," was the Scotsman's blunt reply.

"All right. I'll let you lead," was the rejoinder, and the next day and thereafter Archie McKellar led No. 605 Squadron most brilliantly. Keen sight to the fighter is as important as it is to the peregrine falcon. Without it, neither can detect the prey. The fighter risks being shot down and the falcon risks starvation, so defective sight threatens death to both. Archie McKellar knew this and used to lie upon his bed with pads of cotton wool, soaked in a special lotion, over his eyes in order to preserve his sight.

He refused to go on leave, and as the strain mounted during the Battle of Britain he and Squadron Leader Currant began to get on each other's nerves. "You're due for a week's leave, Bunny," said Archie to his friend. The latter protested, but the Scotsman had his way.

So Squadron Leader Currant went on leave and when it was over, on the morning of November 1, 1940, he returned to the station and found Archie shaving in the bathroom.

"Had a good time?" inquired Archie.

"Fine, thanks," was the reply.

"What are you doing?" asked Archie.

"I'm going on patrol."

"You can't go on patrol directly after leave. Wait here and I'll see you when I come back," said the cheery Scotsman.

He went out and never returned. At half-past seven on that morning of November 1st, the day after the Battle of Britain was officially ended, his aircraft was seen to plunge from a high level after an engagement and fly madly on its back three times round a country mansion before it crashed in a flower bed.

To the general public his name was unknown, but in the Royal Air Force he was recognized as one of the finest fighter pilots of them all, a kind and generous man who made friends wherever he went, one whose skill and valour were an inspiration to all who knew him.

Sir Archibald Sinclair, then the Secretary of State for Air, never forgot the vivid personality of Archie McKellar, as he mentioned during his visit to Glasgow when Sir Patrick Dollan, the Lord Provost, welcomed him on January 16, 1941. ''How greatly are the achievements of your gallant, your magnificent 602 Squadron regarded by your comrades in the Royal Air Force! Apart from those officers who remain with the squadron now, all the officers of this splendid squadron are now serving as squadron leaders or wing commanders in the Royal Air Force. It is a glorious record is the record of 602 Squadron. . . . Not long ago I visited a fighter squadron which was taking part during the dark days in the battle of this island. That squadron had lost its leader in an air fight—and they felt the loss. He had been wounded in combat and had been withdrawn from service. I found in his place, taking the air with daring and resolve, proving himself a leader among leaders, a young Scot. His name was McKellar. He had come from the City of Glasgow Squadron to lift up this squadron in its dark hour and to carry it on to fresh victories and achievement by his spirit. It was quite apparent to me that he had the whole squadron with him. He was regarded with the greatest admiration and affection by his officers. I will never forget the impression he made upon me when I saw him.''

Archie McKellar was a true champion of Democracy, a man of the people who died for the people. In thirteen months his outstanding abilities lifted him to the foremost ranks of the fighter pilots of the Royal Air Force and won for him the D.S.O., the D.F.C. and Bar. His straight shooting played its part in defeating the Germans in the Battle of Britain and his influence helped to deal the Nazis the mortal blow that saved Mankind.

CHAPTER XXX

GREAT AIR FIGHTERS

AFTER the Royal Air Force vanquished the Luftwaffe during the Battle of Britain, the pulses of the world were stirred by other fighter pilots like Finucane and Buerling who ascended into the high heavens and won imperishable fame.

When I first saw Paddy Finucane he was resting on crutches against the back of a bus, with his right leg swathed in bandages as a result of that escapade which led him to jump over a wall in the blackout and land in a basement instead of on the level ground as he anticipated. His eye was keen and blue, his nostril was wide and clear-cut and very sensitive, and his jutting jaw had a touch of the indomitable fighting spirit which drove him into the skies to outwit the Germans and shoot them to pieces. At that moment he was tranquil, but it was obvious how his blue eyes would light up and his sensitive nostrils quiver when he was bent on the chase.

In rather more than a year he rose from the rank of pilot officer to that of wing commander and from being quite unknown his name was news wherever English was spoken or read. Paddy Finucane was as Irish as his name, and if ever an Irishman spoiled for a fight it was he. But there was nothing reckless about him. He was cold, calculating, with swift nervous reactions, and eyes and fingers so attuned that from his first sortie till his last tragic plunge into the English Channel, no German ever got the better of him in combat.

Wing Commander Brendan Finucane, D.S.O., D.F.C. and Double Bar, was born in Dublin on October 16, 1920, and started his working life entering figures in a ledger. His father, who was not well-endowed with this world's goods, had to work hard to keep and educate his family of five, of whom Paddy was the eldest. For a time Paddy was an office boy, but at the age of 17, directly he was old enough, he joined the R.A.F. So in May, 1938, he began to drill and study and absorb the Royal Air Force discipline and training, and in June, 1940, after the miracle of Dunkirk, Pilot Officer Finucane began to fly a Spitfire on operations with the famous East India squadron whose Spitfires were paid for by the people of the East Indies. Quietly, unobstrusively, he began to knock down enemy aircraft until he had five to his credit. He took himself seriously, was a devout Roman Catholic, and to him air fighting was an absorbing art on which he concentrated all his intelligence. Slowly his score was built up. Day after day he swung into his Spitfire which was painted with a green shamrock and his initials B.F. in the centre, while his rigger and fitter stood by proudly to see him roar away in the aircraft which they kept as fighting fit as Paddy Finucane kept himself. His favourite attack was to come up on the tail of his enemy and shoot him to bits. Many a time he watched the enemy aircraft slide into position in the flickering electric ring on his reflector sight. Then he would press the button on his control column while the speed of his Spitfire would be retarded by forty miles an hour as the stream of bullets sped into the enemy's vitals and destroyed him.

Leading an Australian squadron as his twenty-first birthday approached in October, 1941, he was anxious to bring down his twenty-first German by the time he came of age. He achieved his ambition the day before his birthday, when it was also announced that he had been awarded the D.S.O.

Now and again he destroyed two Germans during a sortie, but he remained as modest as ever. He was not only a brilliant fighter pilot, but an exceptional leader whose spirit permeated the squadron. His fighters would have followed him anywhere and he was unselfish enough to see that they got their share of the shooting and that they did not act as so many beaters to drive the Germans into his guns. Sometimes he led his squadron on sweeps over France, at others he went roving miles high with a companion to look for any Germans that were snooping about. There was a day when he swooped down to pump cannon shells into a steamer stealing along the French coast. With a thunderous roar it blew up and in seconds only a black cloud of smoke and a white patch of foam remained.

Another day he was hunting with a companion among the clouds at 20,000 feet when a breath of wind blew the clouds away and he saw they were right in the middle of about twenty Messerschmitts. Much as he loved a fight, he recognised in a glance when it was prudent to go and play elsewhere. This was it. The odds were ten to one, and the enemy could pounce out of the sun which was blinding the Irish pilot. "Come on," he called to his companion, and they went down in a screeching dive for a couple of miles and dropped right through another forty Messerschmitts which they fired at as they passed. Down below they saw two more Messerschmitts giving a lonely Spitfire rather a bad time and Paddy picked off one and watched it drop into the Channel while his companion disposed of the other.

Speeding along just above the surface, the Irish pilot noticed a stream of cannon shells hitting the water, and knew instantly that a Messerschmitt had dropped down out of the bunch above and was coming up on his tail. Carefully noting where the shells were striking and thereby judging the position of the enemy, he made a sudden turn. It was timed to perfection. The Messerschmitt, seeking to follow him, shot ahead and Finucane whipped in behind, put in a burst, and flew home to chalk up two more victories.

His vision was so keen that he could see the enemy while they still remained invisible to the rest of his squadron, and his mental and muscular reactions were so closely correlated that he appeared to think and act simultaneously. That was what made him deadly in the air.

His first Spitfire was very asthmatic, so he dubbed her Wheezy Anna. Sometimes she wheezed her way home with her skin marred by a bullet hole or two, but his rigger Firth and his fitter Moore soon made her presentable again.

From the middle of June, 1940, until February, 1942, he roved the skies fighting battle after battle without receiving a scratch. It was a tribute to the quickness of his brain, eye and hand. Then on February 20, 1942, came the first check in his career. Flying in company with an Australian, Pilot Officer Richard Lewis, he led him down to attack a ship near Dunkirk. Immediately afterwards they saw two Focke-Wulf 190s on which they made a head-on attack. Finucane, feeling something hit him in the leg and thigh, pulled out of the fight.

"Return to base," he ordered his companion.

But Lewis, seeing that Finucane was hit, mounted guard under his leader's tail.

The Focke-Wulfs, knowing they had winged one of the Spitfires, attacked again and again in an attempt to finish him. But Lewis fought them off. Half a dozen times the Focke-Wulfs came in to kill, and twice the wounded fighter pilot turned at bay to help his companion. During these fierce counter-attacks one of the Germans was shot into the sea, but it was impossible to tell who made the kill.

Then the English coast appeared, and those at the base watched Finucane make a perfect landing. They saw the Spitfire with its green shamrock taxi up to the dispersal point as though nothing were amiss; but when the ambulance drew nigh and the rigger and fitter went to the aircraft they found Paddy had lost consciousness.

Fortunately his wounds were not serious. Within three weeks he was in the air again, and on March 13, 1942, he exacted vengeance by shooting down two Focke-Wulfs during a sweep over France. By ones and twos his score mounted until on May 17, 1942, he brought his total of confirmed victories up to thirty-two.

As a fighter pilot he was peerless. Not once was he shot down, not once did he have to bale out, and only once was he wounded. It was strange that this brilliant pilot whom the Germans could not vanquish in the air should fall to a haphazard shot from the ground. Yet so it was.

Leading a big fighter sweep over France on July 17, 1942, he sped along at ground level over the beach when two Germans, who had set up a machine gun on a ridge of sand, fired straight at him. Pilot Officer F. A. Aikman saw the bullets strike the wing and radiator of Finucane's Spitfire.

"You've had it in the radiator, Sir," Aikman warned him over the radio-telephone.

"I shall have to get out of this. Hello! Wing Commander calling. I have had it. Am turning out," Finucane called back.

Pilot Officer Aikman, flying close, saw him open the hood and take off his helmet, after which he fumbled about in the cockpit to prepare his parachute. But he was far too low to jump and had not enough power to climb.

"I'm going to climb to fix your position," called Aikman to the Irishman.

At that time he was about ten miles from the French coast and flying only ten feet above the water.

Then to the Station Commander at base and to Pilot Officer Aikman came Finucane's last words. He was perfectly calm. "This is it, chaps!" he called.

Aikman saw the tail of Finucane's Spitfire touch the water in a shower of spray.

"At about 5,000 feet I circled round watching the spot where he went in. But he did not come up. All I saw was a streak of oil floating to the top of the water," said Aikman, in reporting the tragic end of one of the finest fighter pilots who ever wore the Air Force blue.

Many a pilot has pancaked upon the sea in a Spitfire and had time to get out before his aircraft sank. By the irony of fate, Finucane plunged straight down into the sea and was seen no more.

His death was a blow to Fighter Command, and the whole world poured money into a fund to build the wing of a hospital as a permanent memorial to the fearless young Irishman who gladly gave his life to uphold his Faith and the human decencies.

If Flight Lieutenant J. H. Lacey loomed less in the public eye, he also was in the first flight of fighter pilots, the very stuff of which heroes are made. Wetherby, in Yorkshire, where he was born in 1917 might well be proud of him, but the pride of Yorkshire could not exceed the pride which the fighter pilots of the City of Gloucester Squadron had in this modest pilot who excelled them all.

Lacey started work washing medicine bottles in a chemist's shop and busied himself in helping the chemist to dispense the various prescriptions that were handed over the counter. But he never qualified as a dispenser, and at the age of twenty enlisted in the Royal Air Force Volunteer Reserve. That was in 1937, and by the time war broke out he was a well-trained pilot.

His name was blazoned for the first time when the Germans bombed Buckingham Palace on September 13, 1940, for it was he who dived after the Heinkel and shot it down over Kent before he was compelled to bale out of his own damaged aircraft.

That spectacular piece of work brought from Australia the gift of a silk parachute that was the first parachute made in Australia to be received in Great Britain. And with it came a silk scarf signed by a hundred girls and men who worked in the factory that made and sent the gift. By the time the parachute arrived he had been forced to bale out nine times, so he knew the value of the present.

His name was seldom seen after the swift vengeance he took on the

German who bombed Buckingham Palace, but Fighter Command took a growing interest in the red-haired pilot who attacked so cleverly that the toll of his victims mounted steadily. Early in 1941 he received his commission as a flight lieutenant, and was soon leading the squadron in which he had flown for nearly two years as a sergeant pilot; and by the time he left his old squadron to instil into the pilots of the future the great art of shooting down the enemy on the wing he was officially credited with the destruction of twenty-three aircraft.

Nine times his German antagonists disabled his aircraft and forced him to bale out; nine times a silk parachute saved his life. He had barely finished his spell of teaching and returned to active operations when his former good luck deserted him and he fell a victim to the Germans over whom he had so often triumphed. But the fighting tactics and courage of Ginger Lacy will never cease to inspire the City of Gloucester Fighter Squadron.

Another brilliant fighter pilot, who won his commission in November, 1941, after winning the D.F.M. and two Bars, was Squadron Leader Don Kingaby. The son of the Rev. P. F. Kingaby, of Devizes, Don Kingaby was so keen on flying that he joined the Royal Air Force Volunteer Reserve as a pilot in April, 1939, and when war was declared he gladly discarded the dull routine of an insurance office to seize the chance of coming to grips with the Germans in the air. Many an enemy rued the day when the insurance official, by sheer skill and concentration, transformed himself into one of the deadliest fighters in the Royal Air Force, and by March 3, 1943, when he was awarded the D.S.O., he had flown on 300 sorties and was officially credited with having destroyed twenty-one enemy aircraft, apart from half a dozen probables and seven damaged.

On the day that Paddy Finucane shot down his last enemy Don Kingaby ran headlong into trouble. "I'm in a jam!" he called over the radio-telephone, as the enemy assailed him. But he managed to extricate himself all right. "I dodged all over northern France and through every cloud to get away," he remarked after he taxied in at base.

After that Don Kingaby, whose uncanny sense of air fighting was developed by long experience, led his squadron in many a fierce air battle and gave his fighters the chance of proving to the enemy that they could shoot as straight as their leader.

Whenever photography was mentioned in the messes of the Royal Air Force the name of Squadron Leader Adrian Warburton was bound to crop up. Time and again, when any special photographs were wanted, Warburton was selected to get them. The task called for coolness and nerve of the highest order, for he flew off alone into the heart of the enemy country, relying solely on his speed and skill as a pilot to save him and bring him back safely. Not for him the thrill of the fighter seeking his enemy in the air. His sole object was to go to his destination and obtain pictures. His flair for the work was un-matched. Nothing deterred him. Often he dived through a hell of fire down to ground level and set his camera clicking. He performed some brilliant feats, particularly when he went to photograph the result of the raid made by the Fleet Air Arm torpedo bombers on the Italian battleships and cruisers in Taranto Harbour, and swooped over the ships at a height of no more than fifty feet with enemy guns blazing all round him.

"This officer has never failed to obtain photographs from a very low altitude, regardless of enemy opposition. His work has been most valuable, and he has displayed great skill and tenacity," was the official tribute paid to him in the citation announcing the award of the D.S.O. to him on March 20, 1942. At that time he already held the D.F.C. and Bar for his fine work.

His experiences were legion, and few men in the Royal Air Force can have had more numerous escapes. Born in Middlesbrough in 1918, he dwelt awhile among the spires of Oxford to receive his education at St. Edward's School, whose class rooms echoed to the voices of those other famous pilots, Wing Commander Louis Strange and Wing Commander Douglas Bader. Warburton's first patriotic gesture was to join the Territorials in 1937 as a private in the Royal Tank Corps, but the appeal of the Royal Air Force proved stronger than that of the tanks, and by January, 1939, he was commissioned as a pilot officer.

He specialized in obtaining photographs, in which work he became an acknowledged master. The feelings of the men who studied the photographs in order to assess the air-raid damage done to the Germans can be imagined when they heard in the middle of November, 1942, that Warburton was missing.

It was on Sunday, November 15, 1942, that he left his base at Malta to note anything of interest in North Africa. For a time bad weather rather hampered him, but later the cloud began to break up and gave him a chance of observing what was below. Those breaks also enabled a covey of Messerschmitts to catch sight of him, and before he knew it eight or nine Germans were after his blood. Their shooting was good, for the bullets riddled the hood above his head and made a pattern on the body of his aircraft. Giving the aircraft full boost, he dodged away as hard as he could go. "There seemed to be no future in that sort of situation, so I flew as fast as I could in a very startled aircraft," he said in recounting his adventure some days later.

The cloud cover and his usual superb skill enabled him to escape the Messerschmitts, but not before they had punctured his oil tank. Looking at his instrument board, he saw the engine temperature mounting. How long the engine would run without oil was quite problematical. The one thing to do was to get down quickly. Here was the snag. The American and British troops were just finding their feet in North Africa, and an odd aircraft dropping out of the skies was

likely to be shot to bits. Warburton was not blind to the risks, nor
was he unaware that his engine must already be running on red-hot
bearings. Looking for a landing ground, he saw the aerodrome at
Bone, and in a minute or two touched down without anyone firing
at him.

He ran over his aircraft to see what was wrong, and soon saw there
was no chance of repairing it at Bone. However, a kindly French
admiral, who was about to fly to a conference at Algiers, offered him
a lift.

"Thank you," said Warburton, who duly landed in Algiers. Here
the little god of luck smiled on him once again in the shape of a pilot
who was about to fly a bomber over to Gibraltar. In due course
Warburton entered the bomber and climbed out again on the Rock.

They were, as may be expected, rather strict in Gibraltar, and any
unauthorized person who landed there, whether in Air Force blue or
any other uniform, was regarded with suspicion. The consequence was
that the authorities were rather sceptical about Warburton. Nobody
had told them that he was coming, and it was unwise to drop in without
giving some official intimation beforehand.

Warburton told them frankly who he was, and the polite authorities,
for all their urbanity, were obviously a little dubious. Had Warburton
suggested that they disbelieved him, they would have protested strongly,
but they nevertheless insisted on finding some official who could vouch
for him. So a few messages passed. After a time things were smoothed
out and the authorities realized that Warburton had dropped in as
casually at the Rock as he had dropped in at Taranto.

Using much discretion and any amount of tact, he managed to
wheedle an aircraft out of them in which he could fly back to Malta,
and was not sorry when he headed across the straits for North Africa
in order to make his way home. Landing twice to refuel, he was
flying along the North African coast near the spot where he ran into
trouble a week earlier, when he saw a Junkers 88 whose pilot was
apparently flying in a daydream, for he took no notice of Warburton.
Warburton promptly proved that he could shoot as straight with a
gun as with a camera. Sneaking up on its tail, he set its port engine on
fire before cutting the wing away with his machine guns. It fell blazing
into the sea.

Only his lack of ammunition saved another Junkers, which was
stealing in and out of the clouds, and as it vanished he resumed his
course for Malta.

"Sorry I'm late," he said apologetically when he landed.

His great humanity and courage were never more clearly displayed
than in October, 1942, when he came across the crew of a British
aircraft drifting in their dinghy in the Mediterranean. Warburton,
flying over them, knew they had no chance of being rescued by the
British. But he was determined to save their lives, so he reconnoitred

until he located an Italian destroyer, around which he flew to attract her attention. He knew that his action would expose him to the risk of being shot down; but he knew equally well that if he did not take the risk the British airmen drifting in the rubber dinghy would perish.

As he expected, the gunners in the destroyer, seeing the markings on his wings, instantly opened fire to drive him away. But he would not go. Then one or two Italian aircraft appeared on the scene and did their best to destroy him. The task he had in hand prevented him from shooting back, so he evaded them and flew in the direction of the dinghy and then back again, and by his clever tactics gradually led the Italian destroyer towards the drifting men, who were at length sighted. With the aircraft attacking him, and the destroyer trying to shoot him out of the skies, he persisted in flying round the position until he saw the destroyer pick up the British air crew—a selfless action which won him a second Bar to his D.F.C.—and not till then did he turn for Malta. He was lost over Lake Constance in April, 1944, and the King personally handed his decorations to his widow, Mrs. Eileen Warburton, at Buckingham Palace on February 12, 1946.

Invincible Malta saw the rise to fame of one of the greatest fighter pilots of this war, Pilot Officer G. F. Buerling, D.S.O., D.F.C., D.F.M. and Bar. Buerling's career was phenomenal. Landing in Malta quite untried and unknown, in four months he won four decorations and a commission for shooting down twenty-eight enemy aircraft. His favourite expression for anything which struck him as odd was "screw-ball." "Those Goddam screwballs didn't know the form," he would say after shooting an Italian or German into the sea. And he used the term so often that he soon became known to his fellow-pilots as "Screwball" Buerling.

Buerling's father was a Swede who, going to Canada at the age of twelve, married an English girl, so Buerling, who was born in Montreal, was half English, half Swedish and all Canadian. From the age of ten, when a friendly pilot took him for his first flight, he haunted the local flying field with the determination of becoming a pilot. The boy had flying fever. He was so keen that he worked at odd jobs to save every penny in order to learn to fly. and by the time he was sixteen he used to fly away to a lonely spot to practise stunting on his own. His disappointment was almost unbearable when he passed all the tests for a commercial pilot's certificate and found it could not be granted because of his youth.

Young as he was, he could throw an aircraft about in the air like an old stager; but when he went to join the Royal Canadian Air Force he was rejected on educational grounds. Frustrated at home in Canada, he worked his passage to Glasgow to join the Royal Air Force, only to learn that his birth certificate, which he lacked, was essential. Refusing to be beaten, he worked his way back to Canada and once more back to Glasgow, where he produced the magic certificate which enabled him to join the Royal Air Force within twenty-four hours.

From the time he was accepted by the Royal Air Force he lived for solely one thing—to excel as a fighter pilot. Nothing else mattered. He trained with all his heart and soul, pored over his books, absorbed all the knowledge he could at lectures and devoted every minute of spare time to the subject which obsessed him.

He gained his wings, and it was his good fortune to be taught by that other great fighter pilot, J. H. Lacey, who gave Buerling the fruits of his long experience of air fighting, warned him about the traps the Germans would set and disclosed all the tricks he knew—and Lacey knew a few.

Every waking moment Buerling concentrated on the art of air fighting. He did not drink, he did not smoke, he did not swear; he kept his body in first-class physical condition, and he trained his eyes to see things in a flash. "Everything depends on the eyes," he used to say, as other exceptional fighters have remarked before. His methods of training them were as simple as effective. Locating something small on the ground or the trunk of a tree perhaps a hundred yards or so away, he would look in another direction for a time and then turn quickly and try to locate the little target. He would repeat these exercises again and again until his eyes were trained to pick up things in a glance.

So in June, 1942, he landed in Malta, an unknown fighter pilot, tall and lean, with a shock of corn-coloured hair that was as untidy as the clothes he wore. He was quite unconcerned about his personal appearance. The sleeves of his tunic were too long, but that did not worry him; if he forgot to comb his long hair he made up for it sometimes by running his fingers through it while discussing fighting tactics. "Ginger Lacey told me this," or "Ginger Lacey told me that," he would say, during his discussions with the other sergeant pilots. Lacey's influence on Buerling was profound, and the lessons of this master-fighter sank right home in the mind of the keen young Canadian.

Buerling is one more shining example of a young man who knew what he wanted and was prepared to work for it to the exclusion of all other things. Luck played no part in his triumphs. He was no daredevil who rushed in and took unnecessary risks. When he was after the enemy he remained as cool as a chess player thinking out the moves to defeat his opponent. Everything he did was worked out scientifically. It was no accident that he shot down twenty-eight enemies in four months. He lost no opportunity of studying enemy aircraft, noting where they were armoured and seeking the vulnerable points. He was not content to pump lead at the enemy; he knew the weak spot in each type of aircraft, and he aimed directly at it. A good natural shot, he practised until he became exceptional. He hated to waste ammunition, and never fired a shell or bullet more than was necessary to bring his opponent down.

Not a pilot in Malta could see as quickly as he could. The note of enemy aircraft approaching high up out of sight would come to their ears. Buerling would point with his finger and say: "Look at those goddam screwballs," and count the number of enemy aircraft seconds before anyone else could pick them out at all. His keen eyes, blue as arctic ice, could take in at a glance what was happening in an air battle, and whereas other pilots could tell only what they were doing he could land and give a comprehensive picture of the fight.

He lived for fighting, and was never happy unless he was in the air. Always ready and begging to fly on operations, he was quite depressed if he was given a rest. The Malta pilots will never forget one day when he saw two Macchis approaching the island. Taking off, he went after them. There were two quick bursts, as though a double-barrelled gun were fired, and both the Italians plunged into the sea like dead ducks. Take-off, pursuit, two victories and his return were crowded into twenty minutes.

The other pilots used to watch him planning new attacks, drawing diagram after diagram to work out the best approach. His usual attire was a dirty pair of khaki shorts, an untidy old shirt, and flying boots. Once, after planning a new method of attacking the Junkers 88, he went after one and flew beside it for a time to study it while it was doing 240 miles an hour. Completing his observations, he calmly gave it a short burst and watched it blow up. His detachment and coolness were extraordinary.

He sought neither glory, medals, nor promotion. Indeed, when he was given a commission he drawled: "I don't wanna be an officer. I'd sooner be with the sergeants."

His greatest successes came when hunting with his Flight Commander, Flight Lieutenant Eric Hetherington, D.F.C. "They were magnificent," said their Squadron Leader. "Hetherington was one of the grandest fellows I ever knew. He never said a word about anything they had done, but he and Screwball were unbeatable. Hetherington would just shepherd a Hun into Screwball's sights, and that was the end of the Hun."

"They ought to give the gongs to Hether," Buerling said every time he was awarded a new medal.

His triumphs did not depend solely on his quick eyes and accurate shooting. He was an exceptional pilot, who could always manage to coax a little more speed out of his Spitfire than the rest, and would forge ahead to be first on the mark.

"We would be out in formation and Screwball would report enemy aircraft," his Squadron Leader once remarked. "No one else could see anything, and we would go off chasing purely on Screwball's word. Then after what seemed a long time we would see two black specks. Screwball would shout, 'A couple of 202s!' and then he'd start to leave us behind, as usual, when we were all going flat out."

During one big enemy sweep over Malta he shot down a Messerschmitt 109 before turning to attack a Macchi. After noting his bullets and shells striking the Italian machine, he was forced to turn away, but as he did not see it crash he simply told his Intelligence Officer that he had shot down a Messerschmitt and had damaged a Macchi 202. "I saw strikes in the port wing and the cockpit and the engine," drawled Buerling.

Later a signal came through that a Macchi 202 had fallen on the island of Gozo to the north of Malta, and when it was examined they found that Buerling was only inches out.

Unable to see what happened to it, he would no more have thought of claiming it than a scientist would think of announcing a new discovery that was not fully proved. So they added another to Buerling's triumphs.

On October 13, 1942, he reached the climax of his career by shooting down a Junkers 88 and two Messerschmitt 109s in a single sortie. This triple triumph brought the number of enemy aircraft he had officially destroyed up to 25. The next day the young Canadian whose spectacular air victories over Malta had amazed the world and exacted such stern vengeance from the Luftwaffe and Regia Aeronautica flew head-on to attack a formation of bombers. Calmly he watched his cannon shell shatter a bomber which plunged into the sea. Suddenly he felt a sharp pain in his leg and heel. Almost at the same instant he saw a Messerschmitt making an ugly attack on his Squadron Leader. Completely ignoring his own wound he attacked the Messerschmitt and shot it down, while Squadron Leader M. M. Stephens, D.S.O., D.F.C., took his revenge on Buerling's assailant by shooting him into the sea—in the week ending October 15th this last gallant fighter destroyed five of the enemy and won a Bar to his D.F.C.

Most wounded men after two victories would have pulled out of the fight and gone home. But not Buerling. Putting up the nose of his Spitfire, he climbed to meet another adversary who quickly fell before his blazing guns. By this time Buerling's Spitfire was so badly shot about that it was out of control, so Buerling baled out, and floated safely down to the sea, where he was soon located and picked up. When it was learned that his wounded heel would for the time being put a stop to further flying operations, he was transported from the scene of his triumphs back to Montreal to let him rest and recover.

His rise to fame was amazing. In sixteen weeks he proved himself to be without peer and without fear. Exceptional eyesight, a natural ability to shoot straight, an intense love of flying and the joy of fighting lifted him to the ranks of the great fighter pilots. But the dominating factors were the strength of mind which drove him to devote himself entirely to the scientific study of air fighting and his unshakable determination to excel.

CHAPTER XXXI

MALTA CONVOY

In the summer days of 1942 when Buerling and his gallant companions wrought such havoc among the recurring waves of enemy aircraft, Malta was reduced to a parlous state. Food grew short. Sunken ships blocked the quays. The tireless anti-aircraft gunners, whose fierce barrages made the enemy quail, saw their stocks of shells dwindling. Aircraft losses mounted and reduced the strength of the squadrons. The petrol problem was the worst of all, for without aviation spirit the Malta fighters could not fly and so much was used in meeting the ceaseless attacks that there was a possibility of their being grounded by lack of supplies. This would have laid Malta open to the enemy. So grave was the situation that it became necessary to carry cargoes of petrol to the island by submarine in order to keep the fighters in the air.

The whole world knows of the valour of the men in the Malta convoy who fought their way through to succour the island. The daring of merchant seamen and naval men alike will be remembered long after we are dead, for they saved Malta and won a victory of the first magnitude.

Among those who took part in this victory was Lieutenant Richard John Cork, D.S.O., D.S.C., a fighter pilot of the Fleet Air Arm attached to one of the aircraft carriers, who was born in London on April 4, 1917. No more reticent or modest man ever entered the Navy. Passing through the Royal Naval College at Greenwich, he gained his wings as a pilot, after due training, on January 20, 1940; but his high hopes of fighting the Germans in Norway were frustrated by the evacuation of the British troops. A week or two later came the disaster and miracle of Dunkirk which left Great Britain so vulnerable that Mr. Churchill was constrained to offer the Royal Air Force the help of all the naval pilots who would volunteer. The heavy air losses in France coupled with the impending attack on England by Goering's Luftwaffe made the position so desperate that it was essential to scour Great Britain for every pilot who could fight the enemy. Cork and his fellow pilots were eager to serve and this is how in the greatest crisis in British history officers of the Royal Navy came to fly in the Royal Air Force.

As there was no comparison between the Spitfires and Hurricanes and the slow Gladiators of the Fleet Air Arm, it was necessary for Cork to learn to fly the fastest fighters in the world. He went off on June 17, 1940, for an operational course and in ten gruelling days flew a Spitfire for twenty-five hours and tested out its capabilities as well as his own.

By July 1st he was posted to No. 242 Canadian Squadron which was being taken in hand by the dauntless Douglas Bader, whose spirit fired the whole squadron with enthusiasm. Nearly all the pilots were Canadians with a few exceptions, among them Bader and Cork, who

soon became known to his companions as "Corky." Having played
rugger with the Harlequins before he lost his legs, Bader knew the value
of team work and welded his Canadians into one of the finest packs of
fighters in the Royal Air Force.

To the naval officer, who took only twenty-four hours to get used to
the Hurricane, fighting and hunting the Germans was "grand sport."
He revelled in it as much as he revelled in the companionship of Bader.
The spirit of Douglas Bader touched the imagination of the naval officer
and every man in the squadron. They worshipped their leader, and none
will forget the day when the weather was so foul that he grounded them
all because of the risk and then calmly climbed into his Hurricane to fly
off at 300 feet along the East Coast where he came on a Dornier which
he shot into the sea.

Those dangerous days were happy days as well, for despite discom-
forts and dangers and lack of sleep, no pilot in the squadron would have
missed the dawn patrol for anything, because it was the best time to
catch the Germans and knock them down, or chase them away from the
convoys. As Bader used to say, the Huns went like the hammer of hell
as soon as they saw a Hurricane.

It was Lieutenant Cork who followed Bader headlong into that big
formation of German bombers from which both miraculously escaped
without injury on September 7, 1940, although their aircraft were so shot
about that they had to be scrapped. In a letter written four days afterwards "in this crazy world of continuous flying and very little sleep,"
Lieutenant Cork etched a scene in the Battle of London which is worth
preserving. "I'm not complaining—don't think that," he wrote. "In
fact I wouldn't miss all this fighting for anything—it really is the greatest
sport. We had grand fun last Saturday—we ran into about 200-250
German bombers and fighters. The squadron got 14—my share of the
bag was one Dornier bomber and a Messerschmitt 110—brings my
total to five. Unfortunately or not, I don't know, I was flying in the
first section with the C.O. and before we knew where we were we found
ourselves in the middle of all this mass. Every way you turned all you
could see were German machines—and was there some lead flying
about the sky! Anyway we stuck together and got out of it without
injury except a few scratches from glass and odd bits of bullets, but you
should have seen our machines—absolutely full of holes and they
couldn't even make one whole aircraft out of what was left."

Spending their lives in the shadow of their Hurricanes with the drone
of death above them, Bader and his Canadians nevertheless managed to
get many a laugh out of life and one of the loudest was when Mrs. Bader
sewed his first ribbon upside down on Lieutenant Cork's tunic.
"Nobody thought it was possible," said Mrs. Bader later. "But I
did it."

Another amusing incident occurred when Lieutenant Cork long
afterwards went down to a fighter station while on leave to visit his
friend Douglas Bader who was in charge. "Come with me on patrol,"

said Bader. "I'll lend you a Spitfire." The naval pilot needed no second invitation. Flying across the Channel and over the French coast in search of Messerschmitts, they passed over the golf course at St. Omer. Bader looked down. A moment later his voice came over the radio-telephone to his companion. "The ninth hole looks rather good, Corky."

It was ridiculous. But such courage and humour inspired all who knew him.

That fierce encounter on September 7, 1940, from which Bader and Cork were fortunate to escape alive, eventually brought Lieutenant Cork the award of the D.S.C.

By the end of 1940 Lieutenant Cork was released from the Royal Air Force and posted back to the Royal Navy as Flight Commander to 880 Squadron of the Fleet Air Arm. From then on he wandered far and wide and took a hand in writing more than one page of history. The end of July, 1941, found him taking off the flight deck of a carrier to patrol while the enemy ships in Petsamo harbour were bombed and torpedoed.

The following month found him in the Mediterranean engaged in flying off from the decks of his carrier a number of Hurricanes to Malta to replace the losses which the Royal Air Force had suffered.

A month or two later Lieutenant Cork joined a new carrier which steamed in many seas before arriving in the Indian Ocean to guard the convoy routes. From her decks the Hurricanes flew in secret to Ceylon, where they completely surprised the Japanese and shattered the air attack which the enemy had planned as a prelude to invasion. Those Hurricanes flown from the deck of the aircraft carrier saved Ceylon.

A few weeks later Lieutenant Cork took part in the operations which prevented Madagascar from falling to the Japanese, and it was on May 5, 1942, that he flew off the deck of the aircraft carrier, which was about forty miles off the island, to lead his flight of Hurricanes to clear the road to Diego Suarez and ground any French fighters while the British bombers attacked the aerodrome hangar and buildings. As the bombs crashed home and the hangar went up in smoke, Lieutenant Cork could not understand why there was no fighter opposition, for fighters were known to be in the island. Going over to have another look at the aerodrome that afternoon, he could hardly believe his eyes when he detected the tail of an aircraft in the burned-out hangar. "It wasn't there this morning," he thought, and dropped down to inspect the inside of the hangar, where he discovered several aircraft and a petrol tanker. The French, thinking the British would pay no more attention to the burned-out hangar, concluded that it was the safest place in which to hide their aircraft and flew them over from another station. But the sharp eyes of the naval officer defeated their ruse. Turning his guns on the petrol tanker, he saw a great gush of flame, which destroyed three Morane fighters.

He and his fellow pilots did useful work in attacking gun positions and units of native troops which gave them a good deal of trouble, for the black machine-gunners faced the aircraft fearlessly and stood their ground stubbornly. One good task the pilots of the Fleet Air Arm accomplished was to dislodge and drive ashore the crew of a sloop whose guns dominated the road to Diego Suarez along which the British troops were compelled to march to capture the place.

But it was in the Mediterranean during the Battle of the Malta Convoy that Lieutenant Cork achieved his great triumph.

Early in August the carrier in which he served started out to keep a most important rendezvous and on August 6th she made contact with the units of the fleet that were covering the approach of the convoy which appeared three days later. Ships covered the ocean to the horizon. Each was in its allotted place, keeping perfect station, and they moved on their unhurried way as though one set of engines and one captain controlled them all.

Taking off in his Hurricane, he saw below him the merchantmen and tankers steaming majestically forward, with destroyers nosing round on the outskirts and one of the great aircraft of Coastal Command patrolling ahead looking for U-boats, while far, far away were smudges of smoke to tell of big ships ready to pounce on any fleet that Hitler or Mussolini dared send to obstruct the passage of the convoy. Though invisible to the merchantmen, the mightiest ships in the Royal Navy were standing by ready to strike.

All that day and the next the convoy steamed through the Mediterranean, disturbed now and again by a submarine alarm and the crash of depth charges, but keeping a steady course. On August 11th the convoy reached the danger zone to meet the full force of the Axis air attack. Every aircraft that the Luftwaffe and the Regia Aeronautica could muster, torpedo carrier, bomber and fighter was let loose to grapple with every British aircraft that could be flown from the decks of the aircraft carriers as well as every gun in that immense concourse of ships. The sky was alive with aircraft. The crash of guns and exploding of bombs was a continuous thunderous roar.

During the morning a Junkers 88, shadowing the British fleet at 20,000 feet, was intercepted by Lieutenant Cork's flight of Hurricanes whose pilots all took part in an exciting hunt. Seeking to escape, the Junkers was headed off by a Hurricane in the direction of Lieutenant Cork, who after a long chase lasting half an hour, got within range. By this time they were down to 200 feet and the convoy was out of sight. There was a sharp duel in which the German gunner hit the wings of the Hurricane and put the starboard ailerons out of action; but Lieutenant Cork had the satisfaction of seeing one of the enemy's engines catch fire and bits fly off the cowling as he broke away, although he did not see it go into the sea.

The gunners sweated at their guns all day; the pilots of the Fleet Air Arm flew until they were dead beat. The attacks of the British fighter pilots and the intense barrage of the naval gunners were too fierce for the German and Italian airmen. Time and again they came in and were forced to jettison their torpedoes and bombs before they could get within range. So effective was the defence that when dusk closed down on the smoke of battle and the powerful naval force drew away from the convoy, not one single merchant ship had been lost, though losses came later.

Next day, August 12th, Lieutenant Cork got up at dawn to attend to his duties. Going to the hangars, he found the fitters and riggers were busy preparing the Hurricanes for the fray. It was not long before the aircraft were up on the flight deck and the pilots were taking off on patrol.

About midday a call was made for the Hurricanes to fight off approaching aircraft and Lieutenant Cork took his flight into the air. The sky was full of Junkers 88 seeking to bomb the merchant ships and Lieutenant Cork led his pilots straight at them with machine-guns blazing. Seeing one Junkers turn away, apparently damaged, he gave it a sharp burst and sent it smoking into the sea, sharing it with the rest of the flight. There were hectic intervals. Later out of the corner of his eye he saw another Junkers 88 stealing off in the direction of Tunis and at once went in pursuit. There was a blue sky with a slight haze, and the Junkers was flying at about a thousand feet when the Hurricane sent its bullets tearing into the vitals of the enemy aircraft. For a moment it seemed to stagger in the air, then it dropped into the sea with a big splash. Forty-five minutes after taking off, Cork landed on the carrier with two victories to his credit.

At once the task of refuelling was carried out and an hour later he flew off with his flight on the second patrol, a little after 1 o'clock. They had not climbed very high when they sighted the enemy. Wave after wave of torpedo bombers came flying over the sea to try to launch their torpedoes. They were about fifty feet above the surface, going all out, when the four Hurricanes led by Lieutenant Cork dived to attack. Had the torpedo bombers been flying higher, the Hurricanes would have had a chance to manoeuvre and shoot them down. But they kept so low that any attempt to dive underneath them would have sent the Hurricanes into the sea, consequently the enemy managed to evade the attacks.

When the British fleet opened fire on the swerving enemy aircraft, the British fighter pilots liked it no more than the enemy. The Hurricanes were pulling out of range when a flock of Messerschmitt 110s in Vic formation dropped on them out of the sun. There followed a terrific dog fight not more than a hundred feet above the surface. The odds were three to one against the Englishmen, while the Messerschmitts were also speedier than the Hurricanes, for in adapting the latter to fly from carriers some speed had been sacrificed. Cannon shell and bullets started to fly as the antagonists twisted and turned. Cork saw one of his companions go down into the sea before a Messerschmitt and, turning quickly, managed to get the German into his sights. Trailing smoke, the Messerschmitt climbed to a thousand feet, when the pilot baled out and the aircraft crashed into the sea beside Cork's carrier, whose officers and men cheered as though a goal had been scored at a cup tie.

The fleet was not disposed to stand idly by and see the Messerschmitts worry their Hurricanes. Over the radio-telephone Cork and his fellow pilots received the blunt order to push off before the guns opened fire. The naval pilots at once pulled out and the terrific barrage made the Messerschmitts flee for their lives.

The Hurricanes suffered badly in the fight. One was lost, the pilot of another succeeded in landing his badly damaged aircraft, while the third pilot managed to get back to the carrier after some good work. Of the four which set out on that patrol, only Cork remained airborne.

Flying along, he heard the warning over the radio-telephone that a big formation was approaching. Climbing over the convoy, he counted ten following their usual tactics of flying close to the sea. But one lagged behind. Cork swept in and shot him down near a group of destroyers which all opened fire on the Hurricane at once. Cork did not wait. He sped back to the *Indomitable*.

While the riggers and fitters ran over his Hurricane to see that it was undamaged, he took stock of the position. Only five other Hurricanes in his squadron were airworthy, and shortly after 2 o'clock he led them into the air on their third patrol. Circling over the fleet, he saw a flight of Fulmars being harried by waves of enemy fighters and at once went to the rescue. The sky reminded him of the Battle of London. German and Italian aircraft were everywhere. Formations were driving in from all directions. Dive bombers were aloft at 10,000 feet waiting to dive on their targets. Messerschmitts were swooping all over the place. The torpedo bombers sped in just above the sea, seeking their chance to dodge the naval ships and launch their torpedoes at the cargo ships in the convoy. Italian aircraft dived down to drop bombs about the size of cricket balls, which were dubbed "cricket ball bombs."

Fulmars and Hurricanes dispersed in the ensuing dog fight, and as he drew off Lieutenant Cork saw another wave of torpedo bombers coming in with one courting trouble by trailing after the rest. Diving behind the laggard, Cork pumped bullets into him. The inside of the aircraft began to glow like a red-hot coal, it banked to turn away from the fleet and side-slipped into the sea. Being under continuous gunfire from the guns of the British ships, the naval pilot returned to his carrier until the racket died down.

Young and strong as he was, three patrols in these exacting conditions tired him. But his mental and physical strains were banished by the overwhelming desire to vanquish the enemy. He knew that if they failed to run the convoy through, Malta was doomed. Consequently about 6 o'clock that evening, he climbed into his Hurricane again to make his fourth patrol of the day. The guns of the fleet were firing at sporadic aircraft; now and again a great upheaval of the sea marked the explosion of a depth charge. Through it all the surviving merchantmen steamed steadily for Malta. Smoke rose from some of them. The glow of fires marked several naval craft; the carriers were scarred by bombs; but they were full of fight despite their wounds.

Flying over that gathering of ships on which so much depended, Lieutenant Cork detected in the distance a Savoia trying to steal in to attack. Diving on it unawares, he had the supreme satisfaction of seeing it fall before his gunfire into the sea, one member of the crew jumping out and hitting the water when it was no more than 50 feet up. As he turned away, he saw the crew of the Savoia floating in their rubber dinghy. Bringing his camera-gun to bear, he was striving to take their photograph to confirm that he had shot them down when the sea below him was all churned up by bullets and shells. Four Reggiane 2001s had marked him down as their prey and started to shoot bits off his Hurricane. With ammunition all spent, there was nothing he could do but get away as quickly as possible. Never was he in graver danger. The enemy came at him from every side, Luck and skill alone saved him, for by skimming over the sea he escaped from the Reggiane 2001s, but his aircraft was too badly damaged for him to attempt to reach his own ship, so he signalled to another carrier nearby and landed safely, his engine seizing up while he was just above the deck.

Utterly exhausted, he climbed out of the cockpit. Aircraftmen swarmed round and looked in amazement at the Hurricane. It was riddled all over. The radiator was practically shot away.

"We can't mend that," they said and without more ado dragged the battered aircraft across the flight deck and dumped it into the Mediterranean.

During that nightmare day of fighting, his carrier lost 6 Hurricanes and 2 Martlets, but fortunately four of the pilots were picked up.

He and his fellow pilots of the carrier *Indomitable* made the enemy pay. They destroyed 28 aircraft, they damaged 10; and it is probable that they destroyed 6 others, only they were so busy getting out of trouble themselves that they had no time to see the final plunge.

That night a message was proudly displayed in the ward-room of the *Indomitable* with the words: "Score at Close of Play."

Junkers 88	.	.	.	.	10
Junkers 87	.	.	.	.	3
Savoia 79	.	.	.	.	7
Macchi 202	.	.	.	.	2
Messerschmitt 110	.	.	.	.	1
Reggiane 2001	.	.	.	.	2
Breda	.	.	.	.	2
Cant	.	.	.	.	1
					—
Grand Total	.	.	.	.	28

And six of them were shot down by Lieutenant R. J. Cork—which explains why he put up the ribbon of the D.S.O. as well as that of the D.S.C.

CHAPTER XXXII

FOR VALOUR

OF medium height, slenderly built, with dark eyes and hair, Wing Commander John Dering Nettleton of the Rhodesian Squadron had little to differentiate him from many other officers in the Royal Air Force—except a scrap of ribbon on his tunic to single him out as the winner of the Victoria Cross. Quiet in voice and manner, he was as modest as brave, and it is doubtful if his most intimate friend could have made him talk about Augsburg. Yet in planning the raid and flying his gigantic black Lancaster across France to drop his bombs on Augsburg he and the other gallant pilots shook the German Naval Command as never before, for the bombs fell according to plan exactly on the immense works known as the Maschinenfabrik Augsburg Nurnberg which supplied the Diesel engines for half the U-boats built in Germany.

Born of English parents at Nongoma in Zululand on June 28, 1917, Nettleton was by birth a South African. His career parallels that of the other great South African fighter pilot, Group Captain Malan, for Nettleton also joined the training ship Botha with the intention of going to sea and after some practical experience in the Merchant Service, gave it up, like Malan. For the next three years he followed the profession of a civil engineer, moving about all over the place doing survey work.

At the end of that time he took a month's holiday in England, a holiday which had momentous results, for three days before it ended he suddenly made up his mind to join the Royal Air Force, which he did. He said afterwards that he had not the slightest intention of doing so when he set out for England. From the day he began training he knew what he wanted. Not the slick fighter, but the bomber appealed to him. To sit at the controls of some giant bomber was the height of his ambition. Being intelligent and determined, he did what he set out to do, and in due course graduated until he became the captain of a Hampden bomber. Time after time he flew over Germany in his Hampden, in nights black as pitch or glorified by the moon, in fair nights or foul nights when clouds blanketed everything and made the target difficult to locate, when fierce electric storms played tricks with the Hampden and treated it like a shuttlecock while blue flames licked about the wings and made arcs of fire round the propellers. He ran the gauntlet of searchlights and flak over Berlin and the scars on his Hampden when he touched down at base made him bless his luck. So his natural ability was mellowed by experience.

In July, 1941, he gained his heart's desire and became the captain of the most wonderful bomber in the world, a giant four-engined Lancaster monoplane that could carry eight tons of bombs for 3000 miles at a speed of over 300 miles an hour. The Lancaster, designed by Mr. Roy Chadwick, C.B.E., on the drawing boards of Avro, was an aircraft miracle. With his step up to the Lancaster came a step up in rank to Squadron Leader and the sight of the sleek black monoplane lined up on the grass was a source of quiet pride to him. Great speed, great range and great hitting power were his to use.

So Squadron Leader Nettleton on July 24, 1941, led his squadron into the air to bomb Brest in daylight. The gun defences sought to destroy them, but the Lancasters dropped their bombs well on their targets, and Nettleton touched down at base with a hole eighteen inches square in his tail plane. It made no difference to her handling. Again he took his squadron out in daylight, this time to St. Nazaire, which got a terrific blasting. The German shooting was good, but the speed of the Lancasters saved them, and although something hit Nettleton's aircraft, he flew her home without difficulty.

The Admiralty and Bomber Command were not entirely ignorant of the existence of the Diesel works at Augsburg, but very prudently they said nothing and bided their time until they acquired the weapon with which to strike. Augsburg was near Munich. It was necessary to go in daylight to make sure of finding the works, and that meant a thousand mile flight across enemy occupied country. Four factors were essential to success, surprise, speed, long range and heavy bomb loads, and the Lancaster could supply them all.

On April 13, 1941, Squadron Leader Nettleton was called in to a secret conference at which he learned of the impending raid. No other man who took part in that raid was told a word about it until four days later.

It was a hazardous undertaking. Squadron Leader Nettleton did not delude himself. He accepted the risk, considered all the factors and worked out his plans. On April 15th he led his squadron into the air to do formation flying and carry out exercises. Away the Lancasters went to Selsey Bill, then off to the North of Scotland, carrying out exercises on the way, and eventually they touched down at their station, well pleased with their day's work. Although they did not know it, they had been practising for the raid on Augsburg.

On April 17th at 11 o'clock in the morning pilots and crew gathered in the briefing room and learned for the first time of the task they had been set to do. They laughed and talked and studied their maps and were glad of the great chance of going to Augsburg.

Their time of departure was carefully worked out to bring them to their target at dusk and give them a chance of flying back in the dark to avoid the fighters, for it was patent that if they succeeded in reaching the target unscathed, all the fighters in France would be up waiting to destroy them on the way home. At 3 o'clock that afternoon a dozen pilots sat at the controls of the mighty Lancasters waiting the signal to start. They were divided into two sections of six, the second section being timed to start three minutes after the first. One by one the first section gathered speed along the runway and became airborne, and at

3.10 p.m. Squadron Leader Nettleton set course and led them off. They were heavily laden with petrol and bombs and flew along to the south at no more than 500 feet. Directly they reached the coast, they dropped right down to about 50 feet, which was as close to the sea as they dared to fly.

Looking back, Squadron Leader Nettleton saw that the other five Lancasters in his section were keeping splendid formation. He took them over the French cliffs like horses taking a fence. Hugging the ground as close as possible, they sped on. Soon they tore across an aerodrome. They were travelling so fast and low that Nettleton did not see it. But his front gunner spotted about twenty Germans lined up and saw some fall before his bullets.

As they roared across France, a pack of Messerschmitts 109s and Focke-Wulf 190s looked down and saw the ominous black shapes flashing over the fields. The Germans dived to attack, their guns spitting bullets and cannon shell. The Lancasters fought back desperately, but they offered huge targets to the fighters and stood little chance. One crashed, then another went down. The rear gunner in Nettleton's Lancaster kept the pack off his tail. He blazed away until his guns jammed. He saw a third and fourth Lancaster go down in the fight. Nettleton went flat out, trying all he knew to shake off the attackers, who gradually trailed away, and in about ten minutes he won free. He gave a swift look round and saw that only one Lancaster still followed him.

He stated afterwards that he believes he ran into a pack of German fighters who had been on a patrol and were just about to land when they sighted the Lancasters. It is probably true, for if their petrol tanks had been full, they would surely have continued the chase until they had wiped out the formation.

In the very teeth of disaster his unshakable courage blazed out. His flight had barely started. His target was hundreds of miles distant, yet not for a moment did he think of turning back. He was bent on bombing Augsburg, and so long as he lived and the Lancaster could fly nothing should stand in his way. For an instant the thought of the good companions who had gone down shook him, then he pushed the thought away.

His Lancaster flashed across the fields, over houses and trees, swerving to avoid an occasional church. His whole mind was concentrated on flying the bomber and avoiding the obstructions that seemed to race under the wings. It was a lovely day. There were few people about. France seemed to be dead. Now and again they saw a farmer in the fields wave to them. Those black shapes in the sky were to the farmers below the symbol of *liberte, egalite and fraternite* to come. And miles away lay the wrecks of four black bombers to mark the sacrifice of twenty-four gallant Britons who had fought and died to make that dream come true once more.

Over Lake Constance he flew and sped up river. The aerodrome from which Hess started on his flight to captivity in Scotland loomed up and vanished. Augsburg appeared ahead. It was 8 o'clock in the evening and quite light. The target could not be missed.

The two Lancasters were still a mile away from the town when the guns opened up on them. The shooting was very good, but the British bombers held on. Nettleton flew low over the roofs, swept right across his target and dropped his delayed-action bombs right in the centre of the factory. His companion who followed was badly hit, but still maintained his course until his bombs had crashed down on the Diesel works which gave the U-boats power to wage their deadly campaign. Then, with the Lancaster on fire amidships, the pilot made a crash landing and the crew escaped as the aircraft burned.

The sole survivor of his formation, Nettleton turned for England, with vivid memories of the German children at a school waving to him under the impression that the Lancaster was German, and the farcical scene which ensued when the horses of a lot of German cavalry with horse-drawn guns suddenly bolted in all directions as the thunder of his Lancaster just overhead struck their startled ears.

That raid was cleverly planned and superbly executed. The meeting with the German fighters was a pure mischance, and if the take-off had been set back for another five minutes, the first formation of Lancasters would probably have been as lucky as the second formation, which started three minutes later and did not see a single fighter on the outward or homeward journey. For his courage in going on in the face of his heavy losses, the V.C. was awarded to Nettleton, who lost his life later.

The other Lancasters, led by Squadron Leader J. S. Sherwood, D.F.C., and Flight Lieutenant D. J. Penman, D.F.C., who both won the D.S.O., met terrific flak over the factory, which they largely reduced to ruins. Sherwood, with his controls shot away, came down and was captured. But the other five Lancasters reached England safely.

That devastating long-distance daylight attack won for the following officers the D.F.C.: B. R. W. Hallows, C. S. C. McClure, E. E. Rodley, E. A. Deverill, P. A. Dorehill, G. C. Hooey, E. L. Ifould, D. O. Sands; while the D.F.M. was awarded to the following flight sergeants and sergeants: F. H. Harrison, B. G. Louch, L. H. Mutter, C. F. Churchill, T. H. Goacher, D. N. Huntly, R. P. Irons, K. O. Mackay, D. L. Overton, and J. T. Ratcliffe.

Another factory shattered by a surprise attack in daylight was the Philips Lamp Factory at Eindhoven in Holland, upon which Germany was relying largely for wireless valves and parts. It was an immense works of vast importance to the enemy when Wing Commander Hughie Idwal Edwards, V.C., D.F.C., who became a Group Captain, led the bombers in to smash it on December 6, 1942. The works were previously studied, each pilot was given his target among these modern glass

P—6

and steel buildings which covered many acres. In view of the frailty of lamps and valves and delicate electrical apparatus, the damage must have been enormous. Some of the bombers dived down to the roofs to make sure of dropping their bombs on the right targets, and the enemy fighters they met on the way in and out failed to stop them. The audacious raid brought the D.S.O. to three Wing Commanders, H. I. Edwards, J. E. Pelly-Fry, and R. H. Young, while the following officers were awarded the D.F.C.: R. J. P. Prichard, R. J. N. Maclachlan, J. E. Houlston, E. F. Hart, T. H. J. Cairns, H. H. E. P. Cairns, C. A. Evans, J. M. Rankin; and the D.F.M. was won by G. E. T. Nichols and W. H. C. Leavitt.

If Group Captain Hughie Edwards, V.C., D.S.O., D.F.C., did his best like every other bomber captain to avoid the searchlights, he avoided the limelight still more. He was as elusive as the Scarlet Pimpernel and his innate modesty was such that he was even known to go on leave to avoid meeting anyone connected with the Press. Born in Australia on August 1, 1914, he became a cadet in the Royal Australian Air Force in 1935 and was commissioned as a pilot officer in the Royal Air Force a year later. He flew far and did many fine things after entering the Royal Air Force, and although a nasty flying accident left him with a physical disability, it failed to shake his nerve, as was proved by his decorations.

There was a day in June, 1941, when he led his bombers against a convoy of eight ships whose captains had been foolish enough to anchor off the Hague. While his bombers selected their targets, Hughie Edwards dived down to mast height with machine-guns firing and dropped his bombs right in the centre of a 4,000 ton steamer. There was a tornado of fire from pom-poms and machine-guns, and as Hughie Edwards swung away he saw a big explosion which flung debris high in the air and left a cloud of rising smoke. Thus he won the D.F.C.

At Bremen on Independence Day, July 4, 1941, he crowned his achievements by winning the V.C. So vital was Bremen to the German war effort that its defences were as strong as the Germans could make them. To bomb Bremen at night in the face of its searchlights, guns and night fighters was a hazardous operation—to attempt to bomb it by day was a thousand times more dangerous, yet the U-boat menace made it essential to do everything possible to bomb the Bremen shipyards which built a quarter of Germany's U-boats, and Bomber Command decided that Bremen should be attacked in daylight. To Edwards, who studied the German defences and knew their full weight, fell the task of planning the raid; and to Edwards fell the honour of leading it. If only the weather had been kind and had dropped a blanket of cloud over the port the risks would have been lessened. Instead it was a clear day with not a cloud in the sky to offer any cover. To increase their jeopardy they were sighted on the way over by some German ships which at once reported them. When Wing Commander Edwards saw the ships he knew their hope of surprising Bremen had vanished and that the enemy gunners and fighters would be fully prepared.

Neither odds nor dangers could stop him. All the guns and fighters waiting to destroy them could not deter him.

Crossing the German coast, he led his bombers for fifty miles inland. They raced along close to the ground until they were confronted by the balloon barrage. Dodging between the cables, they roared on. Every gun within range fired at them. To the Blenheim pilots Bremen seemed to be surrounded by a solid wall of flak. But they went through it, lifting over the roofs of houses, swerving round spires until they found their targets and dropped their bombs. One Blenheim after another was hit. Shells and bullets penetrated every Blenheim that flew to bomb Bremen. Four were shot down and those who got back owe their escape largely to the dazzling leadership of Wing Commander Edwards, who sped like one inspired through that wall of fire. One pilot flew so low that he collected some telephone wires in his tail wheel, another saw a high tension cable just ahead and barely managed to jump it in time. This cable nearly brought Wing Commander Edwards to disaster. Too late to lift over it, he was forced to put his nose down to dive under it, and barely avoided crashing into a pylon. "His starboard wing missed a pylon by a couple of yards" said another pilot afterwards.

But the elusive and modest Wing Commander Hughie Edwards did what he set out to do.

On July 7, 1941, three nights after Wing Commander Edwards brought his shell-scarred Blenheims home from Bremen, Squadron Leader R. P. Widdowson of the Royal New Zealand Air Force set out in a Wellington to bomb Munster. His second pilot was Sergeant James Allen Ward, a New Zealand schoolmaster whose parents emigrated from Coventry to Wanganui, where Sergeant Ward was born in June, 1919. Their navigator brought them straight to their target, on which they dropped their load of bombs. They were heading for home over the Zuider Zee at 13,000 feet—about 2½ miles high— when a Messerschmitt 110 swept in below and started to fire cannon shell and incendiary bullets into them. Sergeant A. R. J. Box, the rear gunner felt a bullet strike him in the foot and quickly swung his turret to train his four guns on the Messerschmitt, which fell away before his fire.

"He's gone down, sir!" reported the rear gunner.

The good news was nullified by the sight of a fire starting up near the starboard engine. A bullet had split a petrol pipe and the spirit was gushing out to feed the fire. The wind blowing with hurricane force, acted like a blast furnace and the rapidity with which the fire began to burn up the fabric made them realise that unless they could stop it at once the whole wing would soon be destroyed. Tearing away the fabric covering from the body of the Wellington, they reached out as far as they could with their fire extinguishers and strove to put out the fire, but it was beyond their reach. They even pulled out the corks from their vacuum flasks and shot the coffee over the flames, but it had little effect.

"Get ready to abandon aircraft," the captain warned them.

"Before we bale out, I'll go out and try to smother the fire with the engine cover," Sergeant Ward volunteered. "I'll leave my parachute to reduce wind resistance," he added.

Quite calmly he proposed to discard his one chance of life if he were blown off the wing. His companions would not hear of it, and at length he consented to put it on when he got outside the astro-hatch, after a rope from the dinghy had been tied under his arms to act as a life-line.

Although the captain strove to reduce the wind pressure by slowing down the Wellington, Sergeant Ward found the wind terrific as soon as he got outside the hatch and only with the greatest difficulty could he put on his parachute.

Let Sergeant Ward describe his heroic feat in his own words.

"First I had to hang on to the astro-hatch while I worked out how I was going to do it. Then I hopped out on the wing. I kicked holes down the side of the fuselage which exposed the geodetics and gave me a foothold. I held on with one hand until I got two footholds on the wing. Fire and blast from the Messerschmitt's cannon shells had stripped part of the wing covering, and that helped.

"Then I caught hold of some of the sections of the wing with the other hand and managed to get down flat on to the wing with my feet well dug in and hanging on with both hands. Once I could not get enough hold and the wind lifted me partly off the wing and sent me against the fuselage again. But I still had my feet twisted in and I managed to get hold of the edge of the astro-hatch and worked myself back on the wing again. It was just a matter of getting something to hang on to. It was like a terrific gale, only much worse than any gale I've ever known.

"As I got along the wing I was behind the airscrew, so I was in the slipstream as well. Once or twice I thought I was going. I had the cover tucked underneath me, and as I lay flat on the wing I tried to push the cover down through the hole in the wing on to the leaking pipe where the fire was coming from. But the parachute on my chest prevented me from getting close enough to the wing and the wind kept lifting me up.

"The cover nearly dragged me off. I stuffed it down through the hole, but as soon as I took my hand away the terrific wind blew it out again. My arms were getting tired and I had to try a new hold. I was hanging on with my left arm when, as soon as I moved my right hand, the cover blew out of the hole again and was gone before I could grab it. The rear gunner told me afterwards that he saw it go past his turret.

"After that there was nothing to do but to get back again. The navigator kept a strain on the rope and I pulled myself back along the wing and up the side of the fuselage to the astro-hatch, holding on as tight as I could. Getting back was worse than going out and by this time I was pretty well all in. The hardest task of the lot was getting my right leg in. In the end the navigator reached out and pulled it in."

The wing was saved because all the fabric was destroyed over the area near the broken petrol pipe and there was nothing left to burn. One more anxious moment occurred near the English coast when some petrol which had seeped into the wing suddenly flared up, but to their great relief it quickly went out.

Shortly afterwards Squadron Leader Widdowson brought the Wellington over an aerodrome and touched down safely. That night he won the D.F.C. and the wounded rear gunner won the D.F.M.

Imagine Sergeant Ward miles high in the darkness over the Zuider Zee, burrowing with feet and hands into the wing of the Wellington to prevent the hurricane from blowing him away like a leaf, striving to the limit of his endurance to smother the fire with that waterproof cover in order that the aircraft should survive and his friends might live.

This young New Zealand schoolmaster, who won the Victoria Cross, put away his books in order to fight evil. He was afterwards lost and will never return to his classroom to teach again; but his action over the Zuider Zee will teach a noble lesson for generations to come.

The passing of another fine young man who used to ride the range managed by his father at Brogan Gate in New South Wales stirred the world and brought the following tribute from Sir Arthur Harris, Commander-in-Chief, Bomber Command, to the father of Flight Sergeant Rawdon Hume Middleton, V.C.

"In the annals of the R.A.F. there has not yet been found a more gallant episode than that in which Flight-Sergeant Middleton laid down his own life deliberately in order to save some of his crew and, if possible, his aircraft. On behalf of Bomber Command I offer you my sympathy in the loss of your son, whose stirring example of devotion to duty has inspired not only the crews of Bomber Command, but will for ever remain an inspiration wherever there are white and blue roundels of the King's Air Force overhead."

Thirteen months after war broke out, Middleton, who was born in 1916 at Waverley, New South Wales, joined the Royal Australian Air Force, and after training in Canada qualified in the Royal Air Force as the pilot of a mighty Stirling bomber, from which he unloaded his bombs on many a German city. Duisberg, Dusseldorf, Osnabruck, Frankfurt, Wilhelmshaven and Munich all suffered from his blows, and each time he brought his Stirling back, though not always without difficulty, for on one occasion a night fighter played havoc with a wing and put one engine out of action, yet Middleton landed safely in England.

On November 28, 1942, he was briefed to attack the Fiat works in Turin. Checking up with his usual meticulous care, Middleton set off on his long journey. Usually there is no difficulty in seeing the Alps, the snowy peaks of which generally reflect some faint gleams of light from the heavens; but the night was so dark that the great barrier of mountains remained almost invisible. Moreover, something made the Stirling sluggish in climbing, and in coaxing his aircraft up to 12,000 feet to cross the Alps the pilot saw by his instruments that he had used up so much petrol that he wondered whether there would be enough left for him to get back.

The question of whether it would be wiser to return or go on was flitting through his mind when it was settled instantly by the sight of some flares dropping over Turin far ahead, so he went on, coming down slowly until he was flying over Turin at 2,000 feet. Unable to pick out his target owing to the darkness of the night, he flew to and fro over the city three times before he located it. All the time the flak was coming up at him, but it was not particularly heavy and there seemed little to worry about until a shell hit the wing and made the Stirling more difficult to control.

Then the perspex was shattered as a shell burst inside the cockpit with a blinding flash. Pilot Officer Skinner, the wireless operator, was wounded in the leg and his wireless smashed; the second pilot, Flight Sergeant L. A. Hyder, received nasty wounds in the head and leg which began to bleed freely; but it was Middleton who suffered the most grievous injury, for a splinter of shell struck him on the right side of the face and destroyed his right eye and laid bare the bone of his temple and cheek.

As Middleton dropped unconscious at the controls, the Stirling went down in a dive to 800 feet. Sergeant Hyder, in a dazed condition, grabbed the controls and took her over until he managed to bring her up to 1,500 feet, when he let go the bombs to complete the task which they had flown so far to perform.

Meanwhile the Italian gunners scored hit after hit. The three gunners of the Stirling fought back fiercely until the after turret was knocked out. Middleton, recovering from the first shock and seeing Hyder covered with blood, ordered the others to give the second pilot first aid and took over control of the Stirling again. The second pilot could hardly be persuaded by his colleagues to allow them to apply the first aid dressing, so anxious was he to get back to his wounded captain.

Middleton sat there, his face a gory mask, barely able to see out of his remaining eye and unable to speak without suffering pain and loss of blood. Yet, badly wounded as he was, his quenchless spirit gave him the strength to retain control of the aircraft and discuss the best thing to do. Fuel was short, there was a big climb to make over the Alps in unfavourable conditions. Would it be better to abandon the aircraft on the spot and end in an Italian prison camp or should they land in Northern France? To Middleton both propositions were unthinkable. One idea was uppermost in his mind—to bring the Stirling back to England and save the crew. Probably at that moment, shocked and shaken as he was, the thought of how he had saved his damaged bomber previously stimulated him to repeat the feat.

"I will try to reach England so that you can bale out," he said slowly to his crew.

As they headed for the Alps, Flight Sergeant Douglas Cameron, who before the war was a gamekeeper living near Perth, and Sergeant Harold W. Gough, a Scarborough lad, began to collect everything heavy and movable and jettison it over the side to give the Stirling a chance of rising high enough to clear the peaks. Doggedly the pilot lifted the Stirling over the great mountain rampart and nursed her along. Flying Officer G. R. Royde concentrated on the task of navigating the aircraft and keeping a good course.

For hour after hour Middleton brooded over the controls, still the captain of his soul and his ship. The thought of reaching England must have dominated him while his great will power kept him going. In great pain, gradually growing weaker, hardly able to see or speak, he not only called up the physical strength to fly the heavy bomber on a straight course, but he astounded the crew by swinging about to evade the heavy gunfire which met them over France and which again hit them. He was unconquerable.

Four hours after being hit, the Stirling thundered over Boulogne with all the batteries in the neighbourhood striving to destroy the symbol of Britain's might. The petrol was nearly exhausted. The instrument board indicated just enough fuel to keep the Stirling airborne for another five minutes.

By now Middleton's voice was nearly gone, his physical strength at a low ebb. The men who escaped believed that he could not have survived much longer. Already they knew his plan, which was to fly just over the coast to give them a chance to bale out and then to turn out to sea and strive to "ditch" her, otherwise bring the Stirling down near the shore.

Acting on the captain's instructions, they prepared to abandon aircraft and helped the wounded second pilot to the escape hatch around which they stood waiting to jump. The Stirling was down to about 900 feet and the sea below was very rough.

The bomber swept over the English coast.

"Abandon aircraft!" whispered Middleton. It was his last order the last words they heard their heroic captain say.

They helped out the wounded second pilot and saw his parachute crack open, then four other members of the crew followed on each other's heels and as they floated down safely they saw the Stirling turn out to sea and hit the surface.

Instead of baling out, Sergeant J. E. Jeffrey and Sergeant J. W. Mackie chose to remain with their friend and captain in the hope that they might assist him to bring the aircraft down safely and help him to escape. Unhappily the Stirling crashed in the rough seas and they died with their captain. Their sacrifice was no less than his and they are for ever numbered among the heroes of the Royal Air Force. Their bodies were recovered next day, but the body of Flight Sergeant Rawdon Hume Middleton, V.C. was never found.

"His devotion to duty in the face of overwhelming odds is unsurpassed in the annals of the Royal Air Force," was the exceptional tribute paid to him in the official citation.

On February 11, 1943, the gallantry of the surviving members of the crew was recognized by the award of the D.F.C. to Flying Officer G. R. Royde and Pilot Officer Norman E. Skinner; while Flight Sergeant L. A. Hyder, Flight Sergeant Douglas Cameron and Sergeant Harold W. Gough were decorated with the D.F.M.

On Friday, May 28, 1943, it was announced that Wing Commander Guy P. Gibson had been awarded the Victoria Cross for the heroic part he played in what the Air Ministry described as "one of the most devastating attacks of the war, the breaching of the Mohne and Eder dams." Leading his Lancasters to the spot, he dropped his delayed-action mine accurately against the Mohne dam and then flew up and down to draw the enemy fire while he called in his supporting bombers one by one to attack. The next bomber was shot down, but the three following bombers hit the mark and let loose the waters. Then he led his remaining bombers to the Eder dam, where he again drew the fire while he ordered his men to attack. The floods raced through the Ruhr, inundating towns and villages, sweeping away bridges, power stations and railways and spreading death and destruction everywhere.

This shattering blow was made possible by the Lancaster, which was the only aircraft in the world capable of carrying the load to the target. To achieve the feat Dr. B. N. Wallis, C.B.E., designed a special mine that had to be dropped from exactly 60 feet at exactly 232 miles an hour to rest against the dam 40 feet below the surface. Experiments proved that at a greater height or speed the mine would break on hitting the water. It seemed impossible for the pilots to fly so low at night without crashing into the black lake, until Mr. B. Lockspeiser suggested fitting the bombers with two lamps throwing beams of light that converged at 60 feet into one spot of light. This enabled the pilots to fly at the required height. Of the sixteen aircraft which reached the target eight were lost with 55 airmen. Gibson himself died on a raid on September 19, 1944—the sole survivor of 24 men who enlisted with him. Truly the Royal Air Force paid dearly for air supremacy.

CHAPTER XXXIII

SURPRISING LE CREUSOT

WHEN Bomber Command struck at the Renault Works at Billancourt near Paris on the night of March 3, 1942, it shattered not only the Renault Factory, but the German sense of immunity. Lorries, tanks and other war equipment poured into German hands from the Renault factory, which was the largest of its kind in France. As a target it was ideal, for nothing could be easier to locate than a sharp bend in the river Seine with an island on which the most valuable part of the factory was built. Being completely isolated by the river from the surrounding neighbourhood, the island could be bombed without devastating French homes. The island was joined to each bank by two flying bridges, and a bright moon and many flares enabled the British bombers to see it plainly and pick out their targets with great care. Their bombs practically blasted the Renault works out of existence. Tank shops, repair shops, the power station, engine shops, gasometer, rolling mills, aircraft depot and other sections of the works were pulverized. One tank shop alone was producing 27 tanks a week and the works were producing thousands of lorries a year. In an hour or two the Renault works were virtually blotted out.

Only the previous night of March 2nd, squadrons of Wellingtons and Stirling bombers flew over to destroy the vast Matford Motor Works at Poissy just outside Paris. The bombers made such good time that many of them reached their target ten minutes early. "When we got over the factory we saw another Wellington doing left hand circuits and we joined in on the circuit, too, waiting for ten-thirty," said one of the pilots. "The factory was unmistakable. Nothing happened except that we saw several other Wellingtons and some Stirlings circling round and waiting for the attack to begin. Then some flares went down and someone dropped a bomb or two into the factory which lit it up even better than before. That was the signal for everyone there. They all seemed to let their bombs go then. In a few minutes the place was ablaze."

To complete their destruction of the Matford Works, the bombers returned to make an audacious daylight raid at 4.30 on the afternoon of March 8th.

The Germans cared nothing if half the homes of France were wiped out, but the three raids shook them, for these two factories, in addition to making several thousand tanks and thousands of armoured vehicles, manufactured about 20,000 heavy lorries a year. The Air Ministry, in an official note, placed these raids in their true perspective. "In effect, one of the major tank battles of the war was won by the Royal Air Force in about six hours at a cost of four bombers and twenty-five men. That was not only of immediate and paramount importance to the Allied armies on both Russian and Libyan fronts, it was also one of the finest examples of Bomber co-operation with the army which this war has yet afforded. The denial of this huge output of military machinery to Germany was not the only fruit of the victory. This great and expected flow of tanks and vehicles would have enabled the enemy to stage a great campaign, to defeat which the Allied Armies would themselves have suffered serious casualties and severe losses in equipment. The sudden denial of some 20,000 lorries and great quantities of tanks and armoured vehicles must profoundly affect Germany's future strategy, circumscribe her actions, and cause drastic interference with her military plan.''

These shrewd blows cheered the British people as much as they depressed the Germans, if the vituperation of Goebbels be any criterion. But the great Schneider armament works at Le Creusot still worked on unhindered, as they had done from the moment they came under German control. Of such prime importance was this immense plant to the Germans that they did not drop a single bomb on it or damage it in any way during their attack on France, so it passed into their possession quite intact.

The Staff of Bomber Command looked at the map of France. Le Creusot was 170 miles south-east of Paris. There were no landmarks by which it could be located at night. The houses in the little town were so closely packed that a night attack would probably wipe out a large part of the population. Le Creusot was a difficult problem. Nevertheless Bomber Command had it in mind to destroy the works, and in May, 1942, Wing Commander Leonard C. Slee, D.S.O., was called into conference. Wing Commander Slee, who was born at Lymm, in Cheshire, in 1910, was tall and wiry, with an open face, brown eyes, a retrousse nose and hair already thinning in front and on top. Since the age of 21, when he gained his commission in the Royal Air Force, he had done excellent work in various spheres, and the chance of bombing Le Creusot appealed to him. To make sure of finding and hitting the target, and sparing the little French houses, it was essential to attack in daylight, and that meant a long flight over France in the face of strong anti-aircraft defences and powerful squadrons of enemy fighters.

Bomber Command pondered over a plan to attack with two squadrons. The works were vast, and while two squadrons might do a lot of damage, they could hardly hope to blot the arsenal out of existence. Yet it was complete obliteration that Bomber Command aimed at, and if this were not accomplished in the first surprise attack, the enemy would be fully warned, and a second force of bombers sent in to complete the task would probably suffer crushing losses. After considering the possibilities and the risks, Bomber Command discarded the project.

Although Le Creusot was left undisturbed, it was not forgotten. On October 10, 1942, Wing Commander Slee was again called in by the

Air Officer Commanding his group of Lancaster bombers and asked if he thought he could lead a hundred Lancasters to a small place far, far away and bomb it.

"I think so, sir," he replied.

Opinions about the method of attack were divided, and most squadron commanders concluded that the best way was for each squadron to go independently, but working to a common time-table.

"This won't work, I am sure," decided Wing Commander Slee.

However, the next day they tried out the plan in a dress rehearsal. The various squadrons were told to rendezvous at a certain time at a particular point over the North Sea, then turn to fly up to Scotland before making for Cardigan Bay, where they were all due to arrive together to make their bombing runs over the target.

Wing Commander Slee, aided by his brilliant navigator Grant, got his squadron to the turning point over the North Sea at the right time, but the others were not so punctual. By the time they should have been converging on the target to blast it in one quick burst, they trailed far into the distance, and it was half an hour before the last Lancaster dropped its imaginary load of bombs.

Flying on schedule, Wing Commander Slee looked back. The pilots did their best, but it was the first time they had attempted formation flying on this immense scale, and it was difficult to synchronize their speed and movements; so difficult that instead of them all arriving at the finishing line in good formation, the last home were thirty-five minutes behind time, after their flight of nearly a thousand miles.

The rehearsal was disappointing, yet it served one good purpose, for it proved to the Air Officer Commanding how the attack should not be made. After conferring with all the squadron commanders, he discarded the plan.

"Do you think that you could lead and time things accurately?" he asked Wing Commander Slee next day, October 12th.

"I think I could," the Wing Commander replied.

"All right. Your squadron will lead, and you will be responsible for leading the formations and for tactics and times and signals," said the Air Officer Commanding. Thus Wing Commander Slee was given the task of working out the plans for the daylight raid on Le Creusot, and his squadron, No. 49, was given the honour of leading it. This was no light responsibility. The difficulties of flying a hundred giant Lancasters in formation were many, for if one got out of its course and touched another there might be a series of collisions which would perhaps finish in a major disaster. It was a risk which needed careful consideration. Then it had to be decided how to take off and form up, and while these problems may be easy to solve theoretically, only the old method of trial and error could solve them in practice.

Accordingly, the nine squadrons were split up into three groups, each containing three squadrons, and each group was given a separate rendezvous where they could form up before flying to the final rendezvous to form up behind Wing Commander Slee.

He got to the first point and picked up his two squadrons, whose formation was a bit ragged. At the second point three more squadrons joined up, and at the third point the other three squadrons got into position. "It was fairly satisfactory, though the formation was very loose indeed; but at least it was a definite attempt to form up the whole group into a concentration in the air. This was the first time that any attempt had been made by Bomber Command to mass a large formation of bombers in the air, and as a result, no one had ever had formation-flying practice. Considering this, it was much to their credit that they achieved what they did in the way of formation flying," said Wing Commander Slee afterwards.

On October 14th they prepared to take off in pairs, as on the previous occasion, for another practice flight. Anxious to study how the plan worked out in the air, the Air Officer Commanding climbed into Wing Commander Slee's Lancaster to see things for himself. With the perversity that usually manifests on special occasions, the Lancaster refused to start, and the pilot had to do a little juggling to set his Merlins roaring and get into the air. The other squadrons formed up nicely at the requisite points, and they all raced away down to Land's End, where about thirty Spitfires and Hurricanes made a spirited mock attack to simulate the real attack which they would possibly have to meet over France, and those Lancasters which hung back on the turn were promptly picked off by the camera-guns of the fighters and claimed as casualties.

"Pack closer in your turns! Pack closer in your turns!" came the warning voice of the Wing Commander over the radio-telephone.

Out over the Irish Sea the Lancasters flew at about thirty feet above the surface, to come thundering in over the Welsh coast near Llandudno. More fighters waited to attack them later on, but this time the bombers defeated them. The fighters, faced with a new type of formation, could see no way to attack, with the consequence that the Lancasters escaped. Of course, when the fighter pilots landed and discussed the problem they found out the way to attack, but they were unable to work out their tactics quickly enough in the air to do it.

At 4 o'clock on October 16th Wing Commander Slee received word that the raid was to take place next day—weather permitting. At once he went to the Operations Room to discuss the route and the weather prospects.

"Bomb up the aircraft, and warn all crews not to go out, but to go to bed early," ordered the Wing Commander.

The ground crews got busy bombing up and filling the tanks, and as the Wing Commander watched their activities he realized that the civilians living around the station would see that something was on. But he was fortified by the fact that at that moment only five people on his station knew all about it, and it is worth noting that when he started next day his gunners still had no idea where they were going.

That evening there was an undercurrent of excitement in the mess, and several officers substituted a glass of lemonade for their usual tankard of ale before they packed off to bed to get what sleep they could.

At 4 o'clock in the morning the tinkling of the telephone wakened Wing Commander Slee. ''Will you please come to the Operations Room as soon as you can,'' said a voice at the other end. For a little while he lay there reviewing the situation, wondering how they were going to take off, what would happen if they were picked up early by a big fighter formation, whether Grant would be able to accomplish the very difficult feat of navigation, and what they were going to meet in the way of defences over the target. There were no answers to these questions, so he dressed and went into the mess for breakfast. There was no light badinage this morning. The faces round the tables were serious. All knew there was something big on, but they had no idea where they were going, and were trying to puzzle out the target.

Finishing his breakfast, the Wing Commander went to the Operations Room—to learn that the weather was playing tricks, and that the Air Officer Commanding was rather dubious whether the raid could take place. The trouble was that low cloud at about 1,000 feet was expected over most of the route, and as the hills on the way ran up to 700 feet, there was little clearance for the Lancasters. For half an hour the Wing Commander was kept on tenterhooks. Like all the other men in the squadron, he was all keyed-up, and anxious to go, and he was afraid of the raid being called off. However, at 8.30 a.m. the message came through that the operation was to proceed according to plan.

Slipping out the back way, he reached the Briefing Room, where he and his colleagues checked up to make sure that all their captains, navigators and air bombers were present—the air gunners were excluded in case the raid happened to be called off at the last moment. All waited in silence, wondering what their target was to be.

''Our aim is to blot out the Schneider Works in France,'' came the blunt announcement without any preliminaries.

''Thinking over how we could get off, I decided there and then that the best thing would be to try to take off in formation. To take off eleven four-engined aircraft in this way was rather ambitious, but it was worth a trial,'' said Wing Commander Slee afterwards. ''I stood up and quickly outlined the details. The method of take-off didn't so much as produce a flicker of interest, which was a good thing. I gave them the petrol and the bomb load, how we were to fly, and what to do, as near as I could guess, if we were attacked by fighters, the route, the formation and the bombing tactics, and finished up by telling them that it was only a matter of follow the leader.''

Donning their flying kit, they made their way to the aircraft, where

Wing Commander Slee found Grant, his navigator, already sitting at his table. They were just about to embark on one of the most daring daylight raids ever made, but the remarkable thing is that not for one moment did either of these two men who carried the main responsibility think that anything could go wrong. The only thing that troubled them was the weather. The leader left nothing to chance. He went over the Lancaster carefully himself, saw that the bombs were properly loaded, that the tanks were full and everything in good shape.

"We had done everything we possibly could to make the whole thing fireproof," he stated. "We knew everything off by heart, the times, the route, the turning points, the formation signals and the positions of the various squadrons, where we were to cross the coasts, the big landmarks, the towns and railways, where we were to start to climb and open out formation to attack. Grant and I had pored over the maps until we dreamt about them. We memorized the shape of the target and how it would look to us from every direction, and did everything we could to make the thing a success."

The engines were warmed up. Every clock was properly synchronized. Then Wing Commander Slee started to move down to the other end of the aerodrome, followed by all the others. Taking up his position in the centre, the Wing Commander waited while the others waddled into their proper places to complete the formation on the ground. Two minutes before the time to take off he spoke to them over the radio-telephone. "Everyone ready to go?" he asked.

"Yes!" came the reply from all.

The success of the take-off depended upon every pilot carrying out instructions implicitly and not deviating from his course. The slightest deviation would have been disastrous. As the hand of the clock approached the minute, the hands of the pilots moved forward to the throttles, and at the exact second all the pilots opened their throttles simultaneously, and the giant Lancasters began to race over the aerodrome in formation. It was a magnificent sight, eleven mighty Lancasters, black as basalt, roaring to the high heavens, all racing over the grass in formation, all lifting into the air together, all withdrawing their landing wheels at the same time, as though they had been drilling for years. Nothing like it was ever seen before, nothing like it was ever attempted. It was not rehearsed, but it worked like a charm.

Imagine what an unnerving take-off it must have been for the leader! But his faith in the pilots was justified. They acted in complete unison, and a most difficult operation was carried out flawlessly.

"All airborne, sir," came the message from Sergeant Mills, the rear gunner, to the Wing Commander. He glanced round and saw them all in formation, nicely spaced, and was proud and very thankful.

At the first rendezvous he saw the first two squadrons approaching at his own height, and as he ducked under them and saw them milling round in the skies to form up he wondered whether they could carry out the manœuvre. His relief and delight when he saw them all drop into place can be understood.

He peered ahead. The weather was worsening. There were rain storms in the distance. After a time he saw three more squadrons over the second rendezvous, and they also came round and took up their places without overmuch trouble.

As they flew on to the last rendezvous the weather got worse just as they were approaching the rising ground. The last three squadrons formed up very nicely, and the ninety-four Lancasters headed for the coast, with the clouds steadily getting lower and the ground higher, while flurries of rain came on to add to the dangers. There were four ridges to cross, the last two being over 700 feet high, and the leader did not like the prospects at all.

"On we went, and things got worse," he said when it was over. "I had to lead them along the valleys as far as I could, but you cannot do very much in this way with such a large formation. And each time I saw the next ridge looming above us I wondered whether they would all get through. Sometimes one or two of the squadrons disappeared into rain storms, but then reappeared once more; once or twice we were sailing along a valley while the aircraft on the flanks were sliding just over the top of the ground on either side. And so it went on. There always seemed to be another ridge in front, and it always seemed to be higher than the one we had just crossed, and, of course, it was. Finally we came to what I thought must surely be the last one, and as we topped the ridge and I saw the land drop away I heaved a sigh of relief."

They reached the coast at the exact time and place planned, and Wing Commander Slee led them over the sea, where conditions soon grew worse than ever, for rain and cloud forced him down to forty feet above the surface, while it was impossible to see more than 500 yards ahead. He looked back and could see no more than his own squadron. All the rest were hidden in the murk, and whether the other eight squadrons were following him he could not tell.

Suddenly a small convoy seemed to rush at them out of the rain, and how they missed the balloon barrage remains a mystery. A little later they just had time to fire recognition signals before flashing past two British warships. But what worried the leader was the fact that they were forced to fly so low that there was grave danger of some of the aircraft flying slap into a lighthouse which lay on their course. Later, in the mess, he heard that some of them had a most exciting time dodging it, though he knew nothing about it at the moment.

Flying on in faith, he roared over the sea for mile after mile without seeing any other aircraft but his own squadron. He was very worried. All he could do was to fly by the compass and pray and hope that all the others were doing the same.

After what seemed to be a lifetime, the weather started to lift a little. It became patchy. Sometimes the cloud dropped down to the surface, then it opened more and more until there was a clear belt of 300 feet between the cloud and the sea.

That was the testing time. Very anxiously Wing Commander Slee looked round, and was reassured and rather amazed to find some aircraft still following him. Feeling quite sure that there could not be half the original number, he reviewed the problem swiftly in his mind. "I might do it with fifty," he thought. "But if they fail to do all we want, we shall lose heavily when we attempt to go back to finish the job. On the other hand, if we turn back now, it will probably leak out what we set out to do and we shall meet the fiercest opposition next time."

He was still cudgelling his brains to decide what to do when the voice of the gunner came to him. "Thirty-four behind us, sir."

The great Lancasters roared onward for another fifty miles over a glassy sea. A cloudless sky lay ahead. "Seventy-eight now, sir," said the gunner. A few seconds later he announced triumphantly: "Ninety-one Lancasters all told, and forming up nicely!"

"By this time the formation had closed in and were taking up station, and it was an absolute marvel that they should be there at all. They were all very inexperienced in formation flying, and yet, after a long period of cloud-flying a few feet from the water in a formation ninety strong, they were all in place when we got to the clear. So they must have been there all the time. I cannot speak too highly of their leaders and their individual pilots and navigators, for if the navigation had been at fault they would have been completely scattered and lost. It was a remarkable effort, and by itself no mean achievement," commented Wing Commander Slee when the raid was done.

Every navigator in the force had reason to pride himself on his fine work in following his leader in the cloud and rain for so great a distance.

Thankfully the leader turned over control to "George," the automatic pilot, and settled down to have lunch. Once he imagined he saw a squadron of five warships, but they turned out to be five fishing smacks with a tug making a good deal of smoke. The sea was calm. The smacks were quite still. There was not enough wind to make their sails flap.

In a moment, as the Lancasters roared over, they appeared to go mad. The slipstream from the giant bombers hit them like a cyclone and sent them heeling over and rushing through the sea at a great pace. It was a remarkable sight.

As his Lancasters crossed the French coast Wing Commander Slee looked at the clock. He was too early by thirty seconds. He did not fail to point it out to his navigator, Grant.

"Well, sir, you can't be closer than plus or minus one minute when you haven't seen land for so long," said the Australian navigator apologetically. His navigation was always faultless, and on that flight approached the miraculous, for he brought their Lancaster over the target to bomb at the precise minute that was scheduled, and they also touched down on the return at the exact minute. A memento of that flight of which Wing Commander Slee was most proud was a photograph of the "ops" board showing his scheduled and actual times of arrival and return. They were identical—and his Lancaster was the only one to accomplish such a feat.

Grant was a remarkable navigator. He did not smoke, nor drink, but he loved Shakespeare and delighted in dancing. On a flight he was quite ruthless. Once when Wing Commander Slee was inquiring his whereabouts, Grant seized the opportunity of slipping in a sly dig at his captain: "I can't possibly tell, sir. You fly such erratic courses," he answered politely, and the Wing Commander long remembered and chuckled over it. Flying Officer Arthur Stanley Grant, who won the D.S.O. on that raid, was the first navigator in the Royal Air Force to win this decoration, which indicates what a superb navigator he was.

"Once we made our landfall, it was very pleasant over France," commented Wing Commander Slee after the raid. "There were no people in the streets, no trains—it was like a dead country. I saw only one private car on the roads and one tradesman's van. One or two people rode cycles, but there was practically no road traffic at all— the roads were quite empty. I expected to see lots of enemy fighters— you can't take a big force of bombers across France like that without being noticed—but we did not see a single fighter all the way to the target."

A graphic description of that flight across France by a sergeant pilot who captained one of the Lancasters is worth recording. "As we all took the hedges it was like the Grand National, except that there were no falls," he said. "Some of the French waved to us, some didn't seem to notice us. But the animals noticed us all right. Cows, chickens, horses, dogs—they all bolted as we roared over their heads. There was a farmer ploughing with two oxen which shied and drew their furrow zigzag across the field. But the farmer just stood and waved to us. We saw no fighters on the way, but a duck came through the windscreen. My front-gunner's turret was filled with feathers and the hole in the windscreen let in an awful draught. All the way over there were Lancasters on each side of us, roaring at zero feet over France. It was a wonderful flight."

Following the contours of the ground, leaping farmhouses and woods, Wing Commander Slee saw the Loire with its picturesque chateaux dotting the river banks. Onward the huge bombers roared, keeping excellent formation. Soon he led them on their climb to the attack, only to find cloud which threatened to upset all his calculations. Flying through the cloud, which thinned out a bit, he came out over his target at the exact second, thanks to the faultless navigation of Flying Officer Grant.

Directly they approached the Schneider works, which covered 245 acres, the squadrons split up to carry out their orders to bomb individually and concentrate their attack in the shortest possible time. The sun had just set. The works stood out distinctly below them, with their long buildings and tall chimneys. Load after load of heavy bombs and incendiaries crashed down. "A stick of bombs from another aircraft dropped right across the works," said the sergeant pilot previously mentioned. "Then we dropped our stick parallel to it. The buildings just flopped apart. There was a red flash in the middle of one building and it wasn't there any more. As we turned to come away more high explosives and incendiaries came right down on the target. In a little while all we could see was a cloud of smoke with red fires and bombs bursting inside it."

The weight of bombs dropped was never officially stated, but I estimate that in less than thirty minutes about 500 tons of bombs hit the Schneider works and largely reduced them to a mass of wreckage.

Wing Commander Slee's squadron dropped all their bombs in the quick time of seven minutes. There was hardly any opposition, just a little gunfire. As he flew over the target he saw the six Lancasters dive to make their attack on the transformer station which emitted blue sparks and a gush of flame. It was here that the only Lancaster out of that big air armada was lost.

He thought to turn to see the results on the main buildings. He simply could not do it. The Lancasters were flying after him "like a swarm of gnats," to use his own words, and if he had turned he could not have avoided a collision. So he flew on and, half-turning in his seat, gazed back and saw the whole target wreathed in smoke and flame.

Directly the attack was over the squadrons formed up behind their leader, who took them back across France at 2,000 feet through a little light cloud lit by a good moon, without seeing a single fighter. Bad weather over England, however, drove them up to 7,000 feet to fly above it.

There was one Lancaster which had an exciting duel over the sea. A faulty engine forced it to fly about forty feet above the surface when it was attacked by three Arado float planes. Two of them kept pace below the Lancaster, while one drew in after much hesitation. The rear-gunner of the bomber quickly caught it with a burst and sent it into the sea. Then another of the Arados swept up to continue the fight and killed the flight-engineer before the British gunners shot it down. The third enemy seaplane fled.

The Headquarters of Bomber Command waited eagerly to learn the result of the attack. There was no little anxiety when twenty-three of the Lancasters were reported as possibly missing. One by one they touched down, however, as Air Marshal Sir Arthur Harris said, "without bending a rivet," until only one was missing, the Lancaster which crashed before the eyes of the crews attacking the transformer station.

Historians will rank this great daylight raid as an undeniable proof of the remarkable development of British Air Power after the Battle of Britain.

On October 24, 1942, just a week after leading the destructive daylight raid on the Schneider Armament Works at Le Creusot, Wing Commander Slee led his squadron to take part with other squadrons in the first daylight raid made from England on Milan, the attack on which was planned to begin at 5.9 p.m. "We took off in the morning," said Squadron Leader D. Clyde-Smith, D.F.C., "and as we flew towards the English coast other Lancasters came in to join us until they were stretching on all sides. As we crossed the English coast the fighters met us exactly on time and turned to fly with us across the sea."

Escorting the Lancasters over the coastal belt of France, the British fighters turned back, while the Lancasters, packed tightly together to bring an enormous fire-power to bear on any aircraft which strove to attack them, jockeyed their way for 500 miles across hostile country and the Alps to Milan, which was duly bombed in broad daylight before the Lancasters turned to fly back across the Alps under the full moon to England.

Three, alas, did not return, but considering that the Lancasters flew for 500 miles across hostile country in broad daylight and 500 miles back under the full moon, the first daylight bombing of Milan from England was a triumph.

The remarkable thing about it was that a layer of cloud which would provide the bombers with cloud cover most of the way was travelling fast in the direction of the flight, leaving a clear sky behind it. Cloud cover over hostile country is better than a life insurance, and when the meteorological experts learned what the clouds were doing, the starting time was moved forward by twenty minutes to give the Lancasters a chance of overtaking the clouds and obtaining the benefit of their cover over France—a sensible move that was crowned with success.

CHAPTER XXXIV

HISTORIC NIGHT AND DAY RAIDS

"IF the Germans want to play rough—all right! they will learn that we can play rough, too," said Mr. Churchill when Great Britain was suffering the full fury of the German bombing attack. Eventually the British people who endured so stoically and toiled so hard, waiting and yearning for a turn in the tide of war, began to see what a united nation could accomplish. In the hour of travail, the engineering geniuses of this nation designed the most wonderful aircraft ever conceived in the mind of man or fashioned by human hands, the mighty four-engined Halifaxes and Stirlings and Lancasters with a

speed and range and bomb load far in advance of the most advanced
bombers produced by any other country anywhere. With them,
Bomber Command nightly hammered home the much-needed lesson
to the Germans—the professional war-makers of Europe—that they
could no longer make war to plunder other lands without suffering
the devastation of war in their own homes.

Tirelessly as the Nazis worked to camouflage the damage of the
early British raids, desperately as Goebbels lied to deceive the Germans,
the British raid on Lubeck on the night of March 28, 1942, lit a fire
which opened the eyes of the Nazi nation, a fire which even Goebbels
was unable to conceal.

Built on an island of 570 acres situated at the confluence of the
rivers Trave and Wekenitz, Lubeck lay about thirteen miles from the
Baltic coast. On this island of about a square mile in extent was packed
the old town with its picturesque buildings of which the Germans were
so proud, and fringing the island and the banks of the rivers were the
docks and wharves where the ships from Sweden unloaded their iron
ore, without which the German arms industry would perish, and where
all the cargoes to and from Scandinavia were handled. Submarines
were building in the yards, submarine crews were training in the
training establishment. The port was still icebound and masses of
munitions were piling up to pour into Finland for the conflict on the
Northern Russian front as soon as the ice broke and the laden ships
could move. Lubeck lay undisturbed. It had no fears.

When the Wellingtons and other bombers started on their long flight
across the North Sea the moon was peeping through a thin veil of
cloud which grew more tenuous until it entirely disappeared and left
the sea and sky bathed in moonlight. Thundering through the belt of
searchlights on the German coast, paying little attention to the sporadic
gunfire, the bombers flew on till Lubeck lay ahead. It was about
10.30 p.m. when the first bombs began to go down. At first only one
or two small fires were noticed. But as the bombs continued to crash,
the fires grew until Lubeck resembled one huge furnace. Wave after
wave of bombers arrived over the town and dropped high explosives
and incendiary bombs at the rate of two tons a minute. For three
hours the attack went on.

"We were 70 miles away overland when we first saw the glow in
the sky from the fires at Lubeck, and we knew that the attack was well
under way," said the captain of a Wellington. "As we got nearer,
we saw a great line of black smoke like a smoke screen blowing back
from Lubeck and over the countryside towards Kiel. It must have
been a thousand yards wide. We were flying straight into the wind and
the smoke was underneath us. It blacked out the ground below.
When we got to Lubeck, we found a great area round the docks
completely enveloped in flames. It wasn't a question of counting the
number of fires: the whole area was one gigantic fire, and as we got
nearer it grew and grew."

That was what Lubeck looked like about 1.30 a.m., and the attack continued for about an hour longer. Warehouses, the Town Hall, the Central Electric Station, the Market Hall, were all engulfed. Street after street collapsed and fed the flames, which destroyed a deep belt through the town, a belt from 200 yards to 600 yards wide and three-quarters of a mile long. About 200 acres of the old town were burned and pulverized. A fortnight later the streets were still completely impassable, just masses of ruins and fallen debris. The suburbs of Lubeck straggling along the river banks were hard hit, and in all 42,000 people were rendered homeless.

In the days to come, Lubeck will mark the turning point where Great Britain began to bring home to the Nazis that the Royal Air Force was at last strong enough to hit back harder than the Luftwaffe.

Nor will the Nazis forget that the Staff Officers of Bomber Command were able to invent more than one new method of bombing which completely surprised the German defences. The first revolution was the cascade raid in which the raiders were timed to arrive over the target and drop their bombs almost simultaneously to swamp the ground defences and make it impossible for the enemy gunners to concentrate all their fire upon one bomber after another. These tactics were originally used to astonish and shock the Germans on the night of Saturday, May 30, 1942, when Bomber Command made what was up till then its most powerful raid on Cologne. This raid will rank in history as one of the greatest feats of organisation and timing hitherto performed by any air force. Along with the prospects of a stupendous success it carried the potentialities of a catastrophe, for it was easy to foresee what might happen with a thousand bombers flying above a city if the timing went wrong and the skill of the pilots and navigators were not of the highest order.

With absolute faith in the ability and courage of the bomber crews, Bomber Command made its plans to send the thousand bombers over Cologne to drop their bombs within ninety minutes. Everything was worked out in the minutest detail to prevent the bombers from colliding with each other in the air or dropping their bombs upon each other, and the Staff Officers of Bomber Command who had perfected the plan in secrecy and silence were rewarded with a triumph.

The crews, that Saturday, had a shrewd idea that something was on, but what it was they did not know. Everything depended on the weather and not until the afternoon were the meteorological experts able to forecast that the weather would be suitable. At 6 o'clock in the evening an army of 6,000 or so officers and men of the Royal Air Force were gathered in the briefing rooms of many bomber stations to learn for the first time that there was to be a thousand bomber raid on Cologne. Many were so enthusiastic that they cheered.

A special message from Air Chief Marshal Sir A. T. Harris was read: "The force of which you form part to-night is at least twice the size and has more than four times the carrying capacity of the largest air force ever before concentrated on one objective. You have an opportunity therefore to strike a blow at the enemy which will resound not only throughout Germany, but throughout the world. In your hands lie the means of destroying a major part of the resources by which the enemy's war effort is maintained. It depends, however, upon each individual crew whether full concentration is achieved.

"Press home your attack to your precise objective with the utmost determination and resolution in the foreknowledge that if you individually succeed, the most shattering and devastating blow will have been delivered against the vitals of the enemy.

"Let him have it—right on the chin."

The task of fuelling and bombing-up the thousand bombers was prodigious. It meant handling rivers of petrol and oil and thousands of tons of bombs, but the armourers and riggers and fitters and ground crews generally did a magnificent job and had everything ready by the time the crews were dressed. It was indeed an army of airmen who climbed into the thousand and forty-three bombers at the many stations concerned in the night's operation. At dusk the flarepaths lit up, and the bombers, vibrating with power, were signalled away at short intervals by the clock and like clockwork they became airborne to speed off to Cologne. Lancasters and Manchesters and Halifaxes and Stirlings and all the other types roared along, each flying to a time-table that was worked out as carefully as that of any railway—only there were no signals in the air to prevent them from colliding.

From all the aerodromes in England the great bombers converged on the doomed city whose inhabitants lurked in their shelters and wondered whether the night would bring a raid. Gunfire and the crash of bombs answered their thoughts. As the bombs and incendiaries rained down the city rocked as though struck by an earthquake. Cologne was defended by 500 guns, with 120 searchlights to light up the flying targets, and early on the searchlights formed great cones in the sky to fasten on the British raiders while the guns sent up their shells and tracer. But before long searchlights and gunfire began to die out under the weight of the attack, while the fires began to blaze up and the buildings to crumble.

Before the attack was very old, bombers speeding over the Dutch coast toward the target saw the city glowing like a furnace in the black-out from a distance of 200 miles. One captain of a bomber, deceived by the glare into thinking he was getting near the city, opened the doors of the bombing compartment to get ready to bomb and at length realized it was a vast fire a long distance away, so he closed the doors again and flew on.

"It was almost too gigantic to be real," a pilot said. "But it was real enough when we got there. Below us in every part of the city buildings were ablaze. Here and there you could see their outlines, but mostly it was just one big stretch of fire. It was strange to see the flames reflected on our aircraft. It looked at times as though we were on fire ourselves, with a red glow dancing up and down the wings."

A bomb aimer lying flat in the nose of a Halifax, watching for his target, saw a string of bombers flying ahead, sending down their bombs and turning away in a procession. "There were aircraft everywhere. The sky over Cologne was as busy as Piccadilly Circus. I could identify every type of bomber in our force by the light of the moon and fires."

Around Cologne in the open country were the fires lit by the Germans to try to mislead the British bombers into dropping their bombs away from their target. To-night these dummy fires were like children's bonfires, so small were they compared with the immense fires, acres in extent, raging in Cologne. A great cloud of smoke rose higher and higher over the city until it touched 15,000 feet, or three miles, and when the British reconnaissance aircraft went to take photographs next morning—a most courageous flying feat—that canopy of smoke hung over the burning city like a billowing black fog.

The damage was colossal, for it covered 600 acres. Mountains of debris blocked the streets. The city lacked gas, light and water. All sorts of factories were demolished and burned out. The life of a great part of Cologne was brought to a standstill. No telegraph or telephone messages could be passed for nine days. Nearly 200,000 homeless people were evacuated. In the Ehrenfeld district a vast tract on the river bank a mile long by a quarter of a mile wide was one ugly succession of factory ruins.

That night of Saturday, May 30, 1942, was pregnant with the fate of Germany.

The success of the biggest bomber raid the world had so far known was marked by the following message from Mr. Winston Churchill to Air Chief Marshal Sir A. T. Harris, the Commander-in-Chief of Bomber Command: "I congratualte you and the whole of the Bomber Command upon the remarkable feat of organization which enabled you to dispatch over a thousand bombers to the Cologne area in a single night, and without confusion to concentrate their action over the target into so short a time as an hour and a half. This proof of the growing power of the British Bomber force is also the herald of what Germany will receive, city by city, from now on."

Forty-eight hours later on the night of Monday, June 1, 1942, another force of a thousand British bombers flew off to spread destruction through the Ruhr and bomb Essen. Again the Germans were rocked by the explosion of the big British bombs, once again mighty fires consumed factories and workshops. While these historic raids were in progress many other British aircraft made diversionary raids and sweeps on aerodromes and other towns to keep the German fighters employed and prevent them from flying to intercept the bombers—tactics which achieved their object.

The next thousand bomber raid, on Bremen on the night of June 25,

1942, was hampered by cloud over the target, but great fires were seen through the gaps, and these made the clouds glow a rosy red, while far away to the north was a remarkable display of the Northern Lights. Many night fighters attacked the British bombers, and one Stirling was chased by a German fighter with a searchlight in its nose—it was the German fighter, however, which went down in flames into the sea.

After those record raids Bomber Command shifted its blows from one target to another, sending out aircraft day and night to destroy locomotives and dislocate transport. The damage in Germany mounted. Bomber Command strove to make the prophecy of Mr. Churchill come true. Improved aircraft dropping bigger bombs filled with more powerful explosives began to devastate larger areas of the Reich, and one bomb dropped upon Wilhelmshaven on the night of February 11-12, 1943, created a record by reducing 150 acres to a mass of rubble in a gigantic explosion which made the pilots think that an arsenal had been touched off.

The coolness and bravery displayed by the Royal Air Force raiders was almost unbelievable. A Master Bomber, Group Captain G. L. Cheshire, V.C., D.S.O., D.F.C., for instance, won his D.S.O. during a raid on Cologne on the night of November 11-12, 1940. Flying over the marshalling yard, he had opened the bomb doors and ordered the wireless operator to stand by to drop a big flare to light the target, when the front turret was blown in and a shell splinter exploded the flare, which blasted a ten-foot hole in the fuselage.

Fighting to control the bomber, the captain saw that fire had broken out. A moment later the wireless operator, Flight Sergeant Davidson, came through with his clothes aflame, after most gallantly pushing the blazing flare down the chute to get rid of it. At once the bomb aimer beat out the flames on the wireless operator's clothes with his hands, then he rushed aft to help to throw out the incendiaries.

The captain dropped his bombs and looked at the wireless operator who had fallen to the floor.

"I'm going blind, sir," the wireless operator said. His face was completely black, he could not see, yet his one concern was to get back to his wireless to help them to reach home. With difficulty, they induced him to let them apply first aid dressings to his burns, then he returned to his wireless. Unable to see the dials, he called out the settings to the rear gunner. "Where is the key?" he asked fumbling round. The rear gunner took his hand and guided it to the sending key. There he stood, blinded by the injuries the flare had inflicted, tapping out his messages for forty minutes to inform base that they were on the way, but his aerial was destroyed and the messages never got through. He must have been in great pain, yet he made no complaint during the whole time they were flying home. His noble and selfless action brought to Flight Sergeant Henry Davidson the D.F.M.

That bomber which Pilot Officer Cheshire, as he was then, piloted home had both doors blown from the front turret, there was a large hole in the fuselage, the body of the aircraft was distorted, the whole of the skin and ribs were blown off one side of it and all the rivets were missing on the other, while the tail plane was in danger of falling off. Yet the pilot flew it home and landed safely at his base. Group Captain Cheshire has had many experiences since then, but nothing to compare with that nightmare flight from Cologne to England.

Even more hair-raising was the experience of Squadron Leader E. G. Gilmore during the big raid on Cologne on February 26, 1943, when he won the D.F.C. while his navigation sergeant J. W. T. M. Smith won the D.F.M. Squadron Leader Gilmore had just dropped his bombs when he was picked up by a cone of searchlights. At once the night fighters and anti-aircraft guns caught him. A propeller was shot off, two of the engines were hit and the third had its cowlings shot away. Hits were made on the fuselage, on the wings, on the ailerons, while the astrodome was completely shattered. At the same time a pipe was cut which prevented the bomb doors from being closed.

As the Halifax went down out of control, twisting and turning and finally rolling on its back, all four engines stopped and the flight engineer who was standing immediately below the broken astrodome fell head-first through the open space. By the grace of God his shoulders became wedged in the framework and there he hung head downward with the wind nearly blowing his head off until the Halifax turned on an even keel again.

At the peak of the crisis a parachute broke loose and rolled against the instrument panel, turning on all the lights to make the Halifax a first-class target for the gunners below. By then the Halifax had fallen 14,000 feet with the pilot fighting all the time to start up the engines and regain control. They were down to 4,000 feet with all lights full on when he at length managed to start up three of the engines; and on three engines and three propellers he flew his battered Halifax straight through the cone of searchlights over Cologne safely back to England.

With details of the first audacious daylight raid of the Royal Air Force upon Berlin on January 30, 1943—the historic precursor of the final phase of the air war in which the actions of the Royal Air Force and the United States Air Force became so closely correlated—this book must close. It was on January 30, 1933, that Hitler seized power, consequently the leaders of the Nazi party gathered together in Berlin in 1943 to celebrate the anniversary, not with the usual speech by Hitler, but with a speech by Goering, which was to be broadcast at 11 o'clock and a speech by Goebbels timed for 4 o'clock in the afternoon.

Bomber Command was determined to upset these celebrations. Never before had an attempt been made to bomb Berlin in daylight; for the difficulties and dangers made such an attack impossible. The distance to Berlin was so far, the German fighter squadrons so many, and the German capital's defences so strong, that Goering and Milch were convinced of the safety of the city by day.

Now the difficulties and dangers were nullified by a new factor of which the Germans had no' exact knowledge. This factor was the Mosquito bomber which de Havillands had developed from their old long-distance racer the Comet. This latest wonder could loop and roll and dive and climb like a Spitfire. Berlin was easily within its range, and at full boost it could outpace the German fighters. Its top speed was most jealously guarded by the Air Ministry and its pilots, for it was the fastest aircraft in the world in military operation. Its flawless skin was made of laminated Balsa wood with not a single rivet anywhere to obstruct the free flow of air and retard the speed. Wings, fuselage, the whole body of the aircraft consisted of plywood, and the Mosquito was gradually developed and refined into a phenomenal example of the genius of British aircraft designers, for some Mosquitos were fitted for reconnaissance work deep in the heart of Germany, others carried 4,000-pound bombs and the latest type carried eight 60-pound rockets beneath the wings, four .303 machine guns in the nose, four 20-mm. cannon peeping out of the belly and two 500-pound bombs under the engine nacelles. It was from the beginning a unique aircraft which gave Bomber Command the opportunity of interfering with the Berlin festivities.

At 5 o'clock on the afternoon of January 29th, Squadron Leader R. J. Reynolds, D.S.O., D.F.C., of No. 105 Squadron of Mosquito Bombers was called in and informed that he had been chosen to lead a raid on Berlin the next morning. Reynolds was keen to go. He knew the risks all right—for experience had come to him from many bombing operations earlier in the war—but they did not deter him. ''I thought it would be a sticky job!'' he confessed afterwards, and a frank smile lit his face and keen greenish-blue eyes.

Born in Cheltenham in 1919, he was sturdy, about 5 feet 6 inches tall, just the sort of man to pack a scrum. His first tentative effort after leaving school in Bristol was to settle in an office, but the Royal Air Force proved too attractive and by the end of 1937 he was commissioned as a pilot. Bombers were his fancy, and it was in Bristol Blenheims that he did fine work and gained his D.F.C. in 1940. That he should be selected to fly what was then the fastest aircraft in the world was a tribute to his ability.

Squadron Leader Reynolds on the evening of January 29th discussed the plans with the Group Captain who worked out all the details of routes, speeds, heights, and times; and the next day the captains and crews of the Mosquitoes were sitting down to breakfast by 5 o'clock in the morning. At 5.30 they entered the briefing room to receive their instructions. Every detail of this historic raid was most carefully planned, every phase discussed and it was nearly two hours before the crews left the briefing room.

''We were a bit excited,'' Squadron Leader Reynolds admitted. ''I thought it might be a very tricky job, with a good chance of being shot up.''

"A very tricky job if it came off." added his observer and navigator Pilot Officer E. B. Sismore, D.F.C.

The Mosquitoes, which were fuelled and bombed-up overnight, stood ready, and the crews proceeded to dress in their flying kit before going out to their aircraft. In due course, round about breakfast time, they sped away on their mission. It was a nasty day, with rain and low cloud and a very high wind. The clouds were no more than 800 feet high and the Mosquitoes were bumped about badly. Theoretically it was possible to see about two miles, but during the flight across the North Sea the rain pouring down the windscreen prevented Squadron Leader Reynolds from seeing anything at all. They went over the Dutch coast at high speed and hedge-hopped across Holland. Not a gun fired at them or a fighter came into view. They were determined not only to drop their bombs on Berlin and spoil Goering's broadcast, but also to shake the morale of the Germans as much as they could.

In one little Dutch town, with red roofs, they saw the Dutch flag flying over what was undoubtedly the Town Hall. It struck them as queer that the Germans should permit the Dutch flag to fly in a country which they occupied. A few people were in the streets, but the roads generally were devoid of traffic. Once they saw some cyclists jump off their cycles, but the Mosquitoes were gone before the cyclists had a chance to recognise that they were British. In one place they actually saw a bus, but this was the only one they noticed.

Then a plough being drawn by a bullock caught their eye, and later Squadron Leader Reynolds roared deliberately over a German ploughman whose horses, startled by the noise, reared up so high above the driver that they seemed to be falling backward on him; but whether they did or not, the crew of the leading Mosquito will never know, for they sped by too quickly to see the result.

One sight during that flight will never be forgotten by Pilot Officer Sismore who saw a German in a field crouch to the ground and grab his hat by the brim in both hands and pull it right down over his face and head as though his hat would give him some protection from the aircraft which was coming straight at him. It was very funny.

Then Squadron Leader Reynolds raced down upon a German steam train. "I wish I'd got a bomb to spare for that train," he thought as he flashed past.

The rain ceased and the cloud lifted to above 6,000 feet. At the right point Squadron Leader Reynolds began to lead the Mosquitoes upward to attain their bombing height. The cloud was like a dense fog which obscured everything and as soon as they entered it the Mosquitoes lost sight of each other. But they followed their leader perfectly and did not lose touch. Presently they emerged above the clouds into the bright sunshine and sped onward to their destination above a solid carpet of cloud.

Soon the clouds broke and through a gap Squadron Leader Reynolds saw the smoke of a railway train. Magically the clouds stopped on the fringe of Berlin and the British airmen saw their goal before them.

Flying over their target, they dropped their bombs at 11.6 a.m., the precise minute at which they were timed to arrive, an extraordinary feat on the part of Squadron Leader Reynolds and his navigator, Pilot Officer Sismore, in view of the fact that they had flown for about 600 miles in bad weather with heavy winds that had bumped them about all over the sky.

At that moment the people of Germany in the fighting services, in the factory, and in the home, were listening to a description of the scenes being enacted in the German Air Ministry as Goering was about to broadcast. Suddenly the Germans heard the sound of confused voices and a cry of "Achtung" in the distance. Amid the confusion an announcer said that Goering was delayed for a few minutes, but for an hour the waiting German nation listened to gramophone records and the apologetic remarks of the announcer before Goering dared to face the microphone and make his speech, during which he frankly admitted that they could do nothing to stop the raids of the Royal Air Force on Germany, because the Luftwaffe was stretched to the limit. So the truth eventually came from the lips of Goering, who used to proclaim that not a bomb could fall on German soil.

While Bomber Command dropped their tribute to Goering, he was obliged to pay his belated tribute to the Royal Air Force.

Turning away from Berlin, Squadron Leader Reynolds and his companions raced for home, where they all arrived safely without a gun being fired at them or a single fighter attempting to catch them. Touching down, Squadron Leader Reynolds looked at the clock. He was two minutes early.

At 4 o'clock that afternoon when Goebbels was due to speak, the ceremony was again interrupted by the arrival of more Mosquitoes.

"We flew over the town expecting showers of flak," said Flying Officer Anthony Wickham, D.F.C., describing the afternoon attack. "Nothing whatever came up. I turned on to the bombing run which was to take us over the centre of Berlin. We dropped our bombs, a long stick of them, and watched them go down in a curve. Then at last the flak came up on the outskirts of the city—but nothing like we had been expecting. My navigator counted the shell bursts and there were only twelve of them—all extremely inaccurate."

Among the young airmen who sat so calmly in the pilot's seat controlling with consummate skill one of the world's fastest bombers with its Merlin engines roaring defiance to the Berlin skies was a pilot who not long previously had been a casual labourer in Sheffield. That modest young man, Sergeant Pilot Joseph Massey, soon wore the ribbon of the D.F.M. He was a shining symbol of the old democracy in this New Age. While Britain breeds such men she shall not perish.

This historic daylight raid on Berlin, so brilliantly planned and courageously executed in the face of great danger, was quietly summed up by Squadron Leader Reynolds on his return that morning.

"It was an uneventful trip," he said.

But not to Goering and Goebbels and Hitler. To them it marked a grave danger that was emphasised later by the developments and brilliant improvements in the technique of night bombing which enabled British bombers to bomb an invisible target through layers of cloud by night as accurately as they could bomb it by day in good visibility. "The wonderful semi-automatic bombsight devised by Professor Blackett," as Dr. B. N. Wallis termed it, with other secret instruments, gave Bomber Command improved chances of hitting the target. Yet the target still had to be found. This led to the selection of Pathfinders from the foremost pilots and navigators in the Royal Air Force, who flew in advance of the bombers to mark the target. On clear nights they dropped a new coloured marker bomb, invented by Dr. W. F. Coxon, that sprayed over the target and illuminated it in an uncanny way; in dense cloud the Pathfinders dived through the flak to identify the target before climbing through the clouds to leave their skymarkers blazing in the sky above. By absolute accuracy in speed, time and course the bombers, using the skymarkers, wrought unprecedented destruction on the invisible cities below. A further refinement was the Master Bomber, who controlled the raiders over the target and gave them instructions just as Gibson did at the Mohne dam.

No space remains to tell of the part played by the Royal Air Force in North Africa and Sicily and Italy and the invasion of France. But brief reference must be made to the work of Air Commodore F. Whittle, whose genius gave Great Britain the jet aircraft, known as the Meteor, and enabled the British Government to send a jet engine to the United States for simultaneous development on both sides of the Atlantic. And a tribute must be paid to another British scientist, Dr. B. N. Wallis, the inventor of the geodetic principle of aircraft construction, who gave Great Britain bigger and better bombs, which grew in size from 2,000 pounds to 4,000 pounds, from 8,000 pounds to the blockbuster and armour-piercing 12,000-pound bomb with which Wing Commander J. B. Tait, who won the D.S.O. four times, as well as the D.F.C., sank the German battleship *Tirpitz*. Then came the 22,000-pound bomb, which surprised not only the Germans, but also the American experts. Reuter cabled from New York on March 15, 1945: "America has been stirred by the news of the R.A.F.'s 10-ton bombs. The fact that a four-year-old British bomber is capable of carrying a load twice as heavy as the Super-Fortress on Tokio raids made a deep impression."

The British people may mark with pride that in the tense year when Great Britain stood alone—and afterwards—British discoveries and inventions and designs, unsurpassed by any other nation, furnished the Royal Air Force with the means of frustrating the greatest menace mankind has known and proved to be some of the chief factors in the ultimate defeat of the Nazis.

INDEX

254